CW01659172

Born in Grays, Essex in the UK, James wer
where he started observing people frorr
backgrounds. James came to Adelaide, A
straight from school, travelling extensively and for several years around Australia, before settling in Adelaide where he married and raised a family.

Having made several attempts at writing a novel length manuscript, *The Seven Crowns of Luca Moro* is his first published novel and has been 20 odd years in the making.

James now devotes himself to full-time writing and has several projects in the works.

To the women in my life....

You know who you are.

Bonifacio

Corsica

1999

Chapter One

Tears from the sun

Hard-ribbed and savage, Gaultier's dogs strained at their chains. Their enthusiastic exertions formed sharp crescents in the dust and marked its limit. It was a low clinging dust. Their jaws and teeth said stay away but their tail said play with me. The show was less ferocious when Luca came alone.

'They will kill you as soon as sniff your crotch,' said Gaultier. The canine cacophony was part of Henri Gaultier's bartering process.

Rain would mat the dog's fur, a clay grey on their spindly legs. Rain would also make Gaultier's onions grow. Tears from the sky. The two men, neighbours, were discussing the tanker of pig slurry. When Victor du Plessier, Luca's grandfather said nothing, Gaultier went on.

'But this is all water. Do I not get water free from the sky?'

'And the sky has not provided for ten weeks,' said Victor. 'I will take all this back,' said Victor, referring to the tanker, 'and your onions won't be worth harvesting in September. The Bear knew your mother, and your mother always said to her, before she died, that you never treated her well.'

Luca had wondered how long it would be before The Bear was brought into the bartering process. His grandfather, having stated his piece, lit his pipe. Gaultier's dogs did not tire. The Bear was Victor's mother: Luca's *arriere grandmaman*. A vessel of wisdom, she told young couples if they should marry. The Germans had sacked the village in 1942 and, with the post war upheaval, only the Bear knew which were cousins and which were not. Luca thought it funny she remembered who was related to whom but forgot her own age.

'What would you know of onion growing?' Gaultier said. 'I am an artisan. I grow the finest onions in Corsica. The sweetest in all Europe.' Gaultier felt the need to establish his credentials to the man he had lived next to all his life.

'I know that nothing grows if it does not rain. I have this fine tanker of pig's slurry: the last. It is yours if we can agree a price.'

'And if not?'

'Gaultier my old friend; don't I keep your dogs in pork bones?'

'Yes, but that will all end soon.'

It had already but Victor chose not to bring it up during the negotiations.

'Luca and I will travel to Porto Vecchio. I will sell it to la Fiete.'

'And risk a fine for taking a tractor on the highway?'

'There is a drought,' said Victor working hard at his pipe. 'There are visitors already in the town. The police will be busy with stolen cameras and lost credit cards. The season has started early.'

'The *season*!'

This seemed to enrage Gaultier. Everything else had been posturing and haggling, to establish a price.

'Are you not a pig farmer like your father before you? What is this *season*? You are a *farmer*.'

Gaultier's venom mixed with cigarette tobacco and wafted on a warm breeze sent by the gods.

'I am a second-generation pig farmer. I'm a pig farmer that's retiring.'

'Retiring?'

'I am two summers older than you my, friend. It had to happen. No?'

Gaultier needed to absorb this new fact, there was still a tanker of pig slurry on offer. He stroked his chin and mentioned a new price, a few francs more than his last bid.

'What, you would rob a man so close to his retirement?'

'What are you going to do with your farm?' Gaultier demanded. 'Don't let that wayward daughter take her inheritance to squander in the cities. There is evil in those cities: cars and supermarkets.'

Victor mentioned a price close to his opening bid.

'What? The price is going up. Take it away, earn a fine on the highway. Pigs will shit, I will take the next batch off you at a journeyman's pay. You will see.'

Victor paused and assessed his old friend. As boys they were lithe and fit and agile, they relied on each other. Henri Gaultier's mind was going; that was a certain truth. 'Henri, my life's friend, and neighbour. This is it. This is the last. No more shit because there are no more pigs.'

'No more pigs!'

The truth of it settled on Gaultier but it was a truth he was not happy about.

An unhurried cloud slipped by, and the sun got a better grip on the sky and reminded Victor that he would soon be fetching his hat from the hook behind the kitchen door. Despite hats, Victor's pate would soon be nutbrown like the rest of him. Oddly, the ring of hair he had left on his head was thick, dark, and strongly contrasted with the thatch of grey at his throat. Like a character from a long dead novelist, Gaultier's hair was thin, unwashed, and badly needed cutting. Gaultier's chin was covered in stubble that showed no uniformity of length or colour and reminded Luca of one of Clara's daisy bushes after the goat had worked his spike loose. Victor shaved every day and received kisses as reward from Clara his wife of 47 years. The only thing that gave him away as a man of the land were hands the size of dinner plates stained and grained with soil and toil.

Victor and Gaultier agreed on a price as if each had lost the zest to barter. Payment would be later, over a jug of wine. Luca unfurled his fourteen-year-old body, stood, and stepped down off the tractor's axle. Motion from a new source excited the dogs afresh. Their chains shone in the bright April sun. Luca was a head and a half above Gaultier's withered frame. As with people who achieve great height at an early age, Luca stooped. With his red hair scattered in every direction he had the look of a gangling scarecrow.

Luca would back the tractor as Victor got a twinge if he twisted his lower back for a long period.

Luca threw a leg over the tractor and slid his buttocks on the seat, ignoring the footplate. His genetic fractions included one-quarter *Corte* from the man who had just negotiated the sale of the tanker of slurry. The dark skin that tanned a golden bronze by June was courtesy of Victor also. The red hair must have come from his father's mother's side of the family. They say it skips a generation. His sea green eyes were his mother's, but he did not like to be reminded of that, she had appeared on his ninth birthday in her version of a surprise. It was not until after she had gone that Luca remembered that, in the turmoil of his birthday party, he had forgotten to look at his mother's eyes. The athleticism was all his own. The rugby coach wanted him to play rugby. The rugby coach was a turd. Luca preferred basketball, if he could find an opponent on the island of Corsica, on an island of short stocky *Corte.*

'Don't pass close to the dogs. They will worry the flesh off your bones,' said Gaultier, tying his breeches with a length of twine. 'They can smell the dirty tourists and it incites them.'

A heavy-breasted bitch barked with her head close to the ground and was raising dust with each snap of her jaw. It wasn't even a warning bark.

'Good girl,' said Luca, and received a wag of her tail for his trouble.

'Come away. She is savage - my best breeder - but she will have your hand.'

Chapter Two

Quiet like the grave

That night, Luca saw his grandfather to bed. Then he lifted the human sparrow that grew onions onto his tractor. He let air out of the front tyres, put it in a low gear, made sure Gaultier's head was secure on the steering wheel and let the tractor follow the wheel ruts home.

He climbed to the flat top of the empty slaughterhouse roof and listened for Gaultier's dogs. They would soon earn their scatterings of pork. They would wake their wine-soaked master. Far from killing, or crotch sniffing, they would clamour to lick his hand. Luca had seen it.

Luca enjoyed this time of the evening. His father, Larry, was pecking away at his TV scripts, or whatever it was that held him in that grey-green cathode beam. Victor would be snoring like a diesel and would be up with the larks. Victor's wife, Clara often joked that he would be asleep before his head hit the pillow. She, herself, would use this time to read in English, marking the passages that interested her and the words she did not understand. She read in English because most of the books belonged to Larry. Luca wondered what portion of his genetic fraction came from his father; evidence of family traits were scant and precious.

****

A pigless piggery is quiet like the grave. The two hours before school would be the biggest void, when Luca used to hose down the pigs - outside in the sun - if it was warm. They loved the water playing in their piggy little mouths. They learned to trust Luca and seemed to enjoy having their teeth cleaned. This slurry drained into a huge underground vat and was sold to farmers or stored until its value soared.

Victor announced his retirement after The Bear left the kettle on the Aga one day. No one believed him. But the slaughtered pigs were not replaced. The breeders were sold or slaughtered and the du Plessiers and the Moros had to contend with a new dilemma: silence.

Three sullen blasts on the horn from a distant a ferry pierced this silence now. The ferry had signalled its intention to reverse out of a harbour. The sound was from the south muted by great distance, ethereal and rare. *A ferry from Santa Teresa!* - The birthplace of his bride. Victor, in seven decades on the farm, had never heard such a thing. It was a sign. He started taking an interest in travel programs on the television. He extended the TV aerial so he could enjoy Italian TV but deemed it not worth watching. Larry thought the whole problem could be solved with a little coaxial cable, but Victor had never heard of any such thing, and it was a little late for his son-in-law to start getting practical. Luca suspected that his grandfather had made discrete inquiries in the town. Luca was the family linguist and would look it up if his grandfather asked. This was one of the drawbacks of living on Corsica; one needed to be exact about things like *coaxial cable* and needed to see it written down. Luca could not see the point of television, but anything could be got on the island if you knew what it was, were prepared to wait, prepared to pay and had an idea of where to start looking. A pig farmer's credo was if you can't make it, you don't need it. Luca wondered which would go first - his grandfather's resolve or his passion for Italian documentaries.

'The wind is from the South. The sound carries far this evening,' said Clara in Italian. She had approached unseen by Luca, silently on the concrete stairs.

'Nonna, you're not reading?'

'I have read every book your father has,' said Clara. 'Then I have to study the building estimates again. Your grandfather has employed a German contractor who is using Turkish labourers. We will have to watch them like a fox.'

'We'd better get used to that. We will have all nationalities when we open for business.'

'Not Turks, Luca. They are not the proud nation they once were. They are the strong backs of Europe. They leave wives at home and go abroad to work. It's not natural.'

'Did you hear the ferry?' asked Luca.

Clara heaved a chestful of sweet air. 'I did.'

'It was probably one from Santa Teresa. Tell me of life in Sardinia, a story from your head.'

'Why Luca?'

'Speaking Genoese makes my face sore and taxes the brain,' said Luca wearily. 'I want to hear about the past, elsewhere.'

Clara saw this as a very thin excuse for a story. 'Has Gaultier gone?' Sometimes Luca would nominate a regional dialect. In her youth, Clara moved around Italy with her five sisters and her Anthropologist father.

'I was just listening to see if he got home safely. He passed out, just as we were getting to the part about Bonaparte's return. Speaking an old language is tiring.'

'To speak it was banned for a time, so naturally it is flawed. It has holes. Victor and Gaultier are a few of the original Genoese speakers. I wish you could make friends your own age.'

'I am the bastard son of a tourist. That won't happen, Nonna.'

'You are not a bastard. Your parents were married.'

'And then she pissed off.'

Luca used the English phrase for *'pissed off'*; it fitted well with expressive Italian.

The sound of Gaultier's dogs confirmed his arrival home. If they didn't settle it would mean that Gaultier had fallen off again. And Luca would have to shut off the tractor and find the drunken old sod.

'It was the same for your mother,' said Clara. 'She never fitted in. Victor married me - an Italian, a Sardinian. She suffered because I was a foreigner.'

'Tell me the story of how you and Victor met, Nonna.'

Clara stepped forward to be nearer her grandson who leaned dreamily on the parapet. She slipped her tiny hand into one of her grandson's. His speaking pure Genoese at home was the subject of much anguish. Victor did not hold with the New Book Genoese, taught by people too young to remember a time when it was banned.

'Your grandfather went fishing, off the coast of Sardinia and he caught me. I knew a secret little cove. We didn't bother with bathing costumes then. It was just after the war. Only your grandfather knew it too. He went out for sardines, and he got a *Sardinian*. Of course, he was expected to marry a local girl. The Germans saw to it that there were very few men left to choose from. Migration was very high after the war. The village they rebuilt was soon empty.'

'And they have never let Grandpapa forget he married a foreigner.'

'Gaultier was then the only single man left of his generation, the only rooster left in the hen house.'

'There is nothing left of him, Nonna. I put him on the tractor, and he weighed less than a runt. Why did he never marry?'

'Sometimes there is too much choice and not enough responsibility. Did you catch the smell off him?'

'I did. I thought he was like that because - because he had given up.'

'No. He begged Victor once to take him to the same cove, one day when he was in his cups. He wanted to see my sisters bathing naked.'

'Why?' asked Luca.

'I think Gaultier was a little in love with me.'

Luca had seen pictures of his grandmother when she was young. Even in grainy black and white with the sun behind her, an un-posed photo looking back at the camera, she had the sort of face that incited men to deeds of action.

'Do you know why men fall in love with you instantly, Nonna?' Luca paused to allow time for his question to float. 'Because it saves time.'

Clara kissed Luca's temple.

******

High above an unforgiving terrain, the sickle moon ducked behind a sliver of a cloud. It illuminated the rough terrain in a way that drew its form but not its colour, pure and faithful, like a sepia photograph or a charcoal sketch. The absence of colour showed the cliff tops in an uncluttered beauty that lodged in the memory and crystallized forever. The dogs fell silent; Luca could now go to bed.

'Come inside Luca. I'll show you the signs Victor wants Dernavern to paint tomorrow. He speaks no Genoese you know; you will have to instruct him.'

'Why is he employing Dernavern?'

'We want the signs in English too. You know the trouble we had last time.'

Chapter Three

The flaxen Goddess

The morning saw the sun leak in over the cliffs facing the Tyrrhenian Sea. It cut westerly shadows with the out-buildings and banished all clouds with the promise of drying heat. It would be another day without rain. Clouds had no business in this sky, pale blue and pure. The smell of acrylic paint did its best to fill the space that the pigs left. It was still and quiet - empty.

Luca approached the strong back of Dernavern at his labours. In a singlet, he worked in the shade of the ancient, twisted olive tree. The smokehouse, the oldest building at the piggery, was approaching postcard perfection. A long way from the abandoned ruin of late last year. But for now, it was a makeshift workshop and housed the paints and brushes.

'Ah! The boy they call Luca Moro. Did you write the words for these signs?'

'Dad wrote the English; I wrote the Genoese words.'

'I hope the letters are set out correctly. I charge for my time and mistakes are costly.'

'I have two hours before I go to school. Ask me anything you want about the signs while I'm here.'

'Here's the first one for you - why English?'

'We hope to attract tourist from Italy, France, Germany and England, of course.'

'Your father is English?'

'Australian.'

'Here is the second question. Why me? Why not a tradesman?

The fact was that the local sign-writer, Guy Olivia was militant and rumoured to be in the FLNC. Since the advent of a computer that could cut vinyl lettering for signs, he charged what he felt like for signs painted in Corsu and Genoese and refused to write a sign in French. Another sign writer existed in Corte and he was French born but spoke no Corsu. He was also Olivia's brother-in-law. Whether the arrangement was one of politics or commerce had been the topic of conversation at the du Plessier dinner table.

'Victor's choice. Not mine. '

Luca thought of the planning and forecasting that went into Pension Lazlo. A man had come from the ATF in Paris. Luca's ear tuned quickly to the soft accent and new words: *inbound, package, pre-paid, night's stay, return visitor*. Luca had been fascinated by the plans; the large cumbersome sheets that had to be rolled because they were too large to fold. The lines and words interested Luca more than any art or textbooks. He offered to roll and fetch the plans, as they were needed. He made himself indispensable in the process. *Luca, where are the site plans that show the drainage?* Luca would then fetch the right plan and the mere act of unrolling it brought a welling thrill. The pension meant the world would come and visit Luca. Luca no longer had to escape. But what would Dernavern understand? Dernavern lived on the edge of a forest, atop a high bank of stone and amidst overgrown verdant bush. His house was the place where tourists turned around. A promising looking road ended abruptly at his gate. The trees were said to grow right up to Dernavern's terrace. Dernavern was the topic of many rumours. And he did nothing to dispel them.

'How much to rent this place?' asked Dernavern of the Smokehouse Studio as he completed its sign.

'This place - The Smokehouse Studio - is a steal at just 550 F a night.'

Dernavern whistled. 'I pay less than that a month for my studio.'

'We are in the service industry,' Luca said. 'We are after a different type of tourist.'

Dernavern rolled his thumb and fingers in front of a seen-it-all face. 'Not ferry frass.'

'Pardon?'

'It is an English word; it means maggot shit.'

Luca laughed. 'You are getting the idea,' he said after a while. 'Is that why you live out of the town?'

'I live out of the town because, as you say, there is criticism born of envy. And I can't justify that sort of rent. Anyway, tourists want to gawk and never buy anything.'

'Are they envious of your art? Because I have never seen any; nor has Victor or Larry.'

'I sell in Paris. Here I live simply and do not overtax my gift. Having the right agent sends my prices up. Perhaps the islanders covet my lifestyle.'

'Lifestyle?'

'My friend who stayed all winter, has sudden business in Oslo.' Dernavern's voice was a cigarette paper away from gloating. 'She's from northern latitudes and has skin like toffee - an excellent subject. Naturally she had to work on that tan and would promenade naked on my terrace. Can't do that in the Old Town.'

'Will she be back?'

'Why?' scoffed Dernavern. 'When the warm weather will bring a fresh batch - a brunette perhaps. A feisty Italian who can cook. Whose mother has instructed her well. I enjoyed cooking and reading for Astrid but after a while, it became a chore.'

So, the flaxen goddess's name was Astrid.

'What did Astrid like to eat?'

'Pasta. Pesto pasta.'

'You probably thought – and still do. That you were eating Italian.'

'I was. I am. '

'Well, what if I told you were eating Genevese. Locally made right here. Invented by poor peasants who could not afford meat. *Pesto Alla Genovese.'*

'So, you're telling me it's a French dish?'

'Depends on what century we are talking.'

Dernavern's reaction was a pensive nod and an arrangement of the lips that said: Well- I-never!

Another trait of the Corse was reticence, by any standard Luca was garrulous. This was the longest conversation he had had in a very long time and it felt good.

The sound of the labourer's Turkish banter was a welcome distraction to Luca's ears. The Turks were arriving for work, disgorging from a large white van. They wore low crotched pantaloons of a lowly caste and embroidered vests. The image, except for the Dresden registered Mercedes van, could have come from any century you would care to name, except this one. Luca picked up a paintbrush.

Dernavern continued 'I would have liked to have met your mother, I hear she was a great beauty,'

'She escaped. Twice! I was an unplanned pregnancy in-between. What do you want me to do?' asked Luca.

'Paint the background colour. Do you think you can manage that?'

Luca painted in broad sloppy strokes.

'Like this,' said Dernavern. 'Use the tips of the bristles.'

Luca copied the brush strokes. 'Say yes! It goes on evenly.'

They painted for ten minutes in silence before Luca spoke again. 'My mother met my father on a ferry.' Was this the first time she tried to escape? People island hopped all the time and were called ferry frass; maggot shit.

'No. She had the right idea. The ferries ride low in the water because they are carrying people's hopes and dreams. They come, and are fleeced, and return to their dreary lives to tell their equally dreary work mates what a wonderful holiday they have had. The postcard culture. The truth is they live a mile from where they were born, work in a job that they hate and live in a house they can barely afford.' Dernavern stopped painting. 'Where did she go? Your mother.'

'Milan first, then Paris. As far as my father's money took them. He was working for the summer on an Italian ferry. The second time I have no idea. She showed up on my ninth birthday and I had to ask her name. With her fine clothes and soft accent, I thought she was catering for a feast. I thought she had come to buy cold meat.'

It struck Luca then they had stopped making *charcuterie, jambon* and *pied de porc* the next year. There had been a phasing out and a scaling down of farm activities so gradual he had hardly noticed it.

'Are you going to paint or stand there dreaming?'

'Sorry.'

Luca remembered he used to collect chestnuts for a selection of piglets Victor had chosen to fatten up for weddings and feasts. Collecting chestnuts was one of his tasks. It had started him saving. Planning.

'Milan and Paris,' said Dernavern thoughtfully. 'If she was miserable here, she went to the source. Sometimes, if you are to navigate a waterway, it is good to find its headwaters.'

'Does your art extend to *bullshit* as well as graphic and fine.' Luca used the English word for *bullshit*; it coupled nicely with artist.

Dernavern roared with laughter. Luca's face split into a smile.

'The boy has spirit. Do you learn that potty-mouth English from the tourists? Where is your mother now? Where is she to give you a cuff, for you to learn some respect?'

'That is where you are wrong Mr. Fuck-The-Tourists artist. Respect,' spat Luca, 'is earned, not taught.' Good nature evaporated as quickly as it arrived.

Dernavern painted rapidly. The 22 letters of the Genoese language, its spidery descenders and accents, the special grouping of letters, did not engage his curiosity. He did not ask the meaning of the words he was painting.

After a while Luca said. 'Aren't we both fucking the tourists in our own way?'

Dernavern inclined his head toward the old smokehouse. '550 F a day! Do you use that tone when you are fleecing the tourist out of a pound or a dollar?'

Luca's time spent in the Old Town was as legendary as were his poor grades at school.

'I am civil.'

'Are you?'

'I unlock a few mysteries - explain some of the rude behaviour visitors might have experienced.'

'Example?'

'For example, if they are French, I take the trouble to explain that the people who resent their presence are direct descendants of those that defeated the Italians in 1755 and set up a system of self-rule, only to have the Italians hand them over to the French. If they are Italians, I tell the same story and make the villains the Genoese or Pisans. Almost all of Europe has ruled over Corsica at one point of history - or tried to.'

'You trade in old loyalties?' said Dernavern.

'I trade in History. I trade in what they teach me or, more exactly, what they don't.'

Dernavern looked up from his lettering. 'What, they don't teach you?'

'What do teachers care about history? It would take a Geiger counter for them to find their arse. I live history. In the Citadel, people ask for me by name. But my assignments come back marked in red, like it was at the scene of a massacre.' Luca was warming to his topic. 'They take marks off for each mistake and a few more for poor handwriting. Take the period of Italian rule - Clara has spoken of the version she learned - the outside version. The one which most of the world concurs. If I didn't have a Sardinian grandmother, I might take what they are passing off for history as Gospel.'

'What are they teaching then, Luca?'

'The Corse sanctioned version of history.'

'How is that different?'

'No different. The dates are still the same. Just that any defeat is by an oppressor and every victory must be preceded by the word *glorious*. Take Napoleon Bonaparte - have you seen the statue of his great victories? It is a four-sided obelisk. Four! What happened to Waterloo? Mention Waterloo in a history test and you can guarantee yourself an 'F'.

'That sounds like propaganda, not history.'

'The cafe owners learn this,' said Luca. 'They have it drummed into them. And they think they are settling history's score when they overcharge: a kind of mainlander tax.'

'I must admit I have not learned the local language. I must get myself a phrase book,' said Dernavern.

'Don't trouble yourself. It would be like studying the slide rule. Victor has forbidden it in the house. '

'Why?'

'We have two natural Genoese speakers in my family and Gaultier, a neighbour. The Genoese taught is a sort of composite from all the districts. Victor saw my book and was angry. He said it was the Genoese of scholars who never set foot in Bonifacio. The bureaucrats in Calvi.'

After a while Dernavern said, 'I'm surprised you even know what a slide rule is. We learned how to use them in my day and you know what we used to call them?'

'What?'

'A guessing stick!'

Luca and Dernavern laughed. Luca silently decreed never to use the phrase *'in my day,'* when he was an adult. Luca would add it to the rapidly growing list, which had started with the cost of things when Victor was a boy.

'Well, if you thought learning how to use a guessing stick was ludicrous, imagine that once you had mastered it, it was only ever used in your village. By 3,000 people at the most.'

'Isn't that part of the attraction of Bonifacio? It's a living museum. Tourists can't wait to tell people about this quaint old language spoken nowhere else but here.' Dernavern reached into his pocket and pulled out a wad of French francs. 'This is what it is all about.'

'This is another myth I dispel,' said Luca. 'That overcharging is born of greed. I take the time to explain that every business, even the ferries and agriculture are subsidised. People only see the cafes full and overflowing. They have not seen them boarded up for winter. Every cafe owner has a farm or a fishing boat to help him survive the winter. A second income to make ends meet.'

Dernavern was blocking in the big signs now, confident fluid strokes copying the unfamiliar words.

'A phrase book might be of some use to you outside of Bonifacio, but you are like my dad. You're not a tourist and you're not a local.'

'Is a different language spoken in other parts of Corsica? Or does each region have its own dialect?'

'No,' Luca said, not bothering to hide the melancholy in his voice. 'Bonifacio is Bonifacio. Genoese is Genoese. I wouldn't say this to the locals, or the tourists but it is like living on a movie set.'

'You're quite the professor', said Dernavern wryly. 'How are you going in school?' he asked, not bothering to look up.

'School! They could not make it more boring if they tried. Books are very hard to come by. And very expensive - ask my father. They are mostly in French. And we have to share sometimes.'

'I know why you can speak so many languages and are an underachiever at school.'

'Why?'

'Because language gains your attention. School is for followers, conformists. It bores you because already you can see the end product.'

'What’s that?' asked Luca.

'Another teacher: an academic. School is a production line conceived by academics, run by academics, staffed by academics, for academics. If someone like you comes off the conveyer belt, you know what they call that?'

'What?'

'A miracle!'

They both laughed again.

'Talking of school, I must get there,' said Luca putting down his brush.

'Stay and learn,' said Dernavern to Luca's departing back. 'I have much to teach you. Kids with one parent have had but a single view of the world. You're missing your mother.'

'How can you miss what you never knew?' Luca was shouting louder than he needed to.

After an eternal silence, Dernavern went on. 'I was going to say, you are missing a mother's influence. I see it with painter's eyes.'

Dernavern caught up with Luca who turned at the speed of a ninja.

'The same *artist's eyes* that did not notice that a different language was spoken here?'

'This is France after all.' Dernavern threw his hands up; the gesture was threatening but his voice conciliatory. 'Luca, how can I put this? I am a mirror not a sponge. The locals hate me because of something that happened in history. I can't change history. They will accept me - or they won't.'

Dernavern's words had the base notes of reason. 'I was going to say ... before. You miss your mother's influence. What I see is talent, misdirected, but I see how fluid your brush strokes are. And I only showed you once. I see you communicate well. Teachers will only note your indolence.'

Later Luca wished he had said *'As much as it tempts me to stay and fathom the depths of your wisdom, I already know the breadth of your deceit. I can smell it.'* He thought of that on the bike ride to school. Instead, he said 'You are full of shit!' Strangely it had an American twang.

Dernavern had followed Luca to where he kept his bike. 'You said to ask you questions,' said Dernavern. 'Here's one: why did the Germans shoot every man except Victor?'

'Simple! The Commandant liked bacon. Victor was about my age and could butcher a pig. The Germans found this place convenient with its meat hooks and drains.'

They were in the slaughterhouse where Luca kept his bike. One of the heavy steel drains was at Dernavern's feet.

'Wouldn't want to get Corse blood on those fine German boots. And he was not the only man to survive. Gaultier survived. His mother dressed him as a girl.'

'Here's another question. Why was the village deserted? They rebuilt it but it is no longer there.'

'They rebuilt it, but there was no heart in it. The Germans killed so many; emigration finished the job. Brand new houses standing empty, it was too much to ask. The village was dismantled for scrap. It was before my time. Ask Victor.'

'Is that so?'

'I was never cut out to be a pig farmer, Dernavern, but failing school doesn’t worry me.'

With that Luca stood on a pedal and mounted his rolling bike and then powered his way toward the village.

The land was worth 30 million Francs. Dimitri, a Greek moneychanger, had suggested this figure and Luca was supposed to take the offer to Victor and report back to Dimitri aboard his yacht in the marina. Luca returned instead and told Dimitri that Victor had no quarrel with the land values, he now wanted Dimitri to put a price on the view. Dimitri never got back to Luca. Luca was taking a huge risk that Dimitri did not speak to Victor directly and that his deceit be exposed. It might be called Pension Lazlo, as Dernavern had painted the sign so prettily, but Luca knew his father, Lazlo Moro, couldn't hold the deeds. He was not a French national - neither was Dimitri, but he knew people in low places.

****

Garrod was a man of medium build. He wore a goatee and the tweed of a country gentleman - an English country gentleman. He looked anything but French. As with most teachers, he thought he was a hoot with the children. As with most teachers he was wrong.

'As usual I am saving the worst till last,' said Garrod.

He had married a local girl and was teaching Genoese under sufferance. He was called *Garrotte* because of the way he truncated 250-year-old Genoese verbs. He was qualified to teach French and that made an improvement on the last teacher, who was a natural Genoese speaker, but not qualified at anything except ridicule.

'There is only one thing harder than learning a 250 year old, largely oral, language' Garrod paused for dramatic effect, 'And that is teaching a 250 year old language without textbooks. Copy the text and make lists of the corrected Genoese words you have got wrong. That will be hard for some, as they see fit to hand up blank pages. Sylvie Murat, kindly share with the class your reasons for *not* doing this assignment.'

The new girl, the pretty one from Paris with the looping, sooty locks shrugged in a way that most teenagers would want to go away and practice. Few perfect it, fewer still outside of their own bedroom. Luca sat behind her and made a few moments idly watching the hair cascading to the small of her back. He knew what was coming next.

Garrod stood before Sylvie now and the rest of the class strained to greet her discomfort. There was none. Sylvie hooked an arm over the back of her chair, twisting sideways in the process. The swell of her breast seemed to punctuate her indifference to Garrod, Genoese, the lesson - everything. If a body could pout, Sylvie's was pouting.

'I am waiting,' said Garrod in Genoese.

Sylvie tilted her jaw at a point above Garrod's head.

'We are all waiting, *Miss* Murat.' Garrod positively hissed the 'Miss' in English. Shock spread like a ripple; Garrod had used a hybrid sentence. Sylvie tossed her hair. Luca studied the fine hairs at the newly exposed nape of her neck. Sylvie's pout solidified to a sneer.

'Give me the mark you think it justifies,' she said.

'Then I give it an 'F'.'

'And what mark did you give Luca Moro?'

Luca writhed. The other work Garrod held was Luca's. Every other child had their assignments returned. Luca could read 'F's' backwards through the page. Luca hoped Garrod would exhaust all his scorn on Sylvie.

'He gets an 'F' also.'

'We get the same mark. And there goes an hour we will never see again.'

There was a gut-sucked silence followed by random bursts of whispers. Garrod was famous for his anger.

'Then we shall sit the two of you together so you don't *infect* other students who want to learn, and you can both stay after class until you produce a legible Genoese composition.'

Garrod got red splotches at his temples when he got angry. Luca stole a glance and saw the side of Garrod's face was crimson, he had a white, pinched look about the nose and his lips were pressed tight shut. Luca stared down as Sylvie glided in beside him. Garrod watched the process from just in front of Luca's desk.

'This is the seat vacated by Mr. Roald Pound who went back to Chicago,' said Garrod. 'He learned something of our language and kept Moro company while he rewrote Genoese verbs. ' Garrod turned his head to one side then the other, he was addressing the whole class from near the back of the room. 'Genoese uses the original Latin verbs,' he continued, 'which found their way into American via the English by way of the French. If he were here, it would be a sort of signpost on the literary highway.'

When Sylvie had arrived from Paris a week and a half ago, she had sent the boys all agog. Sylvie's presence evoked strong emotion. She promoted actions and factions. The action from the boys took the form of a display that reminded Luca of one of Gaultier's dogs with a grain sack. The dog knows the sack is dead, but he shakes it for his owner's benefit. This posturing came from behind the toilet block mostly. Luca witnessed a certain polarisation from within the ranks of the girls. Sylvie committed the most heinous crime: she was pretty and foreign.

Luca had talked to pretty girls and foreign girls before in the Citadel. Garrod had unwittingly moved the object of Luca's primary sense within the range of all his others.

The lesson ended with the interruption of the bell and the riotous clamour that it brings.

'Those who have football, go and change. Moro and Murat can bring their compositions to me on the soccer pitch. I look forward to reading them. Then he left the room.

'Arsehole!' said Sylvie in English. She extended an international middle finger.

'At least I get out of soccer practice,' said Luca.

Sylvie reached for her bag and made plenty of noise. Luca was left-handed and was arching his body to that side, the left side, where Sylvie sat.

'See! No books.'

Luca was forced to look up.

'Papa gave me the money for textbooks, but I bought this.'

Sylvie made a great display of applying *Chanel No. 5*. 'Mama has sent the money for books also, but I will charge them to Papa.'

Luca wrote in short punchy sentences that suited the written Genoese Language. He curved his long body around his work as left-handed people do.

Luca wrote: *The Parisian artist, Dernavern pays F350 a month for his hillside studio. He finds rural life simple with an absence of envy. Rather than extend his gift he chooses to meet an established demand for his art in Paris.*

He has not integrated or learned any of our beautiful language in five years.

Island life, for him, signifies an escape from the rigors and high prices of big city living.

Because Luca's mother had left when he was young, his mother tongue was pure. Luca finished his assignment quickly so he could submit it without his grandfather seeing it. In future he would do two version of his homework and hide one from Victor. 'Are you going to do your assignment?' he asked.

'No!' It was a statement and then: 'Here, can you help me?

Sylvie wanted him to take the cap off the nail polish bottle. The act, insignificant to most, was a blip on Luca's sexual telemetry. Luca's telemetry was pheromone driven. Sylvie held her bag open as she returned the bottle of solvent. It was as if she wanted to display the other bottles and clutter in the bag or perhaps the total absence of books.

'You speak French like a mainlander. Where did you learn?' said Sylvie, pouting into a mirror.

'From the tourists.'

'Ah! The tourists.'

'Speaking it is a lot easier than writing it. I don’t learn language from a book; I learn from hanging out in the Citadel.

'How many languages do you speak?'

'Four or five. I can say a few words in Japanese and Korean. To try is more important, to them.' Luca glanced down at his work. 'This is hard.' Luca took a chance. 'This is bullshit.'

'This fucking island is bullshit.'

One of the effects of the generations of Corte, refusing to speak French was the near absence of swear words. It was the first thing Luca noticed about visitors. English was the best; it had the most swear words.

'I refuse to speak the language of pigs,' said Sylvie. 'These misanthropic pack of goat herders hate all Europeans equally. Do you know what they say in Paris?'

'What?' asked Luca.

'If Corsica were *not* so beautiful,' said Sylvie, 'no one would bother to visit it twice.'

'They say that do they? I have a question? What is *misanthropic*?'

'That's the difference between you and me?'

'What's that?'

'I speak one language well.'

'I speak four or five languages well! I can prove it. I will show you at the Citadel.'

'Call for me then! Be sure and let Papa know you are a pig farmer's son. But for now, I must get out of here. Do you know why?

Luca did not correct the feisty girl - a pig farmer's grandson. 'Why?'

'I must swim 2 kilometres. If I am to model swimsuits, I must maintain the figure, yes?' Sylvie smoothed her hand over her chest in a way that dared Luca to look.

'Do you model swimsuits?'

'In Paris. Mama is not so stringent, when I live with her. I get paid work as a photographic model. Regular work in Paris.'

'Don't you have to be 18?'

'When I am in my swimsuit, I pass for 18. No one has ever questioned me.'

'What time?' Luca hoped that the invitation to call had been genuine. The right answer might relieve the tightness in his chest.

'After supper.'

'What do I tell Garrod?'

'Tell him my father called for me. No! Tell him he sent the car,' said Sylvie gathering her possessions. 'I have been summoned. I am a dutiful daughter, no?'

'Ok!'

'One question.'

'Fire away.'

'Why don’t you wear the school uniform?'

'I am too tall. Clothes don’t fit.'

'How tall are you? Stand up.'

Luca stood and Sylvie tilted her Gypsy face, her sooty tangle of curls fell like seaweed in an ocean’s swell at her throat. She levelled her steady sky-blue gaze on Luca, 'I didn’t know they stacked goat shit that high.' Then she blew Luca a kiss and was gone.

Chapter Four

A makeover in a boatshed

'I am going to like working here; your Nonna is a great cook. She speaks French like a native,' said Dernavern.

It was part of the deal. The German contractor saw problems with the Turks. The work looked like taking six months or more. Local contractors had the habit of only working in the winter, weather dependant, and delays could unravel into summer long layoffs. Clara had agreed to cook for the labourers.

This sounded unjust to the Turks, but Luca wanted to put it in a way that Dernavern would understand. The problem stemmed from their need to break for lunch and go into the village. And then there was the issue of Halal meals. Then there was the danger of the Turks not returning.

'Too many distractions in the Old Town.' Luca finally said, picking up his brush.

'Drink?'

'No, I heard Horst tell Victor they are Moslems and don't drink. It's a 20-minute walk and the distractions would be of the female kind, wearing a bikini.'

'Oh! That's alright then,' said Dernavern. 'I think I am going to enjoy working for Victor. I hate to work for a man who does not drink. Never trust a man who doesn't drink.'

'I can help you here until supper; then I have a date.'

'A date. With whom?'

'Sylvie Murat. Know her?'

'Know her? What is she 13, 14? And already been sent down from some of the finest schools in Paris.'

'You know the family?'

'Let's just say that Sylvie's father is a fan of my work since he came to stay with me. Until he found that hideously large place of his. He's more of an investor really. All done with bank money and written off against taxes and then depreciated.'

It sounded terribly complicated to Luca. 'Sylvie refuses to speak Genoese.'

'As do I - and your father; he doesn't even speak French.'

'What are you going to do here? All the signs are painted.'

'Painting - house painting, window frames, door frames. I offered to stay on; there is plenty of work.'

'Does she get on with her father?'

Dernavern stopped painting, his expression and body language a study in thought. He might have been wondering how much to tell the 14-year-old son of his employer. His brush hung like his words in the air. After a time, he said 'Sylvie? Why do you ask?'

'She said be sure and tell Papa you are a pig farmer's son.'

'That's Sylvie. Look if you are serious about this, can I make a suggestion?'

'Sure.'

'Get rid of those sports clothes, you look like an extra in a rap video.'

'I get my clothes sent from *The Big Guy Store* in New Jersey.'

'How did you get onto them? Never mind - do you have anything else?'

Luca and his dad Larry agreed that ordering recognised brand names was a better bet when buying goods over the internet.

'I had a friend who recommended it, why, what's wrong with Nike?'

'Nothing except you look like a tourist,' said Dernavern.

'I will never look like a local, if that's what you mean.'

'Appearance is important if you want the girls to fall for you. They go for this sort of thing.'

'Perhaps Sylvie and I will be just friends. Maybe I just want to be friends.'

'Yeah right!' Dernavern put down his brush. 'Look, I'll tell you what I'll do. I will introduce you to Caroline.'

'Who is Caroline?'

'She is a hairdresser. A salon trained hairdresser. Look I know where she is. We must catch her.'

Intrigue or the tone of Dernavern's voice made up Luca's mind. 'I'll just tell Larry I'm going out. Where shall I tell him I'm going?'

'To get your hair cut.'

'How much money will I need?'

Dernavern smiled and said, 'This one's on me.'

It did not surprise Luca when Dernavern started cruising the beaches looking for a red 2CV with a white roof.

'Here it is,' he said as he threw the car into neutral and pulled on the handbrake. 'Come on.'

Luca followed but the head of Dernavern was already disappearing down the steep path that led to *Plage de sutta Rocca.* Below them the beach was moderately well attended, families probably in small groups. In summer, walking in a straight line was out of the question. On national holidays sunbathers laid towel to towel and the city workers laid out flagged walkways to the cool clear water. From up here, the water was a pale turquoise, but Luca was watching his footing and not the chocolate box scenery.

As he reached the large flat pebbles, he looked around for Dernavern. He was squatting and talking to a girl with a yellow one-piece costume rolled down to her waist. Her tan was flawless, and she wore gold rings on three fingers of both hands plus one on each thumb.

'This is Luca.'

'Luca, this is Caroline,' said Dernavern.

'Hello,' said the nearly naked woman.

'What's this? Have you got yourself an apprentice, Piers?'

'Hello,' said Luca. Her hair was streaked in several shades of blonde and Luca noticed that she wore make up to the beach. The Ray-Bans on her head held her hair back from her face.

'Come closer don't be shy,' said Dernavern.

'He's just a boy, Piers,' said Caroline rolling up her bathing costume. The costume was old and the Lycra thin; Caroline's small breasts were capped with dark, plum areolas that the pale material did little to conceal.

'Luca has a hot date with a girl,' said Dernavern.

'Don't be a tease, Piers,' said Caroline. She was standing now and thrust her hand out at Luca.

Luca noticed the top of her bathing costume was stretched and probably spent most of its life rolled down to Caroline's waist.

'Hello.' They shook hands, 'Oh! I already said that; didn't I?'

'Piers says you are in need of an image change.'

'Well – just a haircut.'

'Caroline, apart from having an incredibly flexible body, is a Paris trained stylist. A man needs be faithful to his hairdresser, only his hairdresser. She comes just below his mother on the catalogue of importance.'

'Don't listen to him, Luca. Come to my house. I'll send this little shit away and we can be alone. A woman may try several hairstyles in her lifetime, a man may stick with one forever, if it suits him.'

She lifted her bag to her shoulder and turned to Dernavern. 'Don't you have some tourists to leer at? Something underage to corrupt?'

'It's too early in the season. It's all families at this time of year. Besides I wouldn't miss this for the world. Besides I'm paying.'

'Why not come back tomorrow for a massage?'

'Oh! I forgot the magic hands. Caroline is very talented,' said Dernavern.

'Piers, there is no way you are coming back with us.'

'You think you can stall me with a massage, and maybe a little afternoon tumble.'

'If, and when, I have three minutes to spare I will be sure and give you a call, Piers.'

Luca walked ahead.

'I'm coming anyway - my car is parked up there. And less of this 'three minutes', didn't you cancel an ocean cruise? Didn't I lie for you so you could keep your deposit?'

'Come on then, if you think you can keep up.'

'You have a lovely little arse... for smacking.'

In the tussle that followed Caroline dared Dernavern to piggy back her up the car park.

'Just to the path. I want to save my strength for tomorrow.'

Luca was quite a way off now.

'Piers, you are embarrassing the boy. Enough!'

Luca's thighs burned when he reached Dernavern's car. He could hear Caroline and Dernavern's banter before their heads came into view. They had linked arms. So, this was the legendary Dernavern at work; perhaps charm was a close cousin to impudence. Luca could tell the way Dernavern was holding his chest that he was trying not to pant. It would be missed by most but the pearls of sweat on his lip gave Luca his clue.

'Come with me, Luca,' said Caroline.

She lived at the back of a boat builder's yard near the new marina. It was a two-minute drive but she insisted on opening the roof of the little 2CV. Luca felt the top of his head very close to the windscreen because the seat was impossibly far forward.

'Who cuts your hair now? Luca?' Asked Caroline.

'The barber near the school.'

'Anyone in particular?'

'No, whoever is free.'

There were a series of gates to negotiate. Luca froze as he saw a huge Rottweiler.

'Relax. That's Mila. She's a *pussycat,*' said Caroline.

At the sound of her voice Mila came over to investigate Luca. The scent of Luca's leg held Mila's attention long enough for her to drool on Luca's foot.

'I'd better chain her up. She's the watchdog for the boat builders. At lot of stuff got stolen. They got Mila and she kept the burglars away, but she chewed things up. She's very destructive and my passage for cheap rent. My job is to keep Mila amused.'

The last gate led to a small garden. High walls prevented lawn from growing but Caroline had done a lot with pot plants by placing them on pedestals.

'Would you like a drink?'

Luca would but he did not know if Caroline meant alcohol.

'A glass of water?' suggested Caroline.

'Yeah! Fine. Thanks.'

'Come up then.'

Caroline went first up the tiny iron spiral stair. Luca had not seen it at first. This was the highest part of the boat builder's shed. The spiral stair might have been built as a fire escape for the offices that would have looked out over the workspace. The offices were placed at the side and up high to give more space for larger vessels. The space below was converted into a living area. Luca saw a TV and a shabby armchair. Next to the shabby chair was a newer one. If Caroline amused Mila, Mila kept Caroline company. Luca was sure the marrowbone and water bowl belonged to Mila.

The room at the top of the stairs was just that, one room, of which the bed dominated half of the space. Caroline's kitchen was behind a set of bi-fold doors.

'Compact living. But the rent is cheap. Actually, it's free.'

Caroline went about making the bed. A strange disquiet came over Luca. It was one thing to be attracted to the prettiest girl in school, it was quite another to be in the bedroom of a sexually accessible one. He was happy when she shrugged on a pair of Calvin's, happier still when she pulled on a T-shirt. The clothes had been on the floor and Caroline's tan lines were undetectable. Her housekeeping was as casual as her dress sense.

'Here. Tap water I'm afraid.'

'Fine. Thanks.'

'I'll cut your hair downstairs, but I'll wash it up here.'

'Wash it?'

'Yeah! Does your hairdresser wash it now?' asked Caroline as if she already knew the answer.

'No. He's more of a barber really.'

'I'm going to have to get you to sit, you're so tall.'

'I thought you said you would cut it downstairs.'

'I will. This is what we call the appraisal. I need to see what we are dealing with. On the bed.'

Luca felt his face colour.

Caroline moved around him darting a hand into Luca's hair at random. She circled him, her hand lashing out like a viper, her finger always came away with sections of Luca's hair. 'When did you last have it cut?'

'Before Easter.'

'What do you use on it?'

'Do you mean today? Nothing today, when it in between it gets hard to control.'

'I'm not surprised,' Caroline stepped onto the bed and fell to her knees behind Luca. She removed his scrunchie. 'How many crowns do you have – six?'

'Seven.'

'Seven! Oh yes here it is. People spend a fortune to get this much volume in their hair. I have clients who would kill for this hair. This colour.'

Luca felt his penis snake up toward his belly.

'Come on, let's get you washed. I'm afraid you will have to kneel at the basin.'

On his knees bent over the basin, Luca thought his arousal had peaked and he was praying it would subside. Close physical contact was unavoidable but when Caroline applied conditioner and massaged it in, Luca thought he would die. When she had finished Luca pretended to have shampoo in his eye as Caroline clanged her way down the iron stair. *When had she slipped on those Dr Scholl sandals?* He rubbed his perfectly healthy eye with the towel Caroline had left wrapped towel around his wet hair. Luca was overjoyed to see the cape and the chair; he carried the towel at his waist.

'Mind if I let Mila in?' asked Caroline with a wry smile.

'No, I love dogs.'

'She'll probably fuss for a while and sleep at your feet.' Caroline brushed Luca's wet hair. Luca wondered if she had forgotten Mila. Then she walked over to the gate and called for the dog. Was that sway, that wiggle for Luca? Luca got an image of Caroline and her mons pubis thinly veiled in yellow Lycra. He shivered.

'Cold?'

'No, I'm fine,' said Luca, glad of the cape.

'Now, Luca I'm going to cut this very short. Your hair will probably end up a shade darker.'

'It goes darker when I put wax in it.'

'You won't need wax or gel with this style, Luca. I'm going to give you a buzz-cut.'

'Ok!'

'Ok, are you sure? Now is the time to say anything. For you it's short or long. Let's do short.

'I'm in your hands.'

'You're so tall. Taller than the locals.'

'I try to blend in, but with this hair they call me matchstick.'

'They are jealous.'

Luca was very aware of Caroline's hands; they were small, supple, fast, and strong. Mostly they electrified him at their deft touch. He closed his eyes and thought of Sylvie's dark cascading hair, her flashing blue eyes. Honourable thoughts, but that image could not dislodge an image of Caroline's pubic hair spoiling the smooth lines of a yellow bathing costume.

'You have a very bold face Luca. This style I am thinking of will suit your face.'

Luca noticed the iron roof. This was where engines and small boat parts would have been painted. It was a room with no sides and Caroline had made it very comfortable.

'How old are you Luca?'

'I'm 14.'

'How old is this girl?'

'She's not yet 14, I think.'

'Your beard is coming in. Do you want me to shave you?' Caroline was very close, and Luca could feel her breath.

'No, I have a razor. 'I'll shave tonight.'

'Big date?' Caroline was untangling an electrical cord. She plugged in the hair clippers.

'It's just as well there are no mirrors,' she said. 'You won't see all your hair disappear.'

'It's not a big date. We could end up just friends. Can't men and women be just friends, Caroline?'

'Sure. Brother and sister.'

Caroline cut a strip of hair up the centre of Luca's head.

'I've changed my mind.'

Caroline walked round to look at Luca. He had a big grin on his face. Luca wasn't sure: was this flirting?

'Too late,' said Caroline.

'How long have you lived here?'

'Nearly a year. I was living in a share house near Porto Vecchio, but I love it here. I would live in town if I could afford it. Then this came up. I sit down here in the summer, and I sit on the bed in the winter. There is no room for furniture.'

'Yes, I noticed.'

'But I like it. Now you are going to have to have your hair cut every three to four weeks. But I think you will love it. Your head's a good shape and you don't have one of those tragic hairlines.'

Mila turned around four times and sank with a sigh at Luca's feet. The sun reached this far; Luca's feet were actually in the sun. Mila lay on her side and in a few minutes was asleep.

'Do you cut hair here regularly,' asked Luca.

'No, I set up under a tree when the tourists hit town. I charge Paris prices; a haircut is one of the few things that are cheaper here in Bonifacio. Actually, I charge less than in Paris but more than here.'

'Any difficulties with the local hairdressers?'

'No, in the height of the season everyone is rushed off their feet anyway. The sort of client that come to me would not put their trust in a provincial barber.'

'Could you get work in Paris? Or set up a shop here and charge mainland prices?'

'Either or both. I could get work in any city in any country in the world. If I set up shop here, I would have very quiet winters. I might open two days a week, but the landlord would still want 7 days rent.'

Caroline had finished with the hair clippers. She put them down next to the TV.

'If I set up shop, I would need an assistant. Then I might lose this place and Mila would start chewing up everything in sight again.' Caroline took up her scissors. 'This is going to look so good.'

'How much do you charge?'

'For a buzz cut – 80 F. For you Luca, I would do it for free. How do you feel about walking Mila?'

'Yeah, I love dogs. Is she trained to walk on a lead?'

'She is but she is so strong. She would pull me over if she saw another dog. Now I have got the shape of this haircut it will be easy for me to keep it looking great. Feel it Luca.'

Luca felt the bristles. They felt strangely sensual against his palm, and at the same time his scalp experienced new, hard to catalogue, sensations.

'Easy to care for,' said Caroline stroking Luca's hair. 'Now do you want to come up and see it? Come and see your new head.'

'Sure.'

'Then I can drive you home. I can get a look at this new Hotel Complex your family are building.'

'We're calling it a pension. Pension Lazlo, which is my dad's real name,' said Luca.

'Won't that upset the locals?'

'The locals are hardly likely to be customers of ours.'

On the drive, Luca kept getting images of Caroline's lithe legs encased now in denim but oh so close. He found it easier to sit sideways. Caroline had already informed him that the seat was stuck in that position due to Mila. On a rough stretch of road, he was sure he saw Caroline's breasts jiggle and desire filled him like an ache. He was stuck facing and close to Caroline as she dragged and pushed the dash mounted gear lever. The proximity of the roof forced Luca to look down in the lap of the driver. Her smell filled his senses and was mixed now with the smell of the lotions she had applied to his head. Luca longed for home and perked up when he saw familiar sights and then the Pension itself.

Caroline engaged him in some banter and Luca promised her a grand tour but when they had opened for business.

'When I need my next haircut.'

'I was hoping for sooner than that.'

****

Luca rushed into the bathroom and looked at his hair. It was short. He heard the sound of his family in the kitchen and decided he could not face them just at that moment. His nerves could not stand it. It was nearly time for the family to gather for the evening meal. Luca made the snap decision to eat in the Citadel. He located the shoebox with his cash and extracted 1000 francs in small bills, he might get the chance to do some money changing tonight. Then he padded to the office which was very close to the kitchen and saw his father's back as he slipped out of the office door and went the long way round to the equipment shed where he kept his bike.

****

'I'm Luca Moro. The *grandson* of a pig farmer.'

'Don't be ridiculous, Luca,' said Murat. 'Your family is undertaking the largest construction in these parts since the war. Are you trying to be funny?'

The housekeeper had shown Luca to Murat's study. Here Murat busied himself while he made Luca wait. Double doors faced out to the courtyard. Sylvie was making faces at Luca from behind the billowing curtains. Murat folded the Paris broadsheet noisily. It was when he had finished this charade that Luca spoke. Murat was sitting stiffly, as if not to put creases in his fine white shirt. The cravat at Murat's neck was black and red paisley and teamed with his well-tailored black trousers. He presented as relaxed and failed miserably. Murat wore clothes like a uniform.

'No, sir, not funny. Your daughter instructed me to say that.'

The study was decorated to impress. It had a calculated air of nonchalance. From the latest gadgets, flocked and busy wallpaper, to the Louis XIII desk. A desk lamp illuminated its allotted space on desk and objects were arranged for their appearance rather than any practical consideration. Luca felt that he could enter this study in a year's time and the desktop would be arranged in the same way.

'Come out, Sylvie; don't hide,' said Murat. 'She actually said *son of a pig farmer*. As she is hiding behind the French doors, I thought I would take this opportunity to correct her mistake.'

Luca knew displays of abject wealth when he saw it. He would have loved to have picked Murat's mind on matters financial, but something told Luca this was not the time. He had in the past sold American dollars to Dimitri but he considered this avenue of transaction closed since the work on Pension Lazlo had begun. Dimitri offered 300% if the notes were clean and unmarked, Luca also considered this avenue of transaction illegal. The shoebox of money in his wardrobe cannily disguised with all the other shoeboxes full of shoes, contained about US$7,800. Luca had not thought what to do with them since he had, for the moment, shelved his plans to escape.

'Look Papa he's cut his hair. I sit next to this giant in class. Papa, this is Luca Moro.'

'What are you children doing this evening?' asked Murat.

'We are going to the Citadel de Bonifacio, sir.'

'Don't call him sir; his name is Fabien,' said Sylvie.

'What time will you be home?'

'10.30, M Murat,' said Luca rather formally.

'Fabien!' interjected Sylvie.

'Sylvie! This boy is showing some manners,' Murat addressed his daughter Luca noticed, without turning.

'How are Victor and Clara?'

'Well, thank you, sir. When the construction is complete, they are retiring - If you can call looking after my great grandmother retiring.'

'I asked him, if he were to sell, to name his price.'

'So did Dimitri.'

'Ah! Dimitri, the moneychanger.' Murat said this in a distracted kind of way, as if his mind was already making the necessary fiscal adjustments to his investment strategies. This was another annoying little trait adults had.

Luca shrugged his shoulders, revealing the bulk and swell of muscle. Sylvie pulled a face at the back of her father's head. The talk of money bored her.

'Go! Have fun.' Fabien handed Sylvie a five hundred-franc note from a billfold of the softest ebony hide.

'Bye, Papa.'

'Goodbye, sir.'

Sylvie kissed her father's coiffed head. She left a pink outline of her lips on the white hair.

Luca felt rather than saw Murat's mind switch up a gear. Behind the doors Sylvie ran and broke into a laugh.

'It's his hairspray - it reacts with my lipstick. His tart is coming down from Nice tonight. That's why he wanted to know what time we would be back. He usually insists I'm back by 9.30 on a weeknight.'

The local use of the French word, tart still meant prostitute in Bonifacio.

'Want to walk?' asked Luca looking of the statuary of the courtyard. He did not want Sylvie to see him colour.

'You've had your hair cut.' It was a statement. But she chose the moment to mention Luca's hair when she was close enough to touch it. For Sylvie this meant reaching up but she squealed as her hand felt the blunt texture. 'I love it.'

Luca was still getting used to the feel of cool wind around his ears.

'We could have Saunders drive us. What do you think?' enthused Sylvie.

Luca had never been in a Bentley.

'Or if we stay out later than 11.00 Papa is bound to send the car.'

The click of Sylvie's sandals echoed off the black shiny cobbles, that Luca recognised belonged to a century of iron-clad wheels and hooves.

The yellow glow of the garage door cut a rectangle in the ivy-clad wall. It was a motor garage now but it was once a fine stable. The rumour was this house was brought stone by stone from another place. Luca longed to take it all in but Sylvie skipped ahead; she was tonight skittish and self-absorbed. Saunders had heard them. It was a still night; the courtyard trapped all the sound and made them its own.

'Your father has given me the evening off, Mlle Sylvie.' Saunders said with regard to what Sylvie had said. Saunders stood and wiped a dipstick on a rag. Bending, he lined it up deep within the engine.

Saunders' voice startled Sylvie. Sylvie flinched and tried to hide it.

'He's probably going to do her in the car. Eh! Saunders.'

'It's his car Mlle Sylvie,' said Saunders, driving the dip-stick home.

'Will you drive us Saunders? Luca has never been in a Bentley, have you Luca?'

'Let Saunders enjoy his day off, Sylvie.'

'Don't be a peasant, Luca!'

'But I am a peasant.'

'What do you expect? What's all this business with 'air doors'? Any fool knows they are French doors.'

'They are French doors in every part of the world, but we are in Corsica.'

'We won't use the car Saunders. I will use the stroll to teach my provincial friend some etiquette.' Then she turned to Luca. 'But isn't this France?'

'If Corsica is left out of Frommer's, then we can call them air doors.' Luca said this for Saunders' benefit.

Saunders smiled at Luca and ducked inside the car to look in the glove box.

'I have a Frommer's, young Sir. Let's have a look,' said Saunders standing. Saunders busied himself with the index.

'Saunders, this is Luca,' said Sylvie.

'Hello, Luca. No, it's not here,' said Saunders. 'It shows it on the map but not in the index,'

'There is a tiny section in Fodors' said Luca, 'and it's lumped in with the Sardinian book, or the book on the Ligurian Coast. Lonely Planet is the best. They have a book dedicated to Corsica.'

'I'm hardly likely to be using it now, am I young Sir? This book was in the glove box when I took the job.'

'Come on Luca. Don't stand around talking to the hired help.'

'Goodnight, enjoy your evening off,' said Luca in English careful of his phrasing. He knew it would have Australian notes to it, which, to the uninitiated, can sound like East London.

'*Bonne nuit*, Luca,' said Saunders.

'Bonne nuit,' said Luca. Impressed. He turned and captured the full blast of Sylvie's pout.

'Is that Chanel Number 5,' asked Luca, sensing that he ought to turn the conversation to Sylvie.

'Well! Luca, you astound me.'

'What astounds you, exactly?'

'You talk about air doors one minute and travel guides the next, and you engage the hired help in conversation. Then you floor me by naming my perfume. Where do you learn all this?' asked Sylvie.

'Well, I'm not used to *hired help*. In fact, when we run the pension, we will be the hired help.'

'Not that, the other. Perfume. Tell me where a farm kid comes up with Chanel number 5.

'Not from books, that's for sure.'

'How do you know then?'

'I have the sort of mind that collates things,' said Luca.

'It collates trivia.'

'Give me your definition of trivia.'

'Useless information.'

'Until *that* trivia is useful, as with the perfume just now. Shall I give you an example?'

'Please do,' said Sylvie, turning a smile on for good measure.

'Have you read the book, The Great Gatsby?'

'I've seen the movie on Encore.'

'Well, it's a classic, F. Scott Fitzgerald. I was reading it and met an American, a student. He had read it also. I was confused at the use of the small 'f' in the word french doors. I had used a small 'f' and been marked down for it by Garrod.'

'Garrod the ramrod.'

'I thought it was a mistake, a very small one, but a mistake none-the-less. I would seem that a small 'f' is used to mark the almost universal acceptance that these types of doors are called french doors. The Americans popularise all things French; they have a love affair with France.'

'I know! I can smell Juicy Fruit some mornings before I dress.'

'Can you?'

'Yes, and we play a game, where we pretend not to understand their French. Or English.'

They played the same game in Corsica, but Luca only participated if they were extremely rude or, the occasional beefy Fraulein who turned up with an Italian phrase book. Every summer would release a fresh clutch of irascible foreigners who believed that the whole world spoke English if you spoke loudly enough and slowly enough. Corsica beckoned also to the geographically inept. And history: history was a can of worms.

'Yes, we have a little fun with the tourists, except we can pretend not to understand far more languages.'

'They are obsessed, no! The Americans are obsessed with France and Paris.'

'Do you know what the Italians say?' said Luca keeping his voice light.

'What?'

'That Napoleon missed out on being an Italian by just one year; now that's just plain rude. They would not let us have self-rule and gave us away - to the French. It was a matter of distance and effort.'

Sylvie's expression told Luca she cared little for history.

'Well, getting back to The Great Gatsby,' said Luca 'it's about an American who is a fake, a sham. The book, being one of my father's, was in English and I thought small 'f' french doors was a subtle clue. Air doors, well, that's just the local name for the doors you open when it's hot and there is an ocean or a gully breeze. For sleeping you know? It was because of F. Scott Fitzgerald that I used a small 'f'; he influenced me.'

'How come you know so much about Coco Chanel?'

'Tourists once more. As for the perfume, it's the one my mother wears. I have a memory for these things.'

'She wears Chanel No. 5? How do you know this?'

'I observe, I watch, I listen. It is one of the truly true things I know about her.'

'Truly true?'

'The different versions of why she left don't add up. I have been spared. Nothing is true unless you find out for yourself,' said Luca.

'You don't speak like any kid I know, Luca,' Sylvie said,' And that's the truth.'

'The truth.'

'That's because I spend most of my time with adults. Chanel No. 5 is not a perfume for teenagers; it is an evergreen. Yet it sits well on you.'

'*Touche!*'

'Why not *Rive Gauche*, or one of the others like *Youth Dew*?'

'This is amazing, Luca. The Chanel was a gift from my father, but how do you know such things?'

'The tourists. They are relaxed, happy to talk. There was a photographic shoot one day in the Citadel. I offered my services as translator.'

'Have you considered modelling?'

'No! Who would I model for?' scoffed Luca.

'You have very beautiful green eyes.'

Luca smiled.

'Anything but hair products.' Sylvie was flirting with him and Luca was beginning to see it worked both ways.

'You'd have to get away from here first.' It was a challenge. The locals hated Sylvie; she hated the locals. Luca had to declare his allegiance.

'I am staying, thank you! I have the money saved up. I was going to run away. But I want to see what happens at Pension Lazlo.'

They had been walking toward the Old Town. On a tall sliver of land with the sea on one side and the clear calm azure sound on the other; in summer they made traffic one way there was one road in and one road out. The Americans, with their Disney World, had the hardest time coming to grips with Bonifacio. This was a real town. This was not a theme park; people lived here and had done for 8,000 years. With its magical and exquisite properties, Luca could understand the American dilemma. Bonifacio might have been a product of the same imagination that conjured up gingerbread cottage in the woods or seven dwarfs. Nursery rhymes for Luca were all set in Bonifacio. It was his stuff of dreams.

The road curled around on itself. Luca knew to stay on the outside of the curve as traffic approached the blind bend. At the top of the rise, where the road levelled out, the marina came into view. Luca guided Sylvie with his hand, he knew the light reflected in the water could take a visitor's breath away. Luca wanted to see his city with fresh eyes. He wanted Bonifacio to work on the pit of Sylvie's stomach, the way a toss of her hair in class worked on him. A small truck sounded its horn, its engine labouring hard, its driver finding a lower gear. The headlights picked out a yellow sign that had been obliterated with shotgun pellets.

'Look at that! Why do they shoot road signs, Luca?'

They pressed into the rock bank for safety and to allow the driver the use of the narrow road.

'They are editing them; only the top half is shot out. See! Only the French.'

Sylvie examined the sign as the synchromesh whine rose another pitch. The bottom sign in Corsu displayed the silvery tones of reflected moonlight, yellow and black. Little did she know she had her back to one of the most breathtaking sights in southern Europe?

'Why would they do this, Luca?'

'Nothing must infect the *Nomi corsi*.'

'But we are in France. I may never understand.'

Luca dusted himself off. Another car was working hard at the hairpin. The tyres protested under the confidence of an experienced driver. As the headlights picked out Sylvie and Luca, the engine note died.

'Why can't they just leave the French,' lamented Sylvie. 'It would make life so much easier if they just left the French.'

It was Dernavern's Fiat.

'Want a lift?' asked Dernavern in French.

'Sure!' said Sylvie. 'Are you going to the Citadel?'

'Yeah, jump in.'

'Do you see my point, Luca? French is the international language.' Then, turning to Dernavern, 'Your accent - you're from Paris?' asked Sylvie.

Sylvie squeezed into the back of the tiny car and sat facing away from the priceless vista. Luca let the seat drop and got in beside Dernavern.

'From Clichy,' said Dernavern over his shoulder as Sylvie was arranging her skirts.

'But I went to school in Lile.'

'We live in Issy les Moulineaux' said Sylvie.

'I know, I've been to a reception there,' said Dernavern.

Sylvie leaned forward from the back seat to get a look at Dernavern.

'No! I don't remember you.'

'You must, I sneaked you half a bottle of champagne.'

'Oh, that was you! You came with Contessa Rosalinda Medici.'

'I did?'

'You did.'

The Fiat peaked at 85 kilometres an hour. Dernavern coaxed every little kilowatt from the tiny engine with the skill of a rally driver and then gave more of his attention to his back seat passenger than the road. The little red beetle shape car clanked and rattled in eager pursuit of the labouring truck. There was no time for pique. There was no time for claustrophobia. Terror sounded like a heartbeat. Even Dernavern would not attempt to pass until the Avenue Sylvere Bohn. Duff, duff, duff, the engine note sounded earnest and longed for another gear. But Luca knew from the position of the gearshift that there were none. Luca gripped a leather strap that hung from the roof of the car.

'The rule of thumb is, any flat land is occupied by humans - everything else by goats,' said Dernavern to the rear vision mirror. They caught up with the labouring truck. Sylvie leaned forward; she seemed mesmerised by its taillights and waiting for Dernavern to attempt to pass. A suicidal move, even in daylight and with a more powerful car.

Dernavern slowed behind the truck and Luca relaxed his grip on the strap but the truck and Dernavern had robbed Sylvie of her first glimpse of the marina at night. This was the reason that Luca had wanted to walk to the old town.

'Do you know they shoot out road signs here? We were just looking at the sign just back there – hey! Mr. Gloomy pants what did it say?'

'Slow down!' said Luca.

They had arrived. Safely. The only danger now came from the crush of the crowd. The Fiat sat squarely in the way at the Rue St Erasme. Tourists and locals alike parted and flowed past the car like water round a stone. Then, with a bark from the exhaust and a squeal of tyres Dernavern was gone

'He was in a hurry?'

'No, that's just the way he drives.'

'How do you know him?'

'Dernavern is an artist but he is working at the site painting signs and doing general painting.'

'I can't remember him but he left Contessa Medici at Mama's, she was furious.'

Sylvie thrust a bag at Luca. Not the large quilted one from this afternoon, but a small evening one. A Fendi. Sylvie fussed with her hair, a few deft twists and it was up in an evening style. Then she slipped a strap over one shoulder.

'Back in two ticks.'

Where she went Luca never saw but she returned in a few minutes with a bottle of Absolut vodka. She materialised at his shoulder and laid her cheek playfully on Luca's bare arm.

'You're so tall. I was going to sneak up on you and blow on your neck.'

'Why?'

'Because it gives me goose bumps. Do you get goose bumps, Luca?'

'Goose flesh, why yes, doesn't everyone? Where did you get the Vodka?'

'Don't be boorish, Luca. Get some coke and some glasses.'

'Where will you wait?'

'How about here?'

'Good idea! I'll sit at the top of one of the flights of stairs. Only tourists bother to climb them.'

Luca threaded his way through the evening crowd. Except for the few families that lived here, Luca was one of the few people who bothered to come into the town in the winter. Oddly he came here to be alone. When the citadel was quiet and eerie Luca became acquainted with every loose stone and patch of moss. With those that lived here safely in front of their kitchen grates, Luca walked the on the same warm stones that would echo to the throng of 30,000 feet in a single day and feel that he was the last soul on earth. In some quarters, passageways not more than a span wide had buildings conspiring to crowd out a cobalt sky. This was the time to look up at the cracked paint and the imperfect masonry. In The Season this same activity would cause you to collide with a perspiring German whose eye was distracted in a viewfinder, or find yourself having to wait or hurry as amateur photographers composed their heart melting memory. Their babble and their tumult could dull the senses to the fact that you were framed between two of the most beautiful stretches of water in southern Europe. When it was quiet, with only the wind as his witness, Luca imagined himself to be on top of the world. It would not be this quiet again until November and Luca dodged the slower moving tourists lest he be stopped and asked to take someone's photograph. Tonight, there was just enough activity to mask the ever-present wind. He saw the freshly sluiced canopy of The Cafe Bonaparte and remembered they sold Coke in cups.

'Two Cokes please.'

'Luca, you honour us with your presence!'

'Pardon?'

'You don't remember me?'

'Remember you? No! I'm sorry.'

'Your grandfather laid me off.'

'Did he? You must have been a casual. I don't remember your face.'

'I was a meat process worker. That will be 28 F.'

'That's a bit steep for two cokes.'

'You can afford it.'

Luca handed over a fifty franc note.

'I hear that you have the first franc that you ever earned. I am Jean Luc. Say hi to Victor for me.'

Jean Luc sauntered over to the cash register. He held up the 50 and checked the watermark. He extracted the change as slowly as he could. Luca remembered a time when Victor was cited for his good farming methods, held up as an example of efficient farm management. It was a strongly if locally held belief that too much success is not a good thing. Larry had warned him that things would get worse after they opened the doors for business.

Jean Luc held the change just out of Luca's reach. 'Go on! What's its serial number?'

'Serial number?'

'On the first frank that you ever earned?'

Luca grabbed at the change, his height a real advantage over Jean Luc who was short dark and swarthy, a typical Corse.

'Where is my tip, Luca?'

'Here's one - be good to your mother.'

'Shame you can't heed your own advice.'

'If I were to put these Cokes down, Jean Luc, I might slop some. Who do you suppose would have to mop it up?'

'Fuck off home, Luca Moro; you were born in the wrong town.'

Other patrons in the queue sent up a small murmur.

'And you were born in the wrong century, mop boy. I bet you get a kick out of wearing that pretty apron; keep it on at home do you? You only got to work for us when we made smallgoods: do you know why?'

'Because the du Plessiers are mean with money?'

'No because you are not fit to keep company with swine.'

'The two-legged kind or four?' said Jean Luc.

A crowd was forming so Luca slopped some Coke as he dodged his way to the door. He looked for Sylvie in the throng. She had made some friends with a young Dutch couple. The three of them were swigging from coke cans. Luca hated that Jean Luc got the last word. He thought his own jibe about being from the wrong century, a little too subtle for Jean Luc, whose family had owned the land where The Café Bonaparte stood for six centuries, which only proved you did not need refinement or good looks to own real estate. Luca recalled a matter of Jean Luc and some missing tools.

'What kept you?'

'I had the pleasure of meeting up with an employee we laid off last year. These are the dearest Cokes in Christendom but I thought it would be good to use the cups.'

'Never mind, Luca, meet Helli and Corny.'

'Hi.'

'How are you,' said Corny in English. 'Shit, man, how tall are you?'

'One ninety two'

How old are you?'

'Fourteen.'

Sylvie kicked Luca in the shin. The Dutch couple seemed at ease with each other and like so many Northern Europeans had a street savvy that come early to those that live in a big city.

'Wow! Do you play basketball?' asked Corny.

'I did with my friend, Roald Pound from Chicago.'

'He was a black man, yes?' said Corny.

'Yes - and he had his own half-court at home.'

'At home in America?'

'No, at home in Porto Vecchio. His father worked in Corse, the capital. I think travelling 55 kilometres is common in America,' said Luca.

'A flat 55 kilometres, yes!'

Time travelled slowly in these parts, as, at times, did the traffic. It was still more of a custom to talk of travel in terms of time lapsed, rather than distance covered.

'Yes, people get quite a shock at the topography of our little but mountainous island. They think it will be a hoot to live in an old town and are not prepared for rock falls and stray goats.'

'Topography?' Sylvie almost shrieked. 'Is that a Genoese word, are you showing off, or using a hybrid sentence; Garrod will give you a detention,' said Sylvie in French.

This was not uncommon in Luca's experience; Sylvie obviously knew enough English to keep pace but answered in French. It happened on a daily basis in his home and was probably the reason he got such low marks in composition and any subject that involved writing.

'Topography is a word we understand. It is a Greek word - I think,' said Helli.

'Holland has no Top Og Graphy; it is very flat, yes!' said Corny springing to Luca's defence. 'As flat as Belgium but then Belgium appears flatter - do you know why?'

'Why?' Asked Luca but Sylvie already looked bored.

'Belgians.'

Tension killed Corny's joke.

'Greek is one of the ancient languages,' said Helli, quickly.

'I thought French was,' said Sylvie. 'The whole world spoke French at some point.'

'No Greek and Latin. The building blocks for all European languages. Latin - or a form of it - is spoken here and no-where else.' Helli felt the chilly pout from Sylvie.

Helli and Corny decided to move on, brandishing a desire to see the sights and soak up the *topography.*

'You scared them off!' exclaimed Sylvie

'They were quite young; they might be back.'

'Don't you know anything? Dutch people always have drugs.'

'Drugs?' said Luca, louder than he meant too.

'It's legal in their country.'

'Were you hoping to score some drugs?'

'Sometimes Luca, you are so thick.'

'What do you want drugs for? You have the Vodka.'

'And why did you have to tell them you were 14?'

'Why did you mention Garrod and detention?'

Night fell and the wind dropped to a land breeze, but as Bonifacio is on its own private finger of land, it became immune to some of the normal night sounds. The marina was lit up like a fairytale and it should have worked its magic on Sylvie - most people find Bonifacio irresistible. Sylvie had left with some German boys for whom Luca had expressed a dislike. Luca not liking them elevated them to the status of irresistible.

Luca sat alone on the wall long after the ache of defeat had entered his bones. Tourists took one look at his demeanour, his long sour face, and moved on. It was close to midnight as he embarked on the long walk home.

Beyond the lights of the Old Town, the undulating black-top flowed like a velvet ribbon. A black macadam gash in the unforgiving terrain. Sometimes Luca thought the road looked out of place because, particularly in the morning, the landscape looked like the first morning of the world. A brush creaked, groaned and squeaked with familiar night sounds. Rats possibly - or a lone bachelor boar, rare in these parts but some rouges had learned to scavenge. Luca had made this journey many times. A bike annihilated distance but then you did not get a chance to absorb the evening sounds with wind in your ears.

Luca was bilious with disgust, vodka and gassy Coke. He was trying to align his mood with the beauty of the night. Letting his woes evaporate when he heard an unfamiliar sound. He heard the Bentley long before he saw it. Other cars worked hard at the incline; the Bentley made a noise like an efficient vacuum cleaner. It sucked up the distance from Villa Murat to Bonifacio. The engine note died as the headlights picked out Luca.

'Get in,' said Saunders in English.

'But I am heading that way.'

'It is hard to turn a big car round on a little road - get in.'

Saunders was dressed in his pyjama's mulberry with latte piping, a crest of some sort on the breast pocket. Luca slid into the back seat and leaned forward on the back of the passenger seat. His elbows sunk into sumptuous leather.

'When did Mlle Sylvie piss off?' said Saunders over his shoulder.

'How do you know she pissed off? I might have left her in the Citadel?'

Saunders let two kilometres act as his reply.

'Will I find her drunk or stoned? - Or both?'

Luca liked the direct, no-nonsense approach of the Englishman.

'She bought a bottle of vodka. She left with some German lads about ten.'

A mobile phone chirped. 'Hello - right - ten minutes - he's with me,' said Saunders in French and snapped the phone shut. 'The police have brought Sylvie home.'

Luca let out a long sigh and sat back in the green leather. 'Just between you and me Saunders, I was not looking forward to the drive home with her. She can be a little difficult.'

'Is that why you waited so long in Bonifacio? You wanted to bring her home.'

'Sort of.'

Luca felt suddenly fatigued.

'Your grandmother is anxious that you return home. She is waiting up. I gather that there is no mother.'

'No.'

'Won't your father be worried?'

'No, I am sometimes out this late, but not on a school night,' said Luca.

'Will he have missed you - eventually?'

'No.'

'He wouldn't miss you?'

'No, when Dad shuts his door that's it. I sometimes find him asleep at his desk, his head on the keyboard.'

'Doing what, exactly?'

'Writing.'

'What sort of things does he write?'

'Writings, scratching and journals,' said Luca getting interested. 'Why?'

'Would I have read anything by him?'

'He sends articles and stories away all the time and when he gets a cheque he is elated for a while and then depressed that the amount is so small.'

'He writes in English?'

'That's his only language, Saunders.'

'I have noticed a hostility – and because I am in service to a Frenchman – well let's just say I had an interesting conversation with a colourful gentleman who claimed to be part of *The Family.*'

'Did you? What did they want from you Saunders?'

'I gather he was looking to sign me up in a membership, as part of the insurrection.'

'Wow Saunders! not many people claim to have spoken to *The Family*, not ones that are still breathing anyway.'

Luca was suddenly no longer tired.

'In every city,' Saunders began, he seemed to be choosing his words carefully, 'in every city there is a certain element. I have driven for some interesting types and in the army too. I told this gentleman, who represented the interests of *The Family*, that I worked for a couple of brothers in London - to whom M. Murat owed money. I was a sort of *insurance*. He seemed to understand that sort of thing. Now don't go losing me my job, I was in a tight situation.'

Luca found after a few sentences he acquired the accent of the person he was speaking to - Saunders had a Home Counties accent. Perhaps it was the excitement.

'Why, if he is President of the bank does Murat live in Corsica?' Luca used the English word for Corsica and in the confines of the car Luca could have passed for a Londoner.

'I'm just a driver, Master Luca. I don't ask too many questions.'

Saunders drove in silence. Luca noticed they were close to the Old Town. Saunders eased the big car around the roundabout, he was indicating but earned some blasts on the horn from other drivers and riders of mopeds that were as much to do with youth and high spirits and envy as much of pique. Now Luca was heading back the right way and the road was empty before them. It opened up invitingly. Saunders accelerated the car with a silent gut-sucking energy and Luca shed his mood that had descended on him while he was in the little Fiat on the journey into Bonifacio. Two impromptu car trips in the one evening did more to transport Luca's mood than his newly shorn physical self. He ran his hand over his jaw and then over his new head. He liked the feel. A thought came to Luca.

'My Dad wrote a TV play perhaps you saw it?'

'What was it called?'

'It was for the BBC. It never aired here. I don't know.'

Somehow the back of the Bentley seemed like the right place for a long shot. 'It was about a man who rushes at his career,' said Luca, 'on the stage, film and TV and finds his best role as a father. I read a draft and he asked my opinion on certain things. Kids things. It was called 'Segues for Life' on Channel Four - very good too.'

Luca knew Saunders would have seen it.

'Dad had the opportunity to go to London and produce it.'

'But he didn't go?' Asked Saunders.

'No. I think he did not trust himself to come back.'

This was bold for the grandson of Victor du Plessier to air family business in public. Perhaps it was the plush opulence. Luca's comment was calculated to produce silence and he filled the void with one of his theories. *Larry did not want to abandon me a second time.*

One of Luca's standard replies was always something to do with school. Mention school and adults shut up straight away. Privately Luca's beliefs fluctuated - his father was a fool one-day and a martyr the next. Sometimes Luca daydreamed that he lived with Clara and Victor alone and sometimes Larry returned to Australia and sent for Luca when he had made his fortune. The idea for Pension Lazlo came out of Larry's one TV success. His accepted drama paid so little Victor stepped in. He floated the idea of Pension Lazlo. He saved the day and announced his retirement plans at the same time. The Bear leaving a plastic kettle on the Aga when she did; her timing was impeccable.

When they were back in the inky blackness of the night away from the light of the city, Saunders broke the silence.

'She's much better when her parents aren't fighting. She's a sweet girl really.'

They had been talking about everything but Sylvie; now Luca snapped his mind around to her now. He wanted to know more but did not know how to frame the question or where to begin. He suspected Saunders was about to tell him something important. Luca had not only resurrected the evening he had made a new ally.

'Her mother has foisted young Sylvie on her father as a sort of punishment for him.'

'He has a tart in Nice – I know.'

'How do you know Master Luca?'

Luca told of the episode where Sylvie planted some lipstick on her father's head. 'Call me Luca. And I can't get my head around Saunders. What do I call you?'

'Call me Saunders in the presence of M. Murat and at other times call me Cyril. That is my given name.'

'Cyril, it is. But is that likely. Me and Sylvie?'

'I happen to know that M. Murat would like Sylvie to get a little summer job. She does not speak the local language, she speaks French and a little English; somehow, I can't see her waiting tables, can you? No one will hold tonight against you. In fact, M. Murat hoped you would be a good influence on Sylvie.'

'A good influence how?' asked Luca.

'M. Murat has asked your grandfather if Sylvie can get work at Pension Lazlo when it opens.'

Luca was silent for the last few kilometres. He let his hand caress the sumptuous interior redolent of England and Empire. 'What as?'

'I'm sorry, Master Luca?' Saunders had cognitively moved on.

'What as? What would Sylvie be expected to do?'

'That, sir, is a very good question. A very good question indeed. Look here is your grandma waiting up for you.'

'She is an owl, Cyril.'

'A what young sir?'

'An owl - nocturnal - in French. Of the night.'

'As it is in English. It's funny how so many of our words are the same as yours.'

'Do you remember William the Conqueror?' asked Luca.

'Battle of Hastings, 1066. Remember it from history, remember it well.'

'He was a Frenchman.'

'Well I never!'

'French is strongly influenced by Latin and Latin is the closest thing to Genoese.'

'The things you learn. No! Sit there; let's do things right.' Saunders made a point of getting out of the car and opening the door for Luca.

'Thank you, Saunders.'

'Will that be all, Master Luca?'

'Yes! Thank you, Saunders.'

'Goodnight, young sir. Goodnight.'

Luca smiled at Clara. The diversion had been largely for her benefit.

'Luca what have you done to your hair?'

'I had it cut this afternoon.'

Clara had on her shawl. Wrapped around her and held by her hand at her throat. She touched his hair, his head. 'It's so short Luca.'

The Bentley crunched slowly out of the driveway. 'A chauffeur in his pyjamas?' Clara shook her head.

'It is his night off.'

'This is not good, Luca; a school night - and it's after midnight.'

The late part of the evening was Clara and Luca's time alone. His quip to Saunders about being an owl was merely repeating words used by Clara. Luca was often up this late but Clara was perplexed and Luca felt he was about to find out why.

'Who is this Sylvie and why does she cause so much trouble?'

'She is a new girl in my class from Paris.'

'Her father wants us to employ her here at the pension.'

'What do you think Nonna?'

'I have never met the girl. She is from a good family and her father is our banker. Your father is the one to make the decision. He will run this place until you are 18.'

This was a surprise to Luca. Things had happened while he was in the Old Town with Sylvie.

'We will discuss it and Victor will tell us what he has decided,' said Luca, trying to make a joke.

Clara was mortified; it showed in her fine Italian face. 'Why do you say that, Luca?'

'It is the way it is,' said Luca, sounding rather abrupt.

'The way it was,' snapped Clara. 'This is no longer a pig farm, Luca.'

Luca realised he had spoken harshly to his grandmother. 'Do you miss the pigs, Nonna?' he said after a while

'I do - give it time Luca. Never make plans on a saddened heart.'

'I'm not sad Nonna, I was sad before but Saunders - Cyril – he cheered me up.'

'It is my heart that is sad Luca.'

There would be no evening chat, no practicing his Italian, no stories from Clara's childhood. Luca saw that. It was with a heavy heart that Luca prepared for bed. He was glad that Victor had not waited up for him. Victor could be surly. Luca heard steps outside his door. He turned as noisily as one can turn to announce his wakefulness. The crack in the door widened to a wedge and Clara padded in. Luca sat up.

'Nonna?'

'We thought - I thought we had lost you. I thought this was a taste of what was to come. I thought you would run away like your mother. Dernavern told us he dropped you and this girl into town and you were not comfortable. He told some of the family history. Luca she is the daughter of our financier and breaks hearts. Don't have anything to do with this girl.'

Luca sat up. 'Run away! Who told you I was thinking of running away?' Luca thought his latest hiding place was the best yet. He was sure no one had found his cash.

'Luca, my beautiful child; every day you earn 130, 150 francs at the Citadel as guide or translator. You never spent a centime. Not like a normal child. What had you planned to do with all that money - one thing - to escape? You are the glue that holds this family together, Luca. Don't go.'

'I don't need to go now Nonna, now Europe will come to me.'

Clara shrieked with laughter one short outburst and she clamped her hand to her mouth, the rest of the family would be sleeping.

'Nonna! Are you spying on me?'

'Spying on you, how?'

'Dernavern, did you send him?'

'No – he cares for you. I think you have made a friend. He told us about your haircut and we thought it strange that you should go off like that. I like him.'

'Nonna?' the tone of Luca's voice forecast the proportions of his question.

'Yes, Luca.'

'Did I ever miss my mother?'

'No,' Clara sat on Luca's bed, 'you were a small child; she was a distant mother. We gave her time, space. Sometimes it is like this after the birth of a baby, one year, two years - nothing. You were a daddy's boy. And then she was gone. You have never asked before. Why now?'

'I don't know. It's been a long day. Goodnight, Nonna.'

Clara ruffled Luca's head and seemed to like what she felt. 'We meet as in clouds.'

'We meet as in clouds, Nonna.'

The strange intimacy of Clara's words dwelled on the adolescent's mind and forestalled sleep. It was delivered in Clara's native Sardinian dialect and was an exchange usually reserved for lovers. It meant that feelings were greater than earthly held ones and often was said about a loved-one who had died.

Luca was not alone long - Larry was the next to visit his son at this late hour.

'G'day.'

'G'day, Dad.'

'You had a date.' It was a statement but Larry had never quite lost the habit of putting the infliction on the end of everything he said, making it a question. A characteristic Luca had noted in other Australians.

'Yeah!'

'Why didn't you say something?'

'I don't know.'

'It's not like you, Luca.'

Luca shrugged in the darkness. Some of that meaning must have conveyed somehow in the darkness. Larry was gathering himself and when he spoke, he was using what Luca called his fatherly voice. 'I thought you'd tell us and we'd talk.'

'We've had that talk, Dad.'

Indeed, they had. Larry was concerned that a tourist might take a shine to young Luca. The blunt way Larry described it, Luca wondered had Larry had casual sex with a horny tourist. There was a certain element of tourist that acted differently when abroad. The English girls forgot to pack their morals. Some girls in Luca's class spent the summers in the hills.

'Were you nervous?' asked Larry

'Sort of.'

'Well, that's good because I was.'

'*You* were?'

'I even had a couple of nips of whiskey.' Luca could smell it. His father drank beer at the Carriage Bar but kept a bottle of whiskey at home for visitors and he and Victor occasionally had a nip.

'Why were you nervous?' asked Luca stifling a yawn.

'It's just something every parent...'

'Dreads?'

'Not exactly. You can never be ready for it. It's inevitable but it still sneaks up on you.' After a while it was evident that Larry was not going to speak again.

'Goodnight, Dad.'

'I just wish your mother was here.'

'What?' Now Luca was really confused.

'I just hope I have been *everything* for you.'

Luca tried very hard to get an image of his mother.

'Goodnight, Son.'

Nothing came to him but it had been one hell of a day.

'Goodnight, dad,' said Luca sounding vague and distracted.

Chapter Five

Millionaires in Training

'Luca, telephone.' Mindful of the early hour, Larry brought the phone to Luca's bedroom.

'Hello,' said Luca rubbing his eyes.

'You still in bed, dozy dork?' said Roald.

'Roald! You length of Yankee camel piss. How the hell are you?' Luca looked at the clock, it was 7.30 and he'd slept in.

'Better than you, snot-for-brains. Guess what?'

'What! You rabid tomcat's gonad.'

'Gonad? Left or right?'

Luca got out of bed and shut his bedroom door. Any conversation with Roald departed from the path of decency and descended smut's wide trail rapidly. After the night's sleep he had had, a little cussing would be therapeutic Luca felt. He got a glimpse of himself in the mirror, the short hair he could live with, he rubbed it as if to reassure himself, but after a date with Sylvie he could do without the red, tired eyes. Ribbing and teasing were bound to follow at school.

'Both? What? What possesses a snivelling reproductive organ like you to ring at this unearthly hour?'

'Unearthly hour? Letterman's not even on yet. I'm going to boarding school in England.'

'What?' Luca calculated it would be the day before in The States.

'Limeyland. Of chestnut trees and fair maidens, of cricket and white flannel'. Roald did lots of voices; The Upper-class Twit was one of them.

'I take it you like the idea,' said Luca.

'Like it? It's got to be better than this Gypsy style of schooling. I hear the food is fawfull!'

'Fawfull?'

'Fucking awful! But dad's pretty good with the allowance. I won't starve. The exchange rate works for me and with the costs of Trans-Atlantic flights, I might have to take my vacations on the continent.'

'The continent?' said Luca. Roald had hinted at this in his last phone call. He was trying to sell his father on the idea of offsetting the prohibitive cost of Trans-Atlantic air travel and those hard-earned dollars being put to better use in the mind expanding arena of continental travel for a young African American.

Roald would have just received Luca's letter about Pension Lazlo; Roald did not mention the letter, as he never sent any himself.

'Somewhere warm, seductive, wild. Lashings of history.'

'The melting pot of Europe,' said Luca.

'Culture, lashings of it, dear chap. Of course, I will need a guide and translator. A land that is ruggedly beautiful and beautifully rugged. Wild yet sensitive to a traveller's needs, a miniature continent perhaps?' Roald was a salesman.

'Azure seas? The seas, shades of azure not yet described in any language. Geographically diverse, culturally stimulating - did I say that?'

'Have you swallowed the guide book or something?' said Luca.

'No! It's good to hear your voice. How goes it anyway?'

'Fine! Well, you came up in conversation yesterday. Listen, Rolly, before I forget. What happened to your basketball hoop and backboard?'

'It's still there in the place Dad rented. The landlord is charging us storage. You could do me a huge favour and go and get it. This guy is a ball-breaker.'

'Consider it done.'

'Listen! Do you think you could clean it up and sell it for me? The Balkan's war is hotting up. Do you see many American servicemen?'

'Every day.'

'It's competition standard; it's not a toy. See if you can get two hundred for it.'

'Bucks?'

'Francs.'

'Sold!' Before sleep came to him last night, Luca had made some decisions.

'What! To you! You never buy anything. The young man with scorpions in his pockets. You had over 5 Gs in cash under your fucking floor boards.'

'I've changed my ways. I was saving for something, but now I'm not.'

'Wonder of wonders. If you buy it, I might have to take some of that money from you, in sporting wagers, dear chap. It's the way it is done, our finest hour. England expects... '

'Roald are you sitting down?'

'Sitting down. I'm lying down. Luca Moro spending money! Circle the date on the calendar. They will make it a national holiday, or something.'

'I had my hair cut really short and I went on a date last night.' Luca had tried to make his voice sound casual, but the line was awkward and silent.

'A tourist?' said Roald. 'It must be tourist. A bit early in the season, isn't it?'

'No! She is from Paris and has moved here with her dad.'

Luca told Roald of his date. Trying to make Sylvie sound feisty made her sound like a bitch. Trying to gloss over the bit about her going off with the German lads was calculated to make her sound wild and untamed. Luca was sounding like a dork and he knew it.

Then, an ocean and a sea away, Luca heard a TV go off. That is, the background noise dropped away. Luca got an image of his friend with a remote control in his hand. The line was silent for some time.

'Who are you and what have you done with Luca Moro's body?'

Luca tried to laugh it off. He could hear the alarm in his friend’s voice.

'She’s a babe.'

'She’d better be.'

'What do you mean?'

'I mean with your family starting the business, maybe this is not the time to get involved.'

'I sit next to her in class. She took your seat,' said Luca. 'It’s going to be hard to avoid her.'

Luca recounted the incident that led to detention. And Roald told him how he was going to knuckle down and try and get into MIT. 'Millionaires In Training,' said Roald confidently.

Luca wasn’t sure what MIT stood for but he was pretty sure his friend was making a joke. Luca had a habit of gathering the orphans and rejects. The Corte were so insular, all outsiders were shunned, friendships started in the womb or before. It was the way in Bonifacio.

'I won't be seeing her again. I think she's got herself grounded! She's mixed up though.'

'Oh, don't do it, Luca'

'Don't do what?'

'I dunno, try and be the big brother thing. Treat 'em mean and keep 'em keen. That's the way it is man.'

Roald's relationship theories were recycled from an older cousin. Who if Luca remembered had joined the navy at sixteen and brought great shame on the family the same year. Roald's claim to fame was his computer knowledge, or to use his own words – words he bandied about with pride *hacker,* and the way to get him to do something was to suggest it could not be done or it was ill advised. The words ACCESS DENIED, for Roald, was the point where it became interesting.

'It's good to hear your voice.'

'Hey! Do you still have my email address?' asked Roald.

'I do - somewhere. I'll write to you - snail mail.'

'Do that! And Luca?'

'Yeah!'

'Leave the Paris babe alone, Ok? For me.'

****

Luca did not feel like facing Dernavern this morning. The phone call had frittered away half an hour, he lingered over his breakfast and let sloth gobble up the rest of the morning. He cycled to school with fresh power in his legs. *Would Sylvie be there or not?*

As Luca locked his bike, he was aware that eyes were on him, at a safe distance and charged with intrigue. He kept his head low and his hand busy with the contents of his school bag. For once it was useful to be so unpopular, lack of familiarity kept curious questions behind hushed lips.

Sylvie was there at her desk and looking the very model of an earnest student.

'You're in a good mood,' said Sylvie.

The lesson was French History. The teacher, Vagnat, was always late. Garrod had sat them together in Genoese, so Luca took a chance and put his books next to Sylvie. She was facing forward; Luca walked round behind her and caught a whiff of her perfume again and climbed over the bench seat. Thus, he sat next to her without having to ask if he could. With some new looking books out and open, Sylvie had written her name on her exercise book. Her handwriting was strong, large and neat. A flush of envy ripped through Luca. No matter how he tried his handwriting was sloppy and forced.

'Yeah, I had a call from a friend this morning. The guy who used to sit here.'

'The American?'

'Yes, Roald Pound. It would have been yesterday there. He cheered me up.'

'What time did you get home last night?' asked Sylvie.

'At a quarter to one. You?'

'Twelve thirty. But in a police car. Someone connected to this school saw me and reported it.'

'Are you grounded?'

'What! You must be kidding. I can make Papa's life hell at home. He would rather me out of the house.'

'Saunders gave me a lift home and then I talked with my Nonna. She and I are always the last to go to bed.'

'Did you find the tart's panties in the car? Her cheap perfume? Did it linger?'

'No, ljst green leather and air freshener. I was practically home, more than half way, and Saunders drove me back to Bonifacio because he couldn't turn the car around.'

'Saunders was looking for me. Papa wanted him to get to me before the cops did.'

'Sylvie, what happened?'

'There was some dispute over the bill. The boys from Berlin left and then some plates got smashed.'

'Are you in deep shit?'

'Hardly! Papa is buying me a mobile phone. I am to ring Saunders if I get stuck. There was a language thing too. The rude little fuckers refused to speak French. They were pretending not to understand, yet asking me to keep my language down!' Sylvie said. 'I said, 'If you can't understand what I am saying; how do you know I am swearing?' That shut them up for a bit and then they tried to reason. The crowd were with me too - until I started breaking plates. Then I told them all to go and get fucked.'

'Larry has an appointment with your Papa this morning. I can't imagine this will go unmentioned,' said Luca.

'You're not fretting over this, are you?'

'No, but I missed painting and I prefer to be forewarned. The workmen will tease me. They will have heard by now I'm sure.'

'Missed painting? When?'

'This morning.'

'Before school?'

'Before school.'

'Who brings you your breakfast?'

Vagnat, who was big on entrances, swept into the room. He stood his coffee on the corner of the desk where it would go cold, and began to roll up his sleeves. Luca's answer would have to wait, as the lesson was about to begin.

Chapter Six

A gift with terms and conditions

'Now that takes care of the international transfers and credit card deposits,' Murat said. 'We treat traveller's cheques as cash and can convert any currencies for you, or deposit them at your bidding. Was there anything else?'

'We need to set up a trust account in accordance with the ATF Charter.' Larry said the words in English, so they came out backwards. He had to clarify things for Murat. *'The French Tourist Authority.'* The eyebrows came down.

'Forgive me! A trust account?'

'For deposits, advanced bookings. It is the law.'

'Forgive me, my knowledge is in international banking, one of our tellers will handle that for you. Please sit, stay. I will attend to this and we will speak of other business.'

Fabien Murat left Larry in the squat little velvet chair whose arms poked up at sharp angles. Larry felt these chairs were designed with *dis*-comfort in mind. He found himself wondering if discomfort was a design specification for visitors' chairs in a bank manager's office.

A door opened, not from the banking chamber, but from deep within the bowels of the bank.

'Coffee, sir?'

'Yes, please. Aren't you the assistant manager?'

'Yes, I am Paoli, Bertrand Paoli, delighted.'

They shook hands but Larry did not get a chance to rise.

'Has Murat got the assistant manager making coffees now?'

'Murat knows you speak no French or Genoese. The first teller and I are the only English speakers and, as you can see, she is busy.'

'Murat is President of the bank, is that right?'

'Correct.'

'I would have thought he was in greater demand in Paris.'

Paoli was scarcely able to conceal his glee as he said, 'Fabien Murat is in great demand in Paris. It is a domestic issue. He may choose to discuss this with you, he may not.'

Paoli, having dispensed his duties, seemed eager to get out of Murat's office. He left the office as if he had suddenly remembered urgent business. Larry tasted his coffee - it was bitter and hot. He was reaching for the sugar when Murat returned.

'It has begun, but for trust accounts we need to notify Paris. If you need to deposit any monies, here is a temporary deposit book for the interim.'

'Thank you,' said Larry.

'Ah! Coffee. I took the liberty of ordering coffee. Are you a tea drinker, Mr Moro?'

'Larry, and no, coffee it is - hot, sweet and strong.'

Larry spooned four sugars into his coffee and stirred it in tiny little circles. Murat's face was a mask of horror. Larry lifted the cup to his lips.

From the top drawer of his desk Fabien Murat produced four theatre tickets. 'Please accept these theatre tickets as a sign of good faith,' said Murat. 'They were given to me and I have to be in Nice that weekend.'

'Romeo and Juliet - thanks! On the 8th, that's a French National Holiday. We open for business on the 30th of April. We will be rushed off our feet.'

'Actually, there are four tickets. I was hoping to entice Sylvie to stay here on Corsica and give my staff the weekend off.'

Larry drained the last of his coffee.

'I was hoping to impose on you,' said Murat. 'A small job? She is, as they say, a pretty thing. Can you find her employment for that weekend?'

'Who?'

'My daughter.'

'Well, M. Murat, the place is mine in name alone. The du Plessiers have employed me as manager but I can't hold the licence. I can't take these tickets. I can't help your daughter or influence Victor's decision.'

'You can't hold the licence?'

'I am an Australian National, married to a local girl.'

'Nationality is not conferred on you as a spouse?'

'It would be in France,' said Larry leaning forward, 'but there are some special agricultural considerations and flat land is so rare, the French government passed laws prohibiting foreigners getting hold of large tracts of it.'

Murat sipped his coffee and Larry wished now he had waited. Spooning four sugars in made it cold and Larry had drunk it straight away.

'Indeed! Keep the tickets; I have no use for them. You will notice they claim the performance will be in the *Original Genoese*,' said Murat. 'Is that some sort of joke?'

'It is a strongly, if locally, held belief that Shakespeare spent his missing ten years in Italy. At least some of them.'

'I can't fault that logic: Two gentlemen of Verona.'

'The Merchant of Venice.'

'Julius Caesar.'

'The Rape of Lucrece.' Murat was warming to his subject. 'And In Romeo and Juliet the play opens with 'In Fair Verona, where we lay our scene, here they speak Corsu or Genoese if you want to give it another name.'

'And Verona is in Genoa,' said Larry.

'I am a humble Frenchman, sadly most of our provincial dialects have died out. Well, the original appeared in Luigi da Porto's, Romeo and Juliet with Mercutio as the character of a Moor. da Porto's was an Italian - possibly a Genoese. Shakespeare, in 1596, made Mercutio a gallant and effervescent gentleman, who died for his Romeo. In Bandello's collection of Italian novels, of which I have a 1554 edition, Mercutio is cold, evil and a lion among maidens. The combination of black skin and Italian speaking has the locals claiming Corsican influence upon Shakespeare.'

'There were no Moors on the Italian mainland?'

'How can I tell? There might have been, but here, the Moors presence is celebrated with the emblem for Corsica being a Moor’s head with a red bandanna. And Shakespeare, as a writer, shall we say he was a backward-looking writer. Some others are forward looking but The Science Fiction genre leaves me cold.'

'I'm still getting my head around the concept of an earlier version of Romeo and Juliet,' said Larry.

'In Italy they say that Napoleon missed out on being an Italian by just one year. It cuts two ways. In 1596, when Shakespeare wrote Romeo and Juliet, Corsica was under Genoese occupation. Shakespeare's missing ten years would have been in the latter part of the 16th century.'

'He might have come here.'

'He most certainly would have travelled by sea. Most of his works were influenced by other writers or indeed by history itself. He would have been aware that Homer's Odyssey was set right here in Bonifacio. He was not published as a writer until after his death. He made his living as a player and later a theatre owner. Shakespeare would have looked for *spicy* references to attract nobility, the clergy and men of words to his plays.'

'Quite the PR man.'

'Find another city in Europe to give you an Italian speaking, black skinned Mercutio.'

'The play opens with: *in fair Verona, where we lay our scene*.'

'Yes, but Shakespeare would have been eager to appease his queen and set Romeo and Juliet in an Italian mainland city with which the British were trading. That part is hard to prove - but you will agree that Corsica has a volatile history. France and England have a volatile history. News then, travelled slowly and plays had long runs.'

'*Ars longa, vita brevis*.'

'Exactly.'

'As long as you are looking after one of my treasures, you may as well borrow this.' From a top drawer in the desk Murat produced the Bandello, it was executed smoothly but had a rehearsed feel to it.

'Thank you,' was all Larry could say.

****

'What is it?' asked Luca.

'It is a very rare book,' said Larry. The book was on the table and both men were standing back as their presence might contaminate the book. Next to the leather-bound tome were four theatre tickets.

'Why have you got it?'

'It's a loan.'

'It looks very expensive.'

'It is. It is very valuable.'

'Then why have you got it?'

'Because I have been out-bull-shitted.'

They were speaking in English and Luca loved the vitality of it – including the swear words.

'What's the deal?' asked Luca.

'We have to give his daughter a job.'

'What?'

'I'll work her like a slave. Luca, what's wrong.'

'Well. Do you remember the girl I was out with; the one that came home in the police car?'

'Oh shit! Is *that* her?'

'That's the one. She's the one.'

'Why didn't you tell me?'

Luca shrugged. It was rare for his father and he to have words. Luca would have told him it was just that the words did not always come straight away.

'I have been ... I wish I was forewarned. Luca I sat in this chair designed by a sadist and had to listen to a man tell me that Shakespeare ... Well let's just say I was biting my lip. He tried to tell me that the original language for this,' Larry pointed to the book, 'was Genoese.'

'And?'

'I happen to know it was Veronese.'

Luca reached over and picked up the book. 'How much do you think this is worth?'

'More than I will ever earn from writing. Luca I'm sorry. I wish I'd known. Is this going to be a problem?'

'What are you always saying Dad? Don't sweat the small stuff.'

****

What Larry didn't know was that Luca was feeling ten-feet-high and bullet proof. Not only had Sylvie accepted his presence in class they had hung out at lunchtime. During this break the school thug, Ingo Fusina had suggested to Sylvie that she might like to leave the swine herder and go with a real man. Sylvie's reply had been both swift and devastating. Delivered in French, it took a moment in the translation but nothing was lost in the rendering.

'Go with you? Not while there are dogs in the street.'

Fusina flushed like a beet. Word quickly spread that Sylvie was a firebrand and Luca had yard-cred. Fusina was the biggest boy in the school but his early growth spurt had been caught up and passed by Luca and a few others. In retribution Fusina picked a fight with a smaller boy and the latest word to Luca's ear was that he had been suspended. The next thrashing would be from Fusina's father when he got out of jail.

****

'Was M. Murat mad at me for keeping Sylvie out late?' asked Luca.

'No; on the contrary. He is going to Nice early in Marsh and wishes to close up his house, give the servants a holiday and foist young Sylvie onto us.'

'We will be open for business then. That will be our first week. What will she do?'

'Think of it as an extra pair of hands. Can she speak French?'

'Fluently.'

'English?'

Luca seesawed his hand in the air.

'She could be our receptionist,' said Larry. 'What are you grinning at?'

'Nothing. Dad, she has spirit.'

'Good.'

'You're feeling confident? You have met the prototype - so-to speak.'

'Her father? If I was forewarned Luca, he might not have put one over on me and I might not have this priceless book for my bedtime reading.' Larry scooped up the book and flicked through the pages. 'Everyone gets a chance, Luca. If she stuffs up, then she is on notice. Just like everyone else. Now is there anything else I should know?'

'I think she's a handful. Judge for yourself.'

'Ok! Just remember she's not yet 14 and her father is our financier,' said Larry. 'Now! Here is a list of hardware items. Small stuff; locks and cup hooks. Do you want to get these things or shall I go and drive.'

'No, I'll go. I'll ride my bike.'

Luca was reading the list when Victor came into the room.

He ruffled his grandson's red stubble. He must have heard the exchange between father and son.

'Don't stand near the sandpaper, or someone will take you home to scrub down a door,' said Victor.

'Shall I charge these things to our account?'

'Yes,' said Larry 'And you'll notice I've included some coach bolts. That's to put up your basketball hoop.'

'Great. See yah!' and Luca was off.

'I have agreed to employ the Murat girl,' said Larry

'She is a classmate of Luca's, no?'

'I think she might be more than that; she was the one he was out late with last night,' said Larry.

'I've heard she is a pretty thing. Have Clara show her the duties of the reception. No, I will tell her myself. It will make her heart light to have a young one to fuss over.'

Victor moved off to find his bride of nearly half a century. She would be tending her herbs or her vegetables. It was not expressly stated but Larry knew that Clara would enjoy the company of another female.

Larry sniffed the leather bound book and examined the bookplate. The book had come from the library of Baronet Milaies. Who was he? And why had he parted with this book? Or was he the last of his line and his library disposed of to pay his creditors? The text was closely set period Italian. Larry set the book down. Perhaps after tea, Clara could be persuaded to give a reading and spontaneous translation. It was time Larry revisited the story of the unhappy lovers of Verona, this time as an historical occurrence.

****

'The English tip big or not at all. And promise to write, they always promise to write,' said Luca.

'England is a small damp island with a literary tradition. Get the English abroad and they flourish like a desert flower,' said Dernavern. They were gardening today.

'And how does a desert flower?' asked Luca.

'Briefly.'

They were working to a plan sketch Dernavern had drawn. A landscaping colour scheme that revolved around purple and white. He seemed to revel in the physicality of manual work. Luca was giving his account of tourists and their quirks. Dernavern had been deflected on matters concerning Sylvie, he assumed she would be grounded or in disgrace. Luca was happy talking about the various visitors he encountered over the years and couldn't wait to see Dernavern's face when Sylvie turned up in a Pension Lazlo uniform.

'This is good to get your hands in the dirt. Fresh air and sunshine, I must do this more often. What about Germans?'

'Germans have scorpions in their pockets.'

'Americans?'

'I think they must go to the bank before they leave and get cases full of one dollar bills.'

'What's the biggest tip you have gotten?' Dernavern was not teasing, it was good-natured banter. His frenetic energy was contagious.

'Getting ten pounds is not uncommon. I can spend half a day with someone as a sort of guide and translator and get a hundred francs.'

'What about the Australians?'

'They have come such a long way and are probably on their way to somewhere else. I like to talk to them to find out about Australia. I wanted to turn the slaughterhouse building into a backpacker's style dormitory.'

'What did Victor say about that?'

'Dad pointed out that it would have to be a dormitory for either boys or girls, not both. And as we don't have a building of similar size, it would not be practical.'

'Practical man, Larry.'

'Yes, I suppose he is.'

'Has he ever been romantically involved with anyone since your mother?'

'There was the time he invited an Italian teacher here for a party. My party. I was nine. That was the day my mother decided to turn up in her version of a surprise.'

'Did the Italian teacher spit chips? They can be feisty.'

'No Dad just never saw her again and she took a job in England.'

'So, he's living the life of an abbot?'

'A what?'

'Never mind. He holds a candle for your mother then.'

'I suppose so.' Luca did not sound certain.

'Come on. No slacking. We have a mound of earth to shift.'

'Some doubt your character, Dernavern. I can vouch for your fitness. You're a slave driver.'

****

'Mme du Plessier, were you good at your studies?'

The question stopped Clara in her tracks. She lost her train of thought. A pair of sky borne blue eyes held her in a steady gaze. She could understand why her grandson worked his shirtless body to a lustre. It was not a case of who and which boy would fall in love with Sylvie; it was a case of how many.

'Why,' Clara began, 'I remember a tutor, dreary and austere. We lived abroad a lot with my father's work. It was up to us, my sisters and I to manufacture our own fun.'

'I say this because you are such a good teacher.'

Clara knew when the charm faucet flowed and she knew when it was a torrent. She was speaking in French with a natural French speaker and of the accents Clara's liked the Paris accent most, it brought back memories of a trip there before the war.

'And a good student becomes a good teacher?' asked Clara.

'I'm not sure. I just know you are the first adult not to talk down to me.'

'The work was never arduous. We made an effort not to be boisterous in the presence of our father.'

'Why?'

'He was a man who lived solely inside his head. We felt, or I felt, that five girls were his life's disappointment. Then Victor stole me away.'

'No brothers?'

'Not one that lived.'

'I'm sorry.'

'My father is one half of my genetic fraction. Study was never hard. But then women were raised to be nurses, teachers, wives and mothers. As an Anthropologist who studied the origins of life, it is sad that it had to end with him. His line - the name.'

'He is still alive then?'

'Yes, but very old and frail. His mind has gone and that was all there ever was of him.'

'And Victor's mother, she is still alive.'

'Very much so. Just a little forgetful.'

'It must be the country air.' Sylvie looked solemn and it was a while before she spoke. 'What do you think of the chances of these men calling the buildings other things?'

'Other than what?'

'The Slaughterhouse - that could startle some guests. The piggery names. I know it will be hard,' said Sylvie, 'but we must try.'

'I say you have about as much chance as getting these men to wear hats and sunscreen.'

'Hats and sunscreen.' Sylvie slid off her chair. 'Well, that's a start.'

Later that day Clara saw her grandson in a T-shirt and hat. Dernavern's skin was slick with, presumably, sunscreen. But what surprised her most was the map someone had drawn of the compound. All the buildings had been re-named. It was stylishly done. Clara presumed the skill of Dernavern's hand had been brought into play.

'Look, Nonna, Sylvie has given me some homework.'

Luca had a list of the new names for the buildings. 'I have to write it out five times.'

****

Larry and Victor surveyed the site. The landscaping gave the edges definition. It was starting to look like a pension.

'I say we have the Grand Opening when the pool and bistro are finished. Next year. We have guests arriving the day after tomorrow. There is much to do,' said Larry

'I'm with you,' said Victor.

'We could have the opening at the beginning of the season,' said Luca. He had approached and was now resting a full wheelbarrow. He wiped his forehead on his shirt.

'What do you call the beginning of the season?' asked Larry.

'Liberation Day, May 8th next year' Luca replied.

'Good idea' said Larry.

'But to matters more immediate. Clara and I will look after the place this weekend. You use those tickets that Murat gave you. But after that, we officially retire,' said Victor.

'Who are you going to invite, Luca?' asked Larry.

Luca threw a gentle punch at his father's shoulder.

Chapter Seven

Laying low in paradise

In a second story flat in London's trendy Maida Vale, two girls sat among the pile that comes when a case has been packed and unpacked, then re-packed several times.

'Leave the pot plants, I can buy new ones when I get back.'

Dee Dee had just given her pet terrapin to the kid next door. Paige Goss had bought Dee Dee that terrapin from Harrods. Paige smouldered. She was not famous for her supermodel tantrums; she was famous as a party girl. Naomi had the market cornered in tantrums but right now Paige was simmering. Simmering was all she had energy for. She was supposed to be sleeping on Dee Dee's couch. Paige wanted to sleep despite it being a few minutes after 3 in the afternoon. But Dee Dee had just emptied the contents of her black leather hold-all onto the couch.

'If you're looking for drugs, The Damocles Centre took them all.'

Paige had just broken up with Christopher Ciccone, one of Madonna's brothers. She needed to sleep. The flight, the one that would become her fourth in three days, was in ten hours.

'Hadn't you better pack?' asked Dee Dee.

'What will I need? I can buy a swimsuit when I get there. How far is this place from Milan? We can buy a whole new wardrobe in Milan, darling. I'm going to take one of my little pills and sleep. Passport and phrase book; just make sure I have those.'

'You haven't unpacked from New York, sweetie.'

'Oh! And tanning oil. I'm going to get my famous little boobs brown.'

Some condoms slid onto the floor. 'Won't need these,' said Paige but slipped them in a smaller bag just the same.

'Go lie down on my bed. I'll book the car to the airport.'

When the bedroom door closed. Dee Dee moved up another gear. She began making phone calls, pacing as she spoke.

-Right

-And I want a full selection of breakfast things

-And black windows.

-They crucified her over there, mate.

-Can you pull some strings at Heathrow and get our driver a pass to the concourse?

- The British press hasn't twigged that she is home yet.

- I don't know what she will eat, or if she will eat at all.

-Croissants - toast the works.

- You look after the food, and I will look after Paige Goss.

- It was not an overdose, all right! Just some bad gear.

- Do it or I'll have your fucking bollocks.'

On Dee Dee's second call she was just a brusque.

-I want a sleepy little village.

-That's right! No dance clubs. No one from the London scene. No! Not Ibiza. Somewhere you'd send your grandma.

-That's it. Perfect! Swing this one and you're a life-saver. No, I'm trying to get her out of the country before the press get wind that she's checked out of rehab.

- Via Canada, but don't worry about that just now. She thinks she is going to St Tropez.

- How far away is that?

- Perfect

- I'll tell her she's barred; that the place is owned by the casino. Yeah! Trashed the place with Naomi.

- Yeah! I'll square it with Jon in St Tropez. And, Josh, leak one word to the press and I'll have your bollocks.

- Do this for me and we'll see about the travel arrangements for the spring and fall seasons, yeah!'

After she snapped the phone closed, Dee Dee cleaned out the medicine cabinet. She had a bin liner of prescription boxes and packets, which she carried to the back door. At the recycling bins Jenny was there, smoking and gushing about the gift of the terrapin.

'Charlie loves his little Leonardo, ever so nice. Off again are you?'

'What?'

'Only, I can hear when you take your suitcase down.'

'No, spring cleaning. Going to have a new house-mate. Share the expenses,' said Dee Dee, hoping she sounded convincing.

'Only, I was only saying the other day, a supermodel! Here in Maida Vale.'

'There goes the neighbourhood,' said Dee Dee.

'Oh! You're ever-so-funny. If she comes back, I must have her over for a cup of tea. And a chocolate biscuit.'

This must have been Jenny's idea of very funny; she laughed without restraint.

'Listen, Jenny, this new house mate is a teetotal. Do you drink gin?'

'Gin and bitter lemon occasionally. I'm a vodka-tonic girl myself.'

'I'll give you them. All of them. There is a litre of gin - unopened. Only you must keep quiet. He's not on the lease.'

'Well. You've been so good to my Charlie. I was only saying the other day... ' but Dee Dee had gone.

Back in the flat, Dee Dee checked that Paige was sleeping and then she went through all her things looking for drugs. The accumulated newspapers went unread into the recycle basket. Then, as a second thought, Dee Dee emptied the basket and put the latest newspapers on the bottom. She put the older papers back on top. Dee Dee had two small packets of white powder to flush down the toilet, The Damocles Centre had *not* found all of the drugs. Now she was ready to face Jenny again.

She snapped the phone open. But there was one missed call for her.

'Hello Paul. Yeah! Dee Dee. I miss you too, baby. Listen, Paul, do something for me.

-Now, don't be filthy.

- I want you to ring me in six minutes.

-No, darling, there is no work for me in London. With Paige Goss in rehab, I might as well lay low.

- And baby, you haven't seen me.

- I wasn't here. Ok!

- Me, I'm in London. And right now, I don't want to talk to the press.

- Six minutes, I'm counting on you.

- I have to convince someone to keep her trap shut but not arouse her suspicions.

- All in a day's work when you're Paige Goss's agent.

Dee Dee thought she had earned a cup of tea. The little phone came out again as the kettle boiled.

'Hello, Reggie.

-Are you still at Heathrow?

- Do they still keep you in that little portable office?

- Well, you get to see the runway. Listen, how would you and Colin like tickets to Alexander McQueen's summer collection.

- Saturday week, darling.

- Paris.

- Under the Eiffel tower, if you please.

- I've got two tickets but Paul and I want to get away.

- That's it sweetie.

-We hetro's are driven by their hormones too.

- I just need the tiniest favour, sweetie.

- I need to get a celebrity on a plane.

- Well, they don't even know she's in the country.

- It's not up to us to do their job for them now, is it?

- Thank you. I'll pop the tickets in the post tonight.'

Chapter Eight

Open for business

'Luca. Luca, wake up. Someone has booked the studio for 14 days. Can you and Dernavern finish it in time?' asked Larry.

'14 days Papa. That's 6,000 F.' Luca stretched and yawned. Sleeping in was rare for him.

'No, it's a private booking. They wanted the best. When I said it was brand new; they didn't want anything else. No discount, no agent fees.'

'They booked direct? Bring my breakfast down to the studio. Have you called Dernavern?'

'He's here already. The call came through last night when you were at Sylvie's; he stayed the night.'

'Stayed? Here?'

'Get used to it Luca, we're running a pension.'

Luca had got a call after the evening meal and had gone over to Sylvie's on the pretext of doing some homework.

Dernavern was washing his upper body in the water butt.

'Did Sylvie Murat keep you out late?' said Dernavern as water dripped off his elbows.

'I was out late - but at least I made it home.'

'Touché!'

'Are you trying to get yourself adopted?' said Luca.

'I was discussing recipes with Clara, art with Larry and Paris with Victor. I remember a jug of wine was poured and that was the first of many. We were also discussing you.'

'Dernavern, are you going to talk or work?'

'You were a great worry to everyone. They thought you were going to run away.'

'With a new, untried, basketball hoop? I think not. Coffee? Who made that for you?'

'Clara.'

'Do you get room service at home?'

'I intend to, Luca. This summer, I intend to.'

****

'Look at this, Paige. It's picture perfect. Or it will be when this vine flowers. What do they call this vine?' Dee Dee.asked Luca

'That's called Morning Glory,' said Luca.

'Morning Glory?'

'It's what my dad calls it. He's Australian. It's a noxious weed in Australia.'

'Are you Australian?' said Paige.

'No, I am a Corse. I was born right here.' Luca waved a hand toward the house.

Clara, setting the large outdoor table for the Turkish labourers waved back. 'That is my Nonna, Clara.'

'This is beautiful,' said Dee Dee. 'The girl in your office, is she you sister?

'No! She's my girlfriend.' It sounded good but Luca still blushed. It was a half-day at school and the village, the island, was getting ready for the Liberation Day long weekend. Sylvie had changed into her uniform, which was a black skirt and plain white blouse.

'Is there a pool?' asked Paige.

'No, next year.'

'We'd better order one then,' said Paige.

'Is everyone here so beautiful?' asked Dee Dee.

'They say the mongrel dog inherits the best characteristics. Sailors from all corners of the globe have visited our ports many times. We are the best of the rest. If Europe were a soup, we would be the crouton,' said Luca

Dee Dee laughed and handed Luca a ten pound note and a card. The card said Rose Underhill and had a phone number.

'What is this?'

'If you are ever in London - you or your girlfriend - give Rose a ring.'

'What does she do?' asked Luca.

'She discovers new talent.'

'I'm sorry?' Asked a confused Luca.

'Models. Do you know Laetitia Casta?'

'Not personally.'

Laetitia Casta was a 15-year-old girl when she was discovered on the beach holidaying with her family in Corsica. She now lived and worked in Normandy and looked like rivalling Napoleon Bonaparte's fame. She was putting Corsica on the map once more.

'She has earned about 10 million already,' said Dee Dee.

Luca was wondering: pounds, dollars, francs, when Paige came to the door. She had been checking out the interior of the studio.

'I get the loft bedroom. Get on the phone to Rose. Tell her to get down here. It's heaven. We could have a party.'

Luca left the studio slightly puzzled. He would rate his English very highly but some of that conversation had gone over his head.

Chapter Nine

Two crazy English chicks

'Do you know who that was?' asked Sylvie.

'A crazy English chick - two crazy English chicks,' quipped Luca

'The one with the light brown hair was Paige Goss.'

'I know. It said that on her case.' A Louis Vuitton with gold lettering.

'Silly. She is one of the world's top models.'

Sylvie stood on tip toe and kissed Luca lightly on the lips. 'You have much to learn, Luca Moro.'

Luca fished the card out of his pocket.

'Who is this?'

Sylvie turned the card around. Other staff at Pension Lazlo made the black skirt and white blouse look like a uniform. Sylvie, her hair swept up in combs, made it her signature.

'It's just a name and a number; who gave it to you?' asked Sylvie.

'The other girl.'

Sylvie returned behind the desk and read the register. 'Deirdre McPhee.'

****

Deirdre McPhee could not sleep. At first Paige being on the phone to people in five continents kept her awake, then the stress that had been in a holding pattern for the past four days came home to roost.

What Deirdre McPhee was at this moment was broke.

Immigration at Corte Airport had taken a long look at her passport. The four entries in four days had looked incriminating to a mind trained to look for drug traffickers. Then his colleague held up Paige's passport which he proclaimed out loud to be nearly full in just ten months. A flight attendant recognised Paige. And a meltdown had been averted.

The Smokehouse Studio apartment at Pension Lazlo had its own private courtyard. The studio was everything Reggie had promised and more. In the five hours she had been in the Smokehouse Studio at pension Lazlo, it had grown dark. The sky was black. It never got this black in the city. Starless and cloudless, this was a shapeless, endless black. The city always had errant light. The streets of London might not be paved with gold, but there was always an abundance of neon. Perhaps that's why Deirdre McPhee had not made her fortune, she was looking down not up. Deirdre McPhee stood in the courtyard and cried.

Deirdre McPhee missed her mammy.

****

It was a warm evening. It seemed that Dernavern was staying for supper. Luca noted that his legs were becoming a common fixture under the du Plessier table. Tonight, they were to eat outside at the large table, an event that evoked memories of summers past when you could take your fill leisurely and be glad of the afternoon sleep. The phone rang; Larry went inside to answer it.

'One of Gaultier's dogs has slipped her chain. The bitch. Luca, can you handle her?'

'Of course, where is she?' Luca hoped he sounded confident. In truth the bitch with pistachio coloured eyes had sniffed his feet when she was at the limit of her chain. She had responded to the tone in Luca's voice, a kindness he had installed for her. How would she react if she were unchained, free, having tasted blood?

'At the milliner's shop,' said Larry, 'she has killed one of her chickens.'

'If she has taken a live bird she must have been hungry,' said Luca. 'Has anyone seen Gaultier?'

'No. He might have fallen, again. He drinks - I think,' said Dernavern.

The subject of Gaultier's sobriety, or lack of it, was usually handled in a less than head on fashion. Life was changing.

'I have some un-smoked lamb belly, it was to be for the Turk's lunch tomorrow,' said Clara. 'Take it Luca, make sure the dogs are fed.'

'Is she savage?' asked Dernavern.

'She's not a house pet,' said Luca. 'Gaultier has nine dogs. There is a three-legged male I wouldn't turn my back on.'

Luca remembered a stagnant memory from childhood, an under the bed bad dream, a reason to leap from the mat to the mattress. Gaultier's dogs were rumored to have been bred with a wolf at one time; the fear had been safely locked away with other black memories. Safe in the vault of daylight reason. Why had it surfaced now?

'Are you cold Luca?' asked Victor. 'You have goose flesh.' Then, mostly for Dernavern's benefit he added, 'Gaultier gets this way in spring. He needs to be weeding or sowing or finding markets. The arrival of tourists always unsettles him.'

'Why?' said Dernavern.

There was a vast silence to digest as Victor sent round the jug. Half a glass was poured for Luca, his second.

After an eternity Luca suggested he restore the milliner with her full complement of hens. No one disagreed.

'I have made impossible pie,' said Clara, 'for my tireless workers who got the studio ready in time.'

Dernavern raised his glass at Luca. 'Bravo!'

'Have you seen the map that Sylvie has coloured with her art pens? It is worth laminating. Luca, where would you get such a thing laminated?' asked Clara.

Luca shrugged.

'The boy's in love, he has no head for practicalities,' said Larry.

Luca noticed his father was worst for the drink and Dernavern was not far behind him.

'I use Lizet's in Ajaccio,' said Dernavern. 'I don't know of another machine at this end of the island.'

'I will fetch the stray bitch and feed Gaultier's nine. As my homework is done, I might be...

'I will drive you,' said Dernavern. 'Where is this Milliners?'

'You have drunk freely. This is a starless night. Let Luca ride his bike,' said Clara.

'No. He has to carry a hen,' said Larry.

'There is always tomorrow,' said Victor. 'Restore the hen in the morning.'

'I have correspondence and newspapers piling up. A few calls to make,' said Dernavern rising, 'to Paris,' he added because he could see Clara about to suggest he use the phone there.

'I'll get a hen and a length of rope,' said Luca.

'Good, wait for me out the front,' said Dernavern.

While Luca was waiting for Dernavern to bring the car round, he thought he heard someone crying. Patches of light escaped chinks in brand new curtains. They had guests under their roof. Paying guests. The thrill entered Luca's bones.

'Jump in. Are you going to Sylvie's?' asked Dernavern.

'That depends on what state Gaultier is in.'

'What's the worst case scenario?'

'The what?' asked Luca.

'What's the worst thing you could find up there?'

'Gaultier mad with the drink holding a shotgun,' said Luca.

'You're kidding?'

'No, I'm not.'

'Has that happened before?'

'It has.'

'What did you do?'

'I was young. Larry was the hero that night, he spoke carefully, so as not to startle him. *'Henri, you might wing one of the dogs,'* he said.'

'Has he always been like this?'

'He went crazy when his mother died.'

'Do you want me to come in with you?'

'No, he is wary of strangers. If I'm in luck, I might find him passed-out-drunk.'

But Gaultier was ill with a fever and had not moved from his bed in days. Luca was back at the car in minutes.

Dernavern was holding the chicken. Luca took the length of rope and reached for the chicken.

'Where are you going?'

'To the Milliner's. The fowl will only slow you down. Gaultier is ill. He has a fever. Drive like you are in a race. Fetch Clara and Victor. They can clean him up before a doctor gets here. Pass me the meat. The dogs will be mad with hunger.'

Dernavern sped off.

Luca knocked at the door of the Milliner's. Her eldest daughter opened the door and held her hands up for the hen. She inclined her head to the left and shut the door, leaving Luca on the darkened porch. The Milliner's cottage was symmetrical with a formal garden out the back. The ramrod path divided the flower beds and herbs. There was a tiny patch of lawn at the front and a stand of fruit trees at the back. Luca would have to navigate the garden by memory and starlight.

Gaultier's bitch was a dusty brown, with light fringes, and naturally camouflaged in this lively garden. From memory, not much happened without this dog's blessing. Then came a bark. One single bark. It was not so much aggressive as assertive. Luca recalled a keen intelligence and strong white teeth. He squatted on his heels. No book learning here.

'Good girl.' Luca loaded his voice with praise. He felt, rather than heard, a tail swish in the dark.

Luca put his hand on the plastic bag of lamb belly pieces tied to his belt. The rustle had a confidence gaining quality to it.

'Come on!' Luca tried again and roughed up his diction running the words together. 'Com-on.' Perfect except for the improvement that 702,000 Gauloises's wouldn't fix.

The dog advanced cowering and sniffing.

'Good Girl,' and then, 'goo-grrrl.'

The bitch circled Luca sniffing his feet. Luca stood slowly, remembering to remain confident. The hairs on his neck bristled and strangely he thought of Garrod. He would have shit himself by now. Luca extended the hand with the piece of lamb and brought the bitches snout up. She had a fringe of white feathers and was wary of the meat.

'Not hungry?'

Luca heard the chain drag and bent to locate the source of the sound.

'Come here girl. Sit.' The dog complied.

'Now, let's get rid of this chain.' Luca said it again and roughed up his voice. He distracted the dog by dropping the piece of lamb. He had to remain the number-one dog. The chain slipped over the dog's head and she immediately stood and shook herself. Not interested in the morsel, she must have been very full.

Luca turned and walked toward the Milliner's cottage; the dog followed. Near a patch of rosemary, she squatted and urinated. A good sign. Luca decided to leave the rope tied around his body. She would follow as long as she could keep up her random olfactory itinerary and punctuate it with the arbitrary bladder deposits. A chemical email for other mammals.

Luca and the bitch walked home at their unhurried own pace.

Chapter Ten

Late night tour of the Citadel

Dee Dee was aware something was happening. Cars came and went and there was far too much activity for this time of night. In the wall of the courtyard there was a little round glass-less window. She moved a chair beneath it and found finger-holds in the rough stone to pull herself up to the window ledge.

A Fiat sat cooling, its engine ticking rhythmically. In the warm air, a man's voice spoke French rapidly into a phone. A door shut firmly. Its glass rattled. An athletic man launched himself up the steps to the waiting Fiat.

'What's going on?' asked Dee Dee.

Dernavern took a while to locate the English voice.

'Up here,' Dee Dee said. 'What's happening?'

'A neighbour is sick,' said Dernavern, locating the source of the questions.

'Have you called an ambulance?'

'No. They will bring him back here. The worst is over.'

'Oh!'

'What's the matter? You sound bored.'

'My friend has jet lag. We should have hired a car.'

'I could call a taxi for you.' Dernavern paused. 'Or give you the late night tour of the Citadel.'

'I'll take the late night tour; when does it leave?'

Dernavern's face split into a smile. 'Now.'

****

Paige slept until noon. She stretched her elfin body like a cat's and spent the next hour on the phone to London.

Luca worked alone. Dernavern had not shown up for work. Larry drove up, an empty trailer attached. Rubbish had been accumulating in the trailer. There was a time when most things at the piggery were re-cycled. Clear plastic became a cloche for Clara's seedlings. Cardboard boxes always found a second tour of duty in Victor's workshop or the old shop that was now the office. Never had they had so many new things at one time. Luca thought Victor would comment or protest. But the trailer went to the tip full and was now empty.

'Dad, I'll need a hand to carry in these mattresses.'

'Where's Dernavern?' asked Larry from the open car window.

'I haven't seen him. Did you take the rubbish to the tip?'

'There is a bloke who will buy things from you. Those plastic bags that the mattresses came in make good covers for chairs for cafes to store their tables and chairs, for the winter. We have people sleeping on these mattresses tonight. We must get them on beds. What could have happened to Dernavern?'

Luca shrugged. Everyone was a little tired with the events of last night. Gaultier, his fever broken and feeling the benefit of Clara's chicken broth, was already clamouring about his dogs.

'After this can you and Sylvie feed Gaultier's dogs? And then I want you two to put this together,' said Larry.

'A computer. Is it ours?'

'It's Pension Lazlo's, yes.'

'Brilliant.'

'Then I need you to put together the service booklets for the rooms,' said Larry. 'You and Sylvie.'

Larry's last writing effort was the service booklet for Pension Lazlo. It showed Luca the work that went into constructing a simple sentence. It also showed the shortcomings of Larry's old computer. Larry thought and composed in English. Luca patiently had to translate the same sentence into French by reconstructing it. Victor had helped with the Genoese and Clara with the Italian. For once being a mongrel family had paid dividends.

'As for Sylvie,' Larry continued, 'I will work her hard. It is what her father would want. She is a natural French speaker. She can help with the service booklet when the new computer is set up.'

It made sense to Luca they had four natural speakers of the five major languages planned for the service books.

Chapter Eleven

Best Use of a Paisley Accent

Dee Dee and Dernavern had breakfast on the terrace. The forest came right up to the house. The twittering of birds had woken Dee Dee. She had no idea that the country could be so loud.

'So, after you left Glasgow, you didn't return to nursing?' asked Dernavern.

'No, I puckered up, headed south, and told the biggest load of bullshit and landed a job as a photographic assistant.'

'Photographic assistant - who? Anyone famous?'

'No, a guy who did a lot of brochures for 18-30's. Travel brochures. But he was hopeless at paying bills. He was always out of the country. He had a studio on the Cromwell Road and one day, the landlord just changed the locks.'

'Did he owe you wages?'

'Yeah! Not a lot. I had the folios of some models who worked for John. I had begun to notice who worked for which agency. I fronted at the busiest, told them I was not neurotic enough to model, and could I get a job as a booker.'

'*Voile*!'

'Then as you get better at your job, they assign one girl to you. Your fortunes are linked - literally. I was handed a skinny, shy 14-year-old who was turned down for most of the jobs she was sent for.'

'Then what?'

'She was picked by Calvin Klein for his jeans commercial and the waif thing began - she never looked back.'

'But you spent all your money to bail her out of a New York detox clinic?'

'The Damocles Centre was in Connecticut.'

Dernavern's eyebrows went up in a way that suggested expensive, without saying it.

'It's an investment. In time and money. If your model is not earning, neither are you. London is so expensive.'

'Do you need to be in London?'

'That's the centre of the fashion industry.'

'But you said it is all phone. They phone you. You phone Paige. Paige phones you from whereever she is.'

'Hey, I never thought of that. But it would be a brave soul who broke away and set up the first booking agency outside London.'

'What did you just tell me? You puckered up and went down to London!'

'I was fresh faced and I'm sure I got the job as a booker because of my Paisley accent.'

'So, how much debt are we talking about?'

'My credit cards are maxed out. I have a small mortgage and next month's salary is already spent.'

'But you have a job and a home. I got out of Paris for much the same reason. I sold my apartment and moved here. I actually work more but sell less. The air is conducive to creativity and there are none of the Paris distractions.'

Dee Dee had wanted to move some of the canvasses in the studio. Dernavern was right. There were 50 paintings stacked around the place. Disarray plentiful. Quality disarray. Chaotic disarray. They were of Astrid mostly. Dee Dee had wanted to put paintings on a chair one by one, stand back and assess them. She suspected the Nordic beauty had gone; the urgency of the sex had confirmed this. The painting in the easel had a final quality to it.

Dee Dee poured the last of the coffee.

'Tell you what. I've had an offer to run a team of bookers for a new agency, a smaller agency. I'll take it if they let me work from home. I'll sell Maida Vale and move out to Herefordshire.'

'Will it mean parting company with Paige Goss?'

'So be it. Some will see it as working my way down the corporate ladder but, hey! Fuck em.'

****

When Paige was bored with telephoning her friends, she came to the office to ask about Dee Dee's whereabouts for the third time. It was like a brainstorm for Larry. He assigned Sylvie as a tour guide for Miss Paige Goss. It got both of them out of the way while he and Luca set up the computer. With the computer progress was slow. Designing the service brochure would not happen today.

'You treated her rather coolly,' said Luca

'Did I? We are running a pension. I treated her civilly. I didn't fawn over her, if that is what you mean.'

This was a new word for Luca, Larry's use of it suggested its use, Luca liked the word. 'Do you know who she is?' he asked.

'Luca, until yesterday you did not know who she was,' said Larry. 'What is a supermodel anyway?'

'Sylvie was impressed.' Luca said in way that inferred he was if Sylvie was.

'She had better get used to it. Did you want to go with them? Is she stealing your thunder?' Said Larry.

'No, they will be talking of fashion and perfume and designers,' said Luca. 'They're not ones for history and architecture I would think. Anyway, I want to get this set up.'

'So, you can email Roald?'

'So, I can email the world!'

'*******

'So, what's the deal with Lazlo?' came Paige's voice from inside the change booth.

'He's Luca's father,' Sylvie said. 'An Australian, I think.'

'Is there a Mrs Moro?' Paige asked, swinging the door open.

'No. Do you think he's cute?'

'Not as cute as Luca. But I've had it with handsome men. They are so much heartache. He's *Korn*. Zip me up.'

'Korn?'

'Fuckable! Now, what do you think of this one?' Paige swirled in the little red dress.

Paige caught sight of herself in the change room mirror and gave herself a profile. Her flat stomach that had sold everything from designer jeans to swimsuits. The bust was flat, but she worked with what she had, she did not have the chest of Christie or Tatiana, but she never tried to be anybody else. She got an image of her cutting up a line of cocaine and someone handing her a rolled-up bank note. Someone always had a bank note. Someone always had cocaine. But she was beyond that now and she thought she knew the reason why. The tingle in her stomach shifted a few feet south and she thought of the little La Perla G string she had slipped in her luggage at the last minute. The one with the lily as a motif: lemon and sky blue.

'I liked the black one.' Said Sylvie.

Paige said to her reflection, 'He doesn't stand a chance.' Then Paige turned her luminous face to the shop owner after exiting the cubicle. The little girl face, the excited one, the face Bailey called 'daddy's home'. She produced a credit card with flourish.

'I'll take them all.'

The shop owner became a flurry of obsequious delight. Paige Goss was enjoying her anonymity.

****

Clara was tending her herbs when the truck backed up. The herb garden was between the back door and the outdoor dining table. It had been installed after the ground had been excavated to extend the kitchen. From the kitchen level, three steps led up to the herb garden. At kitchen window height, it flooded the kitchen with fresh aromas.

'What is this?' asked Clara in French

'Sign here,' barked the truck driver in Genoese. Then he turned on his heel and climbed back into his truck. A cloud of diesel punctuated his distaste at being spoken to in French.

'Larry, Luca, come here and shift this crate.'

'What is it, Nonna?'

'I don't know, it is addressed to a Miss Paige Goss.'

'How did the driver get it off the truck?' asked Larry.

'He levered it off, and left it where it fell; arrogant Corte.'

'Well, it's in the way here, we'll have to shift it,' said Larry.

'Shall I go over to Gaultier's and borrow the pallet lifter?' asked Luca

'Good idea, Luca.'

'What in the world has she had shipped from Harrods?' asked Clara.

Chapter Twelve

Ride to Riches

Joey Cotz was born in Hell's Kitchen. He got as far as ninth grade but found schoolwork seriously cut into the time he spent running numbers. Being a well fed Italian American, he employed his beefy frame collecting a few debts. He once took an Olympus camera, not to break Sonny Ferrone's thumbs. He took the camera and broke Sonny's thumbs anyway. The camera felt good in Joey's hand. He found it opened doors. The right kind of doors. And Joey was always like a schoolboy when he got his films back from processing. One day, assistant Mayor del Gatto was coming out of a brothel the back way, when he encountered Joey and his camera. Joey got five hundred for the photograph and found that the guy he sold it to, syndicated it for fifty times that much. Joey paid him a visit. A new career was born. Premium prices were paid for all Joey Cotz's photographs and he scored himself a byline. Newspapermen, much longer in the business, wondered where this crass *kibitzer* suddenly came from.

Two of his photos of Paige Goss coined new phrases. Joey caught her after a long day's shoot, not long after a bout of the flu, and the photo went out across the wires under the heading 'Heroin Chic'. The waif look was still kicking but it needed more juice. Paige getting sick fuelled the need for more photographs in this vein. Anorexic was the new catch cry. Joey used Photoshop to subtract 15 pounds.

Paige Goss was Joey Cotz's ride to riches.

But Paige Goss had disappeared. Joey drove back to New York with a brand new 14-foot ladder tied to the roof. In tailback traffic, he punched numbers on his cell phone. At White Plains he had a lead. By Yonkers it was strongly rumoured. As he pulled into his parent's home in Jackson Heights he had a confirmation of a sighting at Heathrow. Paige Goss in a limo on the apron of runway two-six-niner.

'Hey Ma! I'm off to London, England.'

'Joey. Eat something.'

Chapter Thirteen

Home Delivered

Dee Dee had 17 messages; 11 of them from Paige Goss. She rang her just after 6.00pm. 'Hello, it’s me. Where are you?' said Dee Dee.

'Dee Dee, your accent, it's come back.'

'I was talking to home. I guess I got a little nostalgic.'

'You left me' pouted Paige.

'The last week just caught up with you, sweetie. When did you wake up?'

'Noon. And I was ravenous. I met Luca's girlfriend and we have terrorised the boutiques. Now we are having a little glass of wine. What happened to you?'

'You slept for 16 hours! I thought if you did wake up it would be in the dead of night. I met an artist from Paris.'

'You don't waste any time. Where did you meet him?'

'I had him home delivered. Now he's out getting more wine and some seafood. It’s a local specialty.'

'What seafood, or taxiing girls straight to the bedroom?'

'We talked for a bit and it was a table.'

'You did it in the kitchen?'

'It's sort of one big room with paintings all around the walls.'

'Dee Dee!'

'And then the bed.' If a phone could crackle with silence it was doing so now. 'Then wine'

'And then you slept?'

'Hardly, then he bent me over a railing on the terrace and we did it in the moonlight.'

'Did you wake the neighbours?'

'That's it: he has none.'

Paige felt a tingling in her thighs and got an image of Larry.

Dee Dee sounded happy and that was the main thing. It was infections. 'This artist is having some friends down from Paris. This weekend is a national holiday. I think he's more your kind of people.'

'What! A man who wants to use your face as a trophy, your body as a trampoline and your heart as a football! No thanks. Time for a change. I've had my eye on something. Someone.'

'It's not like you to be coy. Who is he?'

'He is nobody. A no-one.'

'A no-one? What does he do?'

'From what I can gather very little. But he has his hands full right now. But he has either not read a magazine in ten years or is very coy.'

Dee Dee could see why this might appeal to Paige. 'Luca's girlfriend, will she drive you around?'

'No, sweetie she is only 13.'

'Don't corrupt her, Paige.'

'Corrupt her! She may even corrupt me.'

Chapter Fourteen

Does 'Never' Work For You

Vincent was 26 and travelled to Bonifacio every day in the season to meet with his friend Robert. They would sometimes stalk their quarry for half a day. English girls were easy; they went big on Italian charm and French looks. Vincent had slept with 63 girls last summer, 14 in front of Robert.

Robert had just bet Vincent he could not get the little English girl in bed by the weekend. 100 francs were riding on the fact that he had recognised Paige Goss and Vincent had not.

'What about if I fuck her we go on a pig pull. I select the ugliest girl and you have to fuck her.'

'Tell you what,' said Robert, 'make it two hundred.'

'You have yourself a deal.' Vincent's ears had pricked up when he heard Paige's accent. 'But you have to fuck the other one.'

Robert had noted the novice way Sylvie had handled her wine. He would be surprised if she was 15 and trouble hung over her head like neon. Virgins were a lot of trouble.

'If you don't think you are up for it. The bet is off.'

'What’s wrong with you man? She is pretty, very pretty. I would fuck her myself but I don’t do French.'

Robert knew Vincent’s fiancée well. Vincent had been engaged to Raquel for four years, he was transparent in his infidelities and Robert was ashamed of his high school friend for putting up with Vincent’s ways. Robert hoped that Raquel would wake up to herself but saw this as an easy 200 francs.

Vincent sauntered over, he opened with his big guns; he flashed a maiden winning smile and kissed the back of Paige’s hand.

'When will you be mine?'

'How about *never*, does never work for you?'

Chapter Fifteen

Strumming the gentle bonds of gentle affection

The shed had accumulated two generations of junk. Well sorted and well-stored junk. It was Victor's domain, just as the kitchen and vegetable patch was Clara's.

'What do you want a wrecking bar for anyway?' asked Victor.

'To open a crate for Miss Paige Goss,' said Luca.

'What is she having sent from London? In a crate?'

'Well, we'll know in a few minutes.'

'It will take you longer than a few minutes to open that crate. Do you want a hand?'

'No, I'll catch up on the gossip from London.'

Luca spent each moment he could with the English girls. They seemed to like him and tried his daily tour suggestions. Luca rang taxis for them and told them how to avoid getting ripped off.

'I'll just wipe it down. This is an old wrecking bar. My father would have made it. Rub it down with an oily rag when you are done, to prevent rust.'

Clara entered the workshop. She heard the men down at the workbench on the ground floor. She had entered the workshop on the mezzanine level that opened to the vegetable garden. A shard of southern sun sliced the still air. Dust motes swirled.

The two men were huddled over the workbench conspiratorially. Her husband and her grandson. Her heart was so full of love; it had no room to protest. Victor spent time in here when he was perplexed. Investing hours of time on a new gate latch or fixing a tap that was worth only a few francs.

'Where are Larry and Sylvie?' she said at last.

'Why?' said Victor looking up.

'I cook for six people and when it comes time to serve, no one is here.'

'Larry is fixing a tangled curtain cord in the Eastern Studio. Sylvie has gone home to get her Paris Vogue. Our time and talents are flagged by other uses; our stomachs must wait their turn,' said Victor.

'Then I am glad this is our last weekend. We must make it a feast. Invite The Bear if she is feeling up to it. If we don't, then I'm afraid that you will become one of those husbands that potter.'

'And you, one of those wives that nag.'

It was a light-hearted banter that Luca had witnessed many times. It gently strummed the solid bonds of affection.

'I am going to sell the car. Dernavern has made me an offer. I will become one of those husbands who go out in the morning to buy the paper and will return in time for lunch. After which I will fall asleep, with the paper unread. I will have all the news delivered fresh to my ears on my morning walk. All the news worth knowing.'

'Don't sell the car, Victor. I will learn to drive,' said Clara.

'You, drive, Nonna?' Luca chimed in. 'I will be driving before you.'

'We will see if you are so cheeky with an empty stomach.'

'But you have cooked for six. Who is the sixth?' asked Luca.

'Gaultier. I will send you down with a plate after you have eaten Luca. I have a mind to send you now, with the lot.'

'He would only give it to the dogs,' said Luca.

'I would send it gladly. They wag their tails and not their tongues.' Said Clara.

'I will be along in a minute and fetch Larry on the way.' said Luca. He launched himself up the workshop stairs two at a time. He slowed to kiss his grandmother on the cheek as he slipped by her.

Clara turned to her husband who was wiping his hands. 'Larry! Has he taken to calling his father Larry now?'

'We are running a Pension. We must expect some changes. It's just as well we are retiring, my love.'

'There might be a permanent job for Sylvie, after all,' said Clara. 'She's a lovely girl; a fast learner.'

'There will be a permanent job but not for Sylvie. We must face the prospect of Larry taking another wife.'

'What, now?'

'No. But soon, his days of isolation are over. It is only a question of time.'

'It is best then that we move to Porto Vecchio. I so hate moving but I know you hate it more. Is that why you are naming Luca as your heir?'

'I think Larry will marry again. He believed Genevieve would come back for six years. He hoped she would for another three. I saw the light of hope die in his eyes and I could not bear for him to take Luca away. It is the wrong time in our lives to be moving but I have even employed moving men.'

'Victor, what's wrong have you hurt yourself?'

'No, it was to be my surprise.' Victor moved to the foot of the stairs. 'Ten days touring Italy. Two nights in Roma and then the bus takes us each day to a secret destination in Tuscany. Picnics, wineries, sightseeing. On day ten we are discharged in Pisa and catch the ferry to Bastia. Larry has agreed to pick us up in Bastia.'

'This is so unlike my hard working husband. A day's work done by lunchtime, you always said, and the afternoon left to ponder.'

'I am living my life as I have lived my days. Retire before fatigue sets in with a fresh mind. Before it settles in the bones. I was working here when I was eleven. That's sixty years, Clara.'

'You think I don't know it. Sixty years and no gold watch. No pension.'

'When we return, our furniture will be in Porto Vecchio. Larry will bring us and the possessions we carry will complete the move. I intend to sell the car before we go.'

Clara was wracked with love. No one on earth knew the weight of his sacrifice better than she. They returned, arm in arm to the outside table where places were set for lunch. Clara's eyes were moist, she began to serve as Larry, Luca and then Sylvie came in for lunch.

****

Larry and Luca carried the now empty crate to the wall outside the Smokehouse Studio courtyard.

Inside the courtyard walls the swimming pool filled the space when it was inflated. Larry had solved the dilemma of taking the pool to the compressor or the compressor to the pool. He had made the hose longer.

'The hose needed replacing anyway,' he said.

Luca looked at his father both knowing that 'new' was alien to the way the Piggery was run.

'We might need compressed air in the units,' he continued.

'What, to inflate further swimming pools?' said Luca cheekily.

'No, to drive air tools and unblock drains.'

'The drains are all brand new.'

'You know what I mean,' said Larry.

The patio furniture, bought by Clara, repaired by Victor, painted by Luca was squeezed into the tiny slice of courtyard the pool left. It was dwarfed into uselessness.

'This crate will make good kindling for the winter.'

'It could make a good kennel,' said Luca.

'We can't have a dog. Health and Safety regulations.'

'I was thinking of Gaultier.'

****

'Have you guys finished?' came Paige's voice from the upstairs studio window.

She and Dee Dee had returned unseen, from a day trip to the Aquarium. Now she was changing and Luca got a flash of supermodel at the window.

'Wow! That's big,' said Paige looking at the pool. 'How do we fill it?'

Luca turned to Larry. 'The old hose?' he suggested.

'Good idea,' replied Larry, 'I can attach it to the aerator in the upstairs sink.'

'Won't that take forever?' said Luca

It was all to do with gravity and water pressure. The new water mains from the road were going to cost 100,000 F. This was what Victor and Larry called phase two. About half of the new kitchen and bistro costs were related to the connection of this new water supply. It was hard for Luca to comprehend that seventeen or eighteen humans could use more water than one hundred and ninety pigs

It was all to do with gravity and water pressure. The new water mains from the road were going to cost 100,000 F. This was what Victor and Larry called phase two. About half of the new kitchen and bistro costs were related to the connection of this new water supply. It was hard for Luca to comprehend that seventeen or eighteen humans could use more water than one hundred and ninety pigs.

'How?' Asked Luca.

'I need to make an attachment but I have seen such things made for dishwashers.'

'Dishwashers?'

'Yeah, it attaches to the end of a standard tap. Where the aerator goes.'

Luca was looking puzzled. 'If you like, you can come with me, to Ajaccio, to the dishwasher shop,' said Larry.

Larry had mistaken Luca's confusion to be about the tap fitting; he was making an awful lot of effort for one guest! 'Ok,' said Luca, it would be good to spend time with his father who was today almost garrulous.

Larry was taunting Luca. Washing dishes was his least favourite chore.

****

Larry was preoccupied, Luca could tell. He hardly spoke on the trip to Ajaccio and didnt say anything until they were in the dishwasher shop. There were so many makes and models and they had a display running with a glass door. Larry purchased the aerator connector while Luca watched the apparatus at work.

'Do you think Clara would like one of those?' asked Larry standing behind him.

'No, I think she prefers to stand at her sink and smell her herbs.'

'Come on – home.'

It was rare for any member of the du Plessier family to travel into town for just one item. They were on the town road near the airport before Larry spoke.

'The coast or the mountain road?'

'The coast.'

It was longer, just as spectacular but overall a more relaxed drive. Luca got the impression he had made the right choice.

'This may be our last chance to talk as father and son.'

'How do you mean?'

'I think it's better that you call me Larry in front of the guests.'

Luca had done this already. So, was this what was on Larry's mind?

'This is the last opportunity we have for Victor and Clara to work at the pension. After this we are on our own.'

Luca was as amazed as anyone when Victor announced his Mystery Tour surprise for himself and Clara. Luca had answered some questions for him about passports and visas at the end of last year but he thought it was just a general interest question.

'I think we make it a policy that the office is manned, pretty much all day.'

'Sure.' Luca could find no argument with that. If a guest found no one in the office they went looking for Luca, Larry, Victor or Clara.

'That would be a good job for Sylvie.'

Luca looked over at his father; he was leading somewhere. 'That gets rid of *one* pest.'

The other was obviously Paige Goss. Why had his father made a special trip to buy this plumbing fitting and made filling her pool a priority? Could it be she was the reason for his distracted behaviour? Paige and his father; Luca tried to imagine it.

'What do you think?'

'What do I think of what?' Luca wanted to say who but changed his mind at the last minute.

'What do you think of Paige?'

Luca looked over at his father but before he could answer Larry began a long oration about her looks and how each, if taken individually, were not outstanding.

'But the whole package... I think it's quite alluring.'

This was a word unfamiliar to Luca but he liked it and consigned it to memory.

'She's so small. What makes her a supermodel anyway? Have you seen the mole on her left breast?'

'The whole world has seen the mole on her left breast.'

'Now Sylvie, she's a more arresting beauty. If she were born in another time she would be called comely,' Larry said.

'I hear that you sent them shopping together yesterday. That would have been interesting.'

'Interesting for who?' Larry laughed. 'Sorry, did you want to go with them?'

'No, I don't think I was born with that kind of stamina.'

'Not bad for your first day at work, to be sent shopping with a supermodel.'

Back at Pension Lazlo as they drove down the farm road and past the line of chestnut trees, Luca brought up the subject of flags. It had come to him while sitting alone waiting for Sylvie. Put a flag for each country of guest that they had staying under Pension Lazlo's roof.

'What's the purpose of that,' asked Larry.

'To celebrate the international... 'Luca searched for a word. 'International-*ness* of the place.'

'Look, your grandfather goes on holiday soon and then retires. I like the idea. But let's get the doors open and the place up and running first.'

That was a maybe that sounded like a yes. In his mind, as the car swung around in the gravel drive Luca could already see proud colours of five nations tugging and slapping at their pole moorings. He could hear them flapping but with less of the metal ping that you heard at the marina.

'I'll fit this for Paige and be with you in the office.

****

All morning there was a strange imperceptible hiss. In Larry's haste to get his In-laws to the ferry port he had put it out if his mind. There was a knock on the kitchen door. This was one of the unforeseen drawbacks of running a pension: you were so accessible to your guests. The person at the door was stiff, lanky, Teutonic and Larry could not remember her name.

'It is the reason we book at a small pension.'

'I'm sorry?' queried Larry.

'The noise.'

One hundred to one hundred and ninety pigs and then a gaggle of Turkish workmen had steeled Larry's ears to constant sound. It took him a while to fathom what this immovable guest meant.

Giggles and shouts came from the studio apartment of Paige and Dee Dee. Pool sounds. Sylvie and Luca were there too. The day had started out warm on its way to savagely hot. Larry had suggested that they go for a swim because sometimes the best help you can get is to none at all. Larry wanted to find a way he could get the latest prices for the pound and the dollar, or as Luca had put it go 'on-line.' Easily said, easy to execute but where to go for the source. Some guests wanted to pay for things in the currency they arrived with in their pockets. Some wished to change money with their host, a perfect opportunity to provide assistance and gather some of the strong currencies. Luca had suggested his friend Roald Pound, a computer whiz, a first rate hacker but did he understand the implications of holding large, or for that matter relatively small, amounts of a currency that could de-value overnight or before a newspaper was delivered.

Now Larry had sent Luca off he had probably added to his woes, he could not fob this... what was her name off on him. Luca spoke some

German. Thus disgruntled, he ran more adjectives past his muddled brain but still her name would not come to him.

With meticulous English, she had laid out her complaint. 'The language. It is vulgar. It is constant.'

Determined stoic. What was her damned name? 'It is the heat. Sound carries on a hot still day. Why not shut your doors and put on the air-conditioner?' Larry explained.

'Mr Lazlo, we are from Hamburg. We come to the Ligurian Coast for sun and wildflowers.'

'Yes but there is such a thing as too hot. I'm from Australia; trust me. In the heat of the day shut up the house and take it easy. Open up with the evening breeze. Is your air-conditioner working?'

'Cold air from a machine? Such a thing?'

'Trust me, the natives take a siesta. Or find other ways to keep cool.'

'Will the English girls take a siesta?'

Larry knew that this was unlikely as they had just got up. Paige had padded over bare-foot to invite them for a swim. This turned out to be ill-advised as the ground was too hot to walk on. She had stood on the cool flagstones of the century old kitchen and talked of the production of Romeo and Juliet that night, while Luca found her a pair of flip flops. She wore just a T shirt. Larry and Paige had bantered about what the Australians call thongs and the British call flip flops. Luca returned and the opportunity to ask her to the performance of Romeo and Juliet had passed.

'Will they? - take a siesta' the stubborn German asked again.

'Probably not. It's not an English custom.' Larry had forgotten What-Was-Her-Name standing there.

'Then why are you asking us to conform to Southern European customs, and not the English?'

'Look! If they were making a racket at night I would be right over there - telling them to keep it down. It is a beautiful day.' No, it wasn't. It was oppressively hot.

'What do you suggest we do? To keep cool.'

'The mountains are always cooler; or the beach' It was Saturday, the first day of a long weekend. If you could find a space for a towel, you might have to fight off a hoard to get to it. Larry knew he did not sound convincing.

****

'Look, that German lady is giving your father a hard time.' Paige had heaved her topless torso to the little glassless window in the courtyard. Luca was impaled to the spicy earth with unassailable desires. His back would blister before he moved.

'Don't scratch your famous little boobs,' said Dee Dee.

'That's right, look after your own interests. If I don't work; you don't earn,' said Paige.

'Which German lady?' asked Sylvie getting up.

With all three clamouring to look through the window, Luca took the opportunity to slide into the water.

'Has Larry asked you yet?' Sylvie asked Paige, 'he has four tickets.'

'I think he wanted to. Luca, you were too fast with the footwear,' the girls laughed.

'Would you really want to go?' he asked.

'Oh! Luca, there is not a romantic bone in your body,' Sylvie said. 'The Emperor Theatre Company, Shakespeare on the fresh mown grass, an evening supper, wine, candles. You have the advantage over us, as the play will be delivered in Genoese. It is totally sold out. Larry had better let us know if he is going to use the tickets soon, or you will have to speak to him,' said Sylvie as she slid into the water next to Luca.

'If he doesn't invite Paige soon,' said Dee Dee, 'Luca will have to take the three of us.'

She was met with a blue blade of a stare.

****

Larry eventually discovered the source of the hissing. He had heeded his own advice and taken a little siesta but the noise permeated his dreams. He went to wake his dozy brain with a coffee but no water came out of the tap, not even a dribble – the Aga had run out of water. This usually meant a broken pipe.

The seriousness of no domestic water was punctuated with shouts and cries from the studio courtyard. He had estimated the pool would take 24 hours to fill. It had filled in eight.

He knew his face would be sullen before he fully woke up. He marched to the door of the studio. Paige answered his knock. Larry fixed his gaze on a point over Paige's left shoulder. *It was either that or they stared blatantly at your tits,* he thought.

'How did you fill that pool so quickly?' asked Larry.

'From the tank.'

'That's our drinking water - water for the house.'

'Oops! Sorry.'

'A winter's worth of water.'

Luca padded in from the courtyard.

'Luca, did you help them fill the pool?'

'It wasn't him - it was me' Paige said. 'The water was so slow. We weren't aware it was so precious.'

'If Luca knew, he should have told me. Do you know what happens to an Aga that runs out of water? Come on, Luca. We can fill it manually and find the submersible pump.'

'Go easy on him,' said Paige.

'I want to have a shower. I was going out. I was bloody well going to ask you out!' cried Larry

'Have a *bloody* shower here then,' said Paige, beaming. 'I thought you'd never ask.'

'Sorry I'm a bit cranky. I need a coffee after a siesta.'

'Here, I'll get the coffee,' said Dee Dee.

'Real coffee. Do you mind? Luca will show you where.'

'It's what I live for,' said Dee Dee.

'I will take you up on the offer of a shower here. The units have new solar hot-water systems,' said Larry to Paige when they suddenly found themselves alone. After the longest silence, Larry said, 'It was Dee Dee who filled the pool, wasn't it?'

'Yeah! But she has saved my bacon many a time. Go easy on her.'

'I'll relax when the Aga is filled and I know it's not damaged,' explained Larry.

'A friend of mine sells those things. They build them like tanks.'

'Like tanks?'

Larry was being looked at in a way he found partly disconcerting and wholly alluring.

'Who sold you the swimming pool?' he asked, crossing his arms. He was standing there talking to a half naked supermodel in a pension that bore his name. He felt he had to do something - give his body one simple command - he was smiling from the inside. He was a shove away from giggling. A gentle shove.

'I will tell you tonight,' Paige replied. 'If you can arrange a picnic supper and a blanket, I will organise the champagne. We're in France, so that shouldn't be too hard. But you have four tickets and there are five people who want to go. How do you solve that dilemma?'

'I have asked a local artist to act as night watchman. His name is Dernavern. He is from Paris. Naturally I want to give the other two tickets to Luca and Sylvie. You must understand, we have lived like monks out here. Sylvie is good for Luca. I think she could crush another man's heart like a paper lantern, but she has a soft spot for my son. Do you think you could convince Dee Dee to stay?'

'I reckon I could give it a shot,' said Paige beaming like the over-medicated.

Chapter Sixteen

Low flying in a light aircraft

Joey Cotz was sweating like a pig. He asked again. 'How much to fly me to Corsica? Cor-si-ca.'

'Four hundred dollar. American. Cash.' Joey had heard right the first time. The pilot held up his hands. 'If you don't want...'

Joey peeled off four hundreds. 'Do you have a brother who drives a cab in New York?'

'Pardon?'

'Never mind. How long? The flight, how long?'

'Half an hour.'

'I'm in the wrong business,' said Joey.

Joey had shouted in his brutal Italian, *'Just one - no luggage,'* before the pilot had singled him out from the herd. After that his comprehension got worse. Joey was to sit up front, next to the pilot and had to nurse an engine part on his lap. At least there was no livestock.

'Hey! You have room for one more stick of gum.'

The pilot smiled and mustered up his best English. 'Fuck you, Joe.'

'Damned straight you have.'

But all banter stopped as the plane was now up to full speed and the pilot was pulling back so hard on the stick that Joey thought he saw it bend. Joey prayed; he closed his eyes and moved his lips. The vibration stopped and Joey guessed they were off the ground. He kept his eyes closed for one more minute. They were in the air. Joey allowed himself a normal breath.

The rest of the flight was pretty uneventful. That is if you can count scanning the dials with the concentration of a tax attorney as uneventful. It made the half-hour pass quickly. Joey forgot his apprehension when he saw the Citadel de Bonifacio lit up from below and the harbour with its full complement of yachts.

'Jeeze, Louise,' said Joey, and he snapped off four photographs. They had flown so low Joey had seen a white cap every now and then. The journey, from beginning to end, had all the markings of being an unauthorised flight, so it was no surprise when Joey found himself to be a dusty mile away from the airport terminal proper. The building was festooned with beaconing lights. Some of them spelled out the name Aeroport de Figan. Joey's fellow passengers silently melted into the night as Joey got the blood flow back into his legs. 'I suppose I gotta walk.'

'Damn straight' replied the pilot.

Just for the hell of it, Joey took his photograph. 'Fuck you, Pierre.'

'Fuck you, Joe.' The pilot got all the words right but the inflection wrong.

Joey jogged towards the terminal. Something told him it was imperative to get there soon. He arrived with his legs feeling like hot metal and his jeans clung to his thighs. The doors where electric but Joey could save precious moments by using the disabled ramp on the side of the building. The terminal was air-conditioned. Staff were leaving or hanging around in groups, talking. Joey sprinted to a car hire terminal. The surly girl did not have time to put up the grille.

'Whatayahgot?' said Joey in one breath.

'Nothing.'

'What are those keys, there?' asked Joey.

'A truck. A diesel truck. A Citroen.'

'Is it air-conditioned?'

The girl got a better grip on the grille.

'I'll take it,' said Joey.

'How long?'

'A week. Unlimited miles. Visa?'

Joey relaxed and took in his surroundings. This was a very small airport, Joey was indeed lucky, and in a few minutes it would all be closed up until the next flight. And Joey suspected that would be in the morning. The arrival of Joey's flight would have been timed to coincide with the air traffic controllers finishing for the day.

The girl swiped and produced documents in the same deft movement which Joey signed.

The truck turned out to be air-conditioned and more of a tradesman's van. The surly native had unwittingly arranged accommodation for Joey Cotz, for there was none to be had on the island.

Chapter Seventeen

Straight From The Vine

Some cocktail tomatoes grew wild for Clara. They had ripened early in the unseasonal May heat. Larry picked them last. He remembered how the flavour burst into the mouth when they were bitten. The first bite of spring tomatoes was a special event for Larry. He hoped it would be for this city girl. He had bought some local strawberries, soft cheeses and chestnut bread at a local baker. Bonifacio town was besieged with tourists and best avoided. He was beginning to panic until he heard Dernavern driving his new car -Victor's.

'Hi! If you want to make the first act you had better get a move on. The traffic is like Paris,' said Dernavern bounding from the Volkswagen.

'You'll be Ok?' asked Larry. Dernavern had changed something on the car. It was strange to see another person driving your father-in-law's car. It would not be long Larry thought, before the Volkswagen got the same treatment as the Fiat and became a fire breathing street racer.

'I'll be fine. I've never had to baby-sit a pension before but I have brought my easel and pens.'

'What are you going to paint?' asked Larry.

'Sylvie,' said Dernavern. 'Here, see the sketches.' Sylvie was naked, reclining on a large chair. Sex just oozed off the page.

'You are aware she is only 13?' said Larry, hoping he sounded stern.

'Tonight I'm just preparing the canvas. I don't think this will be a series. If I paint her at all, it will be a one-off.'

The two men's eyes met. Larry would have had much to say but he was late and most of all he was nervous.

****

Joey Cotz was hungry. His nose caught on to the familiar smell of frying potatoes. It was coming from The Cafe Bonaparte. As luck would have it, there was a lull in the flow of customers.

'Can I help you, sir?' asked Jean Luc in English.

'Have you seen this girl?'

'Of course. I have eyes. She is Paige Goss.'

'Have you seen her today?'

'She is here? In Corse?' Jean Luc wiped his hands on his apron. A Paige Goss fan obviously.

'I thought this place was called Corsica' queried Joey.

'What do you call the mainland?'

'France, Italy, why?'

'Locally that is *Française* and *Italia.* Get it?'

'I do. I could use a good man like you. What's your name?'

'Jean Luc.'

'I could go for a burger and fries, Jean Luc.'

'Coming up.'

When Jean Luc brought Joey's meal, he looked at the photograph again. 'If she is here, she has kept a low profile. Where are you staying?'

'That's it, I'm not. This place is like Coney Island on the 4th of July. I have to sleep in my car.'

'Eat here. Report in. I will know soon if she is here.' Jean Luc was rubbing his finger and thumb as he spoke. He spoke Joey's language.

The evening had arrived with a cooling breeze as Joey sat outside the Cafe Bonaparte and ate his hamburger. Idly, he scanned the faces of the crowd.

'What's going on here?' Asked Joey when Jean Luc cleared away his plate.

'Romeo and Juliet - it the Festival of Three Cultures, one of busiest weekends.'

Not a stone's throw away was one of the only level bits of ground in Bonifacio. Near the centre, in the largest expanse of its verdant grassed geometry, stood the Emperor Theatre. The outdoor theatre, with its brick balcony and trained ivy, was awash in the pale yellow of a spotlight. The same spotlight picked out the web of pristine, white gravel. Blankets of differing hues, like autumnal fall-out, were dotted on the grass. Candles were tonight's twinkling house lights. In deference to technology, two giant screens projected the events as they unfolded on the tiny stage. Portable radios relayed the sound to the audience. Luca had been given the task of getting fresh batteries for the portable radio.

To Joey Cotz, it was all just one milling crowd.

The Moor got a big cheer. He wore the traditional red bandana.

'What are they saying, Luca?' asked Paige.

'*You are a lover: borrow Cupids wings*. I can't translate every line. Watch. Listen. Hear the language as it was when this play was written.'

Paige popped one of Clara's cocktail tomatoes in her mouth. 'This is heaven.'

Larry followed suit. They were his tomato bushes now. '*If love be rough with you, be rough with love*,' he said when his chewing was done.

'Do you follow Genoese?' asked Paige.

'No, I know the play and follow the action.'

'We did this play at school,' said Paige, moving closer.

'Which part did you play?'

'None. I didn't. I just listened in awe as Tara Sullivan played Juliet to Andrew Patterson's Romeo. I just let the bare beauty of the words flow over me.'

The anxiety of earlier in the evening had given way to an enveloping calm.

'Tell me about the swimming pool?' Asked Larry. 'Who sent it for you?'

'A friend of mine called Opium.'

Paige moved so her face was ten inches from Larry's. She turned to follow the action on the stage.

'Opium?' asked Larry.

'A slow working dope!'

Larry laughed. He was trying to negotiate a piece of soft cheese onto a cracker with one hand. He was leaning on the other. Paige helped him, and popped the morsel in his mouth.

'Opium is a slow working dope and Truth is her creepy boyfriend - stranger than fiction. Get it? Opium's real name is something un-pronounceable in Latvian. Not all girls who come to London as models make it. Not all of them have nine 'O' Levels. Truth is a Prince or a Shah or something.' Paige held Larry's gaze while he chewed. 'Don't hate her.'

'Opium? How could I hate her?'

It was a genuine question born of interest. Paige studied Larry's face before answering. It was so refreshing to find someone so far behind on current affairs.

'Beauty evokes strong feelings,' she said and watched Larry's reaction. He was inert, so she went on. 'There is never any getting to know you. People have decided they want you - before they have met you. You are a bitch if you sleep with them and a slut if you don't. I haven't told anyone this, but Opium had only two choices: defeat or the needle. A lot of people put the hopes of their tiny fishing village up their arm.'

'Did you introduce Opium to Truth?'

'No, I introduced Opium to methadone.'

'Why are you telling me this?'

'Because there is a very real chance of you meeting the real me. Do you know why? Because you haven't read a tabloid or magazine - in how long?' She did not wait for an answer. Touching Larry's temple gently she continued. 'This is a blank canvas. That's all I ask. That's all any girl can ask.'

Larry picked at his food. Paige got close enough for her hair to brush his face.

'Is this difficult for you? Your son so close,' she whispered.

'Yes. I want him to learn about the world. But not all in one day.'

They looked up at Luca and Sylvie sitting as close as two people can on a balmy summer's night. Luca was explaining the significance of Chestnut Bread. Sylvie wore a halter dress. Her hair cascaded to the waistband of her bare back, the way only hair washed and left to dry naturally can. As Luca turned to say something to her, Larry noticed Luca had shaved.

'How quickly they grow up,' he said.

'I was his age when I started.'

'What? Modelling? Or shaving?'

Larry got a high beam smile as his reward. Good food, good wine, good company. This is what life is about.

Life was good again.

They talked until the eastern sky was yellow grey with the promise of another fine day. It was an irresistible impulse for Paige to tell the true tale, separate fact from exaggeration and fill in the fact behind the chatter. She did not gloss over the fact that she was a party girl, that she smoked sixty cigarettes a day and liked a drink – occasionally. Larry had only seen her smoke moderately and they concluded that Paige's lifestyle was conducive to her habits.

A few feet away on another blanket Sylvie was telling Luca how she wished that she had had a brother. 'A boy for papa. If I had a brother, Mamma and Papa would have gone their separate ways.'

Luca thought of his mother. In an average year he thought of her once, maybe twice. She was much in his thoughts these days. She had gone without a backward glance and left Larry to cope with a small child in a foreign land. He ought to broach this subject with him but not now, they had a play to watch.

'Do you regret being an only child?' asked Luca.

'No, I feel responsible for them staying together.' She turned to Luca, 'That's an awfully big responsibility.'

A new scene was beginning, the lighting changed to a single spotlight that picked out the lone figure of Romeo.

'What's he saying Luca?'

Can I go forward when my heart is here? Turn back dull earth, and find thy centre out.

'Where is your heart, Luca?' said Sylvie reaching for his chest.

Luca's heart was at this moment splitting in two. It was beating double time because he was having impure thoughts about his hairdresser. One girl filled him with desire and this girl – the one he should be falling for – filled him with optimism. She felt like the sister that he never knew he missed.

I have to go out with Sylvie; she is every boy's dream, thought Luca.

Luca had seen envy behind even grown men's eyes, he had watched them suck their guts in and walk into parked cars.

'It's in there.'

'It's beating awfully fast.'

'Thank God - I'm not dead then.'

Sylvie cuddled into Luca's chest and watched most of the performance using him as a backrest.

Paige watched the back of Luca, or rather the absence of Sylvie's silhouette, and decided that Sylvie had the right idea, it was just the sort of evening to cloak yourself in a good man. She decided she had better take the initiative with Larry.

'Have you finished eating?' asked Paige.

'I might pick some more, why?'

Paige inclined her head to the young couple. 'They seem to have the right idea. Don't worry I won't smoke.'

'How's that?' Larry made space for Paige in front of him. 'I thought all super models were supposed to be of Amazon proportions.'

'Not me. No bust. No amazon proportion legs. No surgery – completely original, me. Have you seen the mole on my left breast?'

'Paige, the whole world has seen the mole on your left breast.'

She turned her back to him and settled in. Smoke from a cigarette drifted past Larry and Paige.

'You don't feel the need?' asked Larry.

'I do – and I might even have a ciggy after.' Larry and Paige laughed. 'I haven't smoked – let's just say I'm only lighting up to satisfy my addiction. I'm only feeding my addiction. Did you ever smoke Larry?'

'No, I couldn't seem to get the hang of it. I'd go green and puke.'

'You did the drawback straight away.'

'Lucky me, how long before you should try the drawback?'

'Straight away – I felt sick too but the thing is after one packet you no longer feel nauseous. Then you are hooked; it goes from a social experiment to an addiction in one packet. It's good for me being around you, it's another reason not to light up.'

There was a pause that seemed to last forever.

'What do you say?'

'What do I say to what?'

Paige looked over her left shoulder as she leaned right. She was inches from Larry's face. 'I'm a shallow person, with a short attention span, a compulsive personality and twenty two credit cards. Larry, be my addiction.'

'Well, I thought this chap was the king of romance' said Larry meaning the play and Shakespeare.

'Larry, I need a good man bad or a bad man soon.'

Chapter Eighteen

Welcome to my World

In the crush after the play, Larry and Paige got separated from Luca and Sylvie. Larry and Paige made their way to the roundabout as most patrons were also doing. Anyone who dared to bring their car into the old town would have a fight to get to it - a fight to get through the throng of people and then a fight on the exeunt roads.

'What shall we do?' asked Paige and sat on the bonnet of Larry's car and rummaged in her bag.

'Wait for them here. Are you having a cigarette, after all?'

'No,' Paige held up a flask of Scotch. 'Can't expect me to give up all my vices at once.'

Larry took the bottle when offered and took a swig. 'This isn't local, it isn't even duty free, and where did you get it?'

'London. I haven't had a drink since I have been here, it must be the bracing sea air. Come here.'

Larry complied.

'Kiss me.'

'What?'

'Larry, I can’t wait forever, kiss me.'

'Aren’t you afraid that someone will see us?'

'In Milan, I had a camera poked under the door when I was on the toilet.'

'What?'

'Welcome to my world.'

Chapter Nineteen

Saying goodbye to an old vice

The traffic thinned and was no longer a nose to tail tailback. Paige and Larry had retired to the warmth of the car, it had been a warm day but the cloudless night had given up the day's heat too readily.

'They must have gone home alone. Luca does this all the time. Walks. God, to be that fit again. He's probably at home.'

'He's probably bringing Sylvie to a sweet orgasm now' Paige laughed, but from the look on Larry's face, wished she hadn't.

Luca was at home but Larry would never have thought of looking for him on the roof of the slaughterhouse. Paige followed Larry from room to room he left the lights on as he went.

'Where the hell is Dernavern?' asked Larry.

'I think I might know where he is – I'll go. I'll tell him to meet you in the kitchen.

'Right.'

****

Paige realized her evening was over - the romantic portion anyway, and made lots of noise as she entered Dernavern's studio.

'Dee Dee, it's me.'

Dee Dee appeared followed by a shirtless Dernavern.

'How was the play?' asked Dee Dee.

'The play was good, but Luca has gone missing. Never double date with a father and son. Dernavern make yourself scarce.'

Dernavern's English was not up to this. 'You think I should piss off?'

'Yeah. I think you should go.'

Why did foreigners pick up the bad words first? 'And, Dee Dee, take my advice and lay low,' said Paige.

Dernavern returned with his shirt and sketch pad and folding easel. He left with a casual over the shoulder departing wave on his way to the door. *Don't have to ask him twice,* thought Paige. When the door closed on Dernavern's back, Dee Dee's face had shut down behind a don't-ask-me mask.

One neurotic person was enough to deal with for the evening, Thought Paige. 'I'm off to sort Larry out, I will wait up with him until Luca gets home.'

Paige's nicotine craving descended like an avalanche. She lit up standing outside the pension she was renting for God knows how much. Until a few days ago she knew very little about this country, she was a blank canvas – carte blanche – she knew nothing. Each new fact was unfettered and disseminated without prejudice. There was an anything-goes defiance about these little dark intense people. And the overall result was she went about in flip flops from the One Pound shop to designer dresses and no one gave a damn. Genuine indifference, people weren't even curious. No one fawned over her either, no cameras in your face – *I could get used to this.*

Her first drag consumed half an inch of her only cigarette since breakfast. She clamped her lips down on the filter drawing her fine, $10,000 a day, cheeks hollow. The cigarette brought on a headache not unlike an ice cream headache and with alarming speed. Paige blew the smoke to the stars and swore. The second drag dulled her headache; her third filled her with loathing. She ground the cigarette into the gravel with a Prada sandal.

'There are two types of people, Paige: smokers and non-smokers. What's it gonna be?'

Would she give up smoking for the man who was now prowling the sheds and cleaner's cupboards leaving lights burning in his wake? This man who had never heard of Prada or had the tiniest inkling of how much they would cost if she was ever forced to pay for them? Never gonna happen – but, could she give up smoking?

They *were* her favorite shoes. *I would have worn them anyway.*

'Stuff it! I'll do it for me. I'll give up for me. I am *now* a non-smoker.'

Paige started out towards Larry's trotting silhouette. *Calling out or running, which was less dignified?* But Larry stopped at the sound of her fine sandals on the gravel.

'Oh! It's you.'

'Come on Larry, he'll be alright.'

'Yeah! Do you think so?'

'Let's turn some of these lights out and have a coffee; maybe he is with a friend.'

'He doesn't have any friends. He spends most of his time in the Citadel.'

'What?' *He's flipped; he's distraught thought Paige.*

'He passed the six foot mark at 12. That makes him a sort of freak. Not quite part of the human species.' Larry spilled the words out and he looked like he was not quite finished. 'He's acting strange, he went and got his hair cut and went out with Sylvie without telling us.'

'He's just a teenager, raging hormones and all that.'

'Sylvie could chew his heart out just for practice,' said Larry. 'Just to warm up.'

Paige found this logic hard to argue with. She had not had to deal with an irrational man before – not one that was sober and clean. Most of Paige's friends fell into two categories: under and overmedicated.

'Sylvie's parents?'

'Her father is away in Nice, house locked up, servants given the weekend off. Her mother lives in Paris'

'Wouldn't the best course of action be to wait by the phone?'

'Yeah! I suppose.'

'Get yourself a mobile and put the kettle on there's a good boy.'

Far too bright in here thought Paige, as she systematically turned off the lights, and thought of the thousands she had spent on rehabilitation. She thought it very house-wifey.

She was beyond wondering why apparently sane and rational men would pay her thousands of dollars just to wear *their* dress to a party. She needed to find her off button. All that money in therapy had taught her that. Larry was a sweat pant kind of guy. She just wanted to darn his socks.

On an impulse, Paige walked into the garden, snapped open her phone and pushed the speed dial for Rose. Rose, her Agent had assigned Dee Dee to Paige as her booker, but the unspoken truth was that Dee Dee had to keep Paige out of scrapes and for tabloid damage control. She had to tell someone of her decision.

'Hello Rose, were you sleeping?

-Rose, I've met this amazing man and I just want to put my feet up in front of a roaring fire with him after I have darned his socks.

-Seriously!

-Yes, just as well you were already lying down.

-No, I'm fine. Very fine and very sober. Clean and sober. Get used to it. This is the new Paige Goss.

-No, I've never darned a thing in my life. Well iron his shirts then.

-You know what I mean.

-Rose, it's this place, it's a fairyland. Post card views at every turn. And attitude, it's their *fuck you* attitude, perhaps it's contagious.'

Paige snapped the phone shut. She had tried to give up smoking before but this time she thought she could make it stick. Her heart was light as she hastened to get back to the warm glow of the kitchen.

Chapter Twenty

Not Quite of the Human Species

'Have they gone?' asked Luca.

'Yes,' said Sylvie as she squirmed inside their sleeping bag. They were up on the roof and curiosity had got the better of Sylvie when Paige had gone outside for a cigarette. It was a still night and most of the exchange between Paige and Larry was not lost to Luca.

Larry had said those words - *'Not quite part of the human species.'* And Dernavern was in the shit. And Paige wanted to darn his father's socks. Damn, his father did care, Luca could not have summed it up better himself. Luca pulled the second sleeping bag around his shoulders. If his father looked closely in his room, he would notice the spare pillows missing. Sylvie had asked about Luca's special place and they had decided to give Larry and Paige the slip and come here to the slaughterhouse roof. Luca had gone into great detail about how they would create a rooftop dining room for Pension Lazlo's guests, a sort of respite from walking and sightseeing. A bistro serving international foods; open all year round.

Sylvie and Luca had agreed that they would not have sex out here on the roof and would wait until they had some guarantee of privacy. Luca was relieved as he was in too much of a turmoil about Sylvie and

Caroline. He was an emotional typhoon; would he have to make a choice, was he ready for this?

****

Larry slept fitfully on the bed; Paige was in it and sleeping soundly. Before she fell asleep, Paige had astounded Larry with her astute observations of Corsica and its people. It sometimes took an outsider's eyes to see the small detail. At about 2.00am Larry got up and padded to the door. Paige had not moved so he went into the kitchen first. Then he sat in Clara's herb garden until just before dawn. This strange sensation that Larry was feeling was *alive.* Larry felt alive, for the first time in 9 years. What Larry had was nothing and he was prepared to risk it all. It felt good. With the sun formulating for a full day of splendor in the Eastern sky, Larry gave in to fatigue and got under the covers sometime towards dawn.

****

Luca did not like to wake them. He stood at the door of his grandparent's room, why had his father and Paige slept in here?

'Dad we have to connect the tank to the well.'

The fog lifted from Larry's mind. His thoughts turned to Paige. In the moment before wakefulness, Larry often found his mind worked on complex themes and issues. What was happening? Where was Paige now? It was time to take stock: did he find Paige intoxicating? Yes. Did he love her impish smile? Yes. She had a fuck- you attitude that he found wholly alluring and so, so tempting. Could he live in her world.

Could he abandon his privacy and live with a camera pointed in his face? Yes.

'Where the bloody hell were you last night?' asked Larry.

'We slept on the roof of the slaughterhouse.'

Luca was going to add fully clothed, but he saw that his father and Paige had slept fully clothed also. Luca had indeed been up early, called to duty with odd job around the new pension. A door off its rollers in unit six and a tangled curtain cord in unit nine had kept him busy for an hour. Sylvie had manned the phones and both Sylvie and Luca could now do with a break so they could have some breakfast.

'Shit, it's ten o'clock,' said Larry. 'I'll deal with you later.'

Two people were waiting at reception, so Larry went to help them and Luca joined Sylvie in the kitchen for a bowl of corn flakes. Paige walked in, her clothes looked slept-in, Luca and Sylvie exchanged a look.

'Any coffee?' asked Paige, tipping the pot and sloshing some black liquid in a cup

'I'll make a fresh pot; that's this mornings,' said Luca.

'Why? What time is it?'

'Ten.'

'That's still early; I'm going to run a bath.' Paige yawned and stretched. 'What happened to you guys last night? You had your father worried sick.'

'We slept on the roof of the slaughterhouse.'

Paige shuddered visibly and left, abandoning her stewed coffee. She left the kitchen via the office and spoke to Larry. Luca saw him visibly relax and turn round, catching Luca's eye, he smiled. Sylvie finished her breakfast and went to change and take a shower in vacant apartment seventeen.

When Larry finished with the guests at reception he came in as the fresh coffee was filling the kitchen with irresistible aromas. Luca relieved him on reception as he was popping some bread in the toaster.

'When did you start drinking coffee?' asked Larry through the open door when he could see that Luca was on his own and not on the phone.

'Sylvie brewed it, and it was hot and smelled inviting. So...'

'What do you think?'

'It's an acquired taste, I think,' said Luca trying to gauge his father's mood.

'Why didn't you ring? To let me know you were all right? Why did you slope off yesterday without your tea?' The phone in the house was in Victor and Clara's room and the room next to the kitchen. Had Luca really caused so much aggravation?

'Dad, it was my first date, I didn't need you to be nervous for me.'

Larry ordered his son into the shower. At some level, every parent - especially a single parent - prepared themselves for this day. Luca was right. *Damn, Luca was right. He had been nervous.* Sylvie had all the composure of a self-absorbed teenager but she gave off a calm aura and she was damned pretty.

Luca returned from the shower his pate showed white through his hair that was darker but otherwise unchanged from being wet.

'Comb your hair you scruffy sod. My turn,' said Larry heading for the shower. 'Tell you what, Luca I didn't think it would be this busy, this soon. We may need a full time receptionist. Can you think of someone?'

Larry left the kitchen, left Sylvie and Luca to fathom his new chipper mood. When Larry returned showered and shaved, there had been a large booking on the fax machine. Sylvie and Luca were transcribing the booking to the day sheets when he came in.

'Come on, Luca let's find that submersible pump.'

****

With her hair wet and slick from her shower, Paige crept up behind Larry in the workshop. She knew wet hair accentuated her cheekbones, she had taken off her rings and worn a plain pink jumper. In the kitchen, before her shower, she had decided to give Larry the minimalist look when she saw the tousled Sylvie, raw and sensual. Larry was trying to get to the large aluminium ladder, hanging from an oak rafter. He saw her shadow on the floor.

'G'day,' he said over his shoulder.

'G'day yourself,' said Paige when her stealth had been exposed. She may as well have worn a trench coat. 'What happened in that kitchen?'

Larry halted his exertions for a moment. 'My son is growing up,' said Larry and resumed his wrestle with the ladder.

'He needs his space.'

Larry's laugh was vicious and short. It shocked Paige into silence. She knew a little about teenagers, as most of the people in her industry were not much older than Sylvie and Luca. At 24, Paige was a ten-year veteran.

'We've had nothing but *space* here on a bloody pig farm.'

Paige took a deep breath. 'Well, you are going to get a full-time receptionist, that's for sure.

'What? You? You fancy a change of career? In case this modelling thing doesn't work out.' Larry was at full stretch for the big ladder. 'Bloody Murat, it's a hell of a responsibility to rush off to Nice and dump his daughter on us.' Larry was getting frustrated at the ladder.

'*Hello!*' said Paige. 'Why not use this small one?' Paige put her hand on a smaller wooden ladder. *Was Larry teasing her?*

'It's rotten and full of worm.'

'But it's so quaint,' Paige said.

'It was made by Victor or his father. Besides, it doesn't comply to workplace health and safety.'

'Come on, Larry. Relax! Don't try to be a manager and father 24 hours a day.'

'I'm not, I think the best thing to do is nothing,' said Larry turning at last.

Paige knew her light was good from the open door; she gave Larry a half profile. She paused and brought all of her training to bear.

'Look, last night - the play' she said, 'Romeo and Juliet, wasn't it about two young kids who were, after all, just 14.'

'Yeah! And look how it turned out.'

Paige crossed her arms. 'Your work here is done' she said emphatically.

'My work here is what?' said Larry but his anger was spent, the corners of his mouth wanted to turn up.

'I don't know much about raising kids, but I know that it's too late to start being a parent *now!*' Paige allowed a wry smile to escape and saw it returned tenfold. 'Luca seems like a nice kid. Perhaps the hardest thing to do now is to stand back and watch him make his own mistakes. For a parent, that is.'

'Oh! For a parent.'

'Not that I am a parent, but I was Luca's age when I started. Larry, you have been his mother and father for all this time,' Paige said. 'I can tell you that if two young kids are going to have sex, they will. Throwing them together under one roof is merely underwriting the deal.'

'Underwriting the deal. Where do you come up with this stuff?'

'I work in an industry where predatory men live out their sexual fantasies. Underwriting The Deal is a sort of late nineties version of the casting couch.'

'Were you one of them?' asked Larry.

'No. This is happening now. A woman, Rose Underhill, discovered me. And used me in a Calvin Klein jeans ad. They were looking for a face that said 'innocent'. And strangely I wasn't. The photographer was gay. I guess I had a dream run. It's lucky Juliet was not born today; she'd be in a Coke commercial or something.'

'On Lammas-Eve at night shall she be fourteen,' said Larry in a far-off voice. 'What is this fascination with young, extremely young girls?'

'I guess I started that. I mean why not? I have been blamed for everything else,' said Paige. 'When is Lammas-Eve?'

'August the first.'

'When is Sylvie's birthday?'

'I have no idea.'

'Larry, don't beat yourself up. You relaxed and let your hair down one night and the world didn't end. If Sylvie and Luca had sex under your roof, does it matter? Or the fact that we didn't, does that worry you more?'

Larry finally wrestled the ladder from the rafter. 'Not knowing.'

'What?'

'Not knowing. You asked me what worried me more.'

'It's time you had that talk with Luca; if you haven't already. And make condoms available in the bathroom cabinet.'

'They are. We have and they are.'

Larry carried the new ladder to the water tank. Luca had the pump lowered and ready to connect.

'The old ladder, it's so pretty. Why don't you put geraniums on it?' said Paige.

'Because it is rotten and would collapse. Sorry to sound so cranky, I will be half human after a coffee.' Larry poked his tongue out.

'Then I am going to get you away from this place. Can Luca look after the shop for an hour or two?'

Larry was up the ladder with a flashlight in his mouth.

'Sure,' said Larry, on his knees.

No one else had anything to add so Paige turned on her heel and headed for her unit.

Chapter Twenty One

Snakes and Ladders

Joey spoke at length to Jean Luc after his breakfast. He decided he needed a map of the layout of Pension Lazlo. The sound of the layout meant Joey would need to check things out under cover of darkness. The place also sounded isolated, which was good. But a lone car on the road would not go unnoticed.

'The brochure. It is not available at the Tourist Authority?' asked Jean Luc.

'I don't know, where is that?'

'I will go for you, on my break.'

Joey wanted information, Jean Luc wanted hard currency and revenge. It was a match made in heaven.

'Can't you pretend you want to stay there and walk up and just ask for a brochure?' asked Joey.

'No, it is not like that. Have you stayed in a motel in your hometown?'

Joey had but his 'hometown' was home to some 18 million people. He thought about his options. 'Ok! We could get a tourist to check it out.'

'Sure, but I hear it is up-market. Don't ask anyone who looks like he is down on his luck.'

That's how it was. Joey sat in the sun and watched the faces. He would have to make arrangements for shaving and bathing. Jean Luc, so fond of the folding stuff, would help him there. Joey was so deep in his thoughts that he did not see the stranger approach.

'Hey, fellah. Are you an American?' he asked.

'New York, New York. How'd you guess?'

'The Hanes shirt, a dead giveaway. Would you take a photo of my wife and I, near the steps to the ferry? With the sound in the background.'

'I'd be happy to. Where are you from?'

'Yonkers.'

'Yonkers? Smile,' Joey said. 'A little closer please. One more?'

'Sure, why not? Say, fellah, where are you staying?'

'I'm staying with friends. This place is booked solid. Say! Do you guys have a car?'

'Sure do. We are staying at the Place Hotel de Ville, in Batista. Stop by for a drink, anytime. They have Budweiser.'

'I might just take you up on that. I know where I am staying next time.'

'Where is that?'

'Pension Lazlo. It's brand new. Hey, I don't suppose you guys, being from Yonkers and all, could help me out.'

'Sure. What'd you need?'

'Well, I need a brochure of this new Pension. I stayed there and I'm writing a travel piece.'

'Why didn’t you get one when you were there?'

'I told you it was new. I was there before it was even open for business. It is a mass of old buildings converted to self-contained accommodation.'

'I thought you said you were staying with friends.'

'I am. You meet a lot of people in this business. And I check in as a regular guest and write the travel guide.'

This intrigued the woman from Yonkers. She had been shy at first. 'Say, what a swell job. How'd you get a job like that? I could do a job like that.' If anything, her accent was stronger.

'You need to be pretty handy with one of these,' said Joey, tapping his own camera.

'Oh, we are, aren't we T.J.' T.J. nodded enthusiastically. 'And with the kids grown up and off our hands...'

'Hey, don't work my patch. I waited for someone to die to get this job.'

'It would be a pretty good line of work,' said T.J.

'Who do you work for?' asked the female Yonkite.

Joey mentioned the name of the agency who bought his photographs in London. Lies flowed readily from his tongue. But it was true about waiting for someone to die to get the job with the London agency. Joey filled a void after a British photographer took his own life. Photos of Paige Goss were paying a premium then. Joey dropped all his other interests and concentrated on Paige.

****

Work on the well was under way. Paige had got Larry away from Pension Lazlo for an hour. He drove and they strolled the beaches, climbed the steps to the Old Town and got lost in the narrow lanes, where the buildings tried hard to close out the sky.

These were the views that were gobbled up by so many video and film cameras. With the viewfinder held up close, many camera owners hoped to capture some of the fairytale magic that is Bonifacio. The brothers Grimm could not have conjured up a town like this. No one would have believed them.

There are other walled cities in the world, some half as beautiful in the man-made component. Similarly, there are many natural beauty spots in the world. Bonifacio was both, with history icing. It felt the most natural thing in the world for Paige to hold Larry's hand. It also aided walking in the small spaces.

'These buildings are so close together. We think we're crowded in London,' said Paige.

'Some of these homes have been in the same family for ten centuries,' said Larry.

Paige waved at a woman towing a continuous line of washing three stories above their head. The old woman muttered something that sounded totally unpleasant.

'What did she say?' asked Paige.

'Sometimes I'm glad I never bothered to learn the language. Insults are universal. I did understand the phrase, *go home*.'

'What is it like to live here in Paradise?'

'Hey! Wait a minute. You live in London. Every year hordes of tourists descend on London. What do you feel when you see them?'

'I get driven everywhere these days. But when I was young, I used to try and guess where they were from.'

'And now?'

'Now I couldn't care less. They clog up the transport systems with their back packs and - your lot - the Aussies take over a region, take work in a pub. That seems to be the norm.'

'I never quite got to London,' said Larry.

'What happened?'

'I met Luca's mother.'

'Where did you meet her?'

'I was working for an Italian Ferry company, as a deck hand. I was going to work the summer and head off to Goa.'

'Goa?'

'Do you know Goa?'

'Are you a drug crazed hippy?' asked Paige.

Larry laughed. A big hearty laugh for a small, confined space. Paige wondered if he would kiss her.

'This was in 1984.'

When Larry spoke, it was in a quiet voice. This alarmed Paige. She felt the silence shift. If they were privy to the people who lived in these houses, an odd glimpse of a room here, a blind flapping there, they were probably on full view to the people who lived in these tightly packed houses. They would be able to be heard.

They had come full circle. The houses in the Old Town kept a lot of their secrets, with steps and paths worn smooth.

'I never got to Goa. Look, I need to get back and get this pump connected.'

'I thought Luca was doing it.'

'Luca can't wire it up. After the weekend I will have Horst connect proper pipes and put a permanent line in for the pump.'

'Who is Horst?' asked Paige, not liking this shift in mood.

'The contractor.'

'You mean make it permanent.'

'You know that avenue of chestnut trees?'

'Very pretty. Who planted them? They had to be planted because they are so straight.'

'Victor planted them. One of his specialities was Chestnut fed piglets. But that's where the new mains water has to come from. We can't go ahead with the bistro or the pool until we have a 150mm mains. I won't tell you what that'll cost. You probably make that much in a day.'

'You won't get rid of the Chestnut trees?' worried Paige.

'No, the mains will come in along the fence line.'

'One drink,' pleaded Paige. 'Then we'll go back.'

Larry wished he had not mentioned how much she made in a day. He noticed how Paige revelled in the quaint, the rustic and the charming. She had shied away from a drink in the Carriage, where expatriates hung out, preferring the local ambience of a small cafe where old men in singlets played dominoes.

Chapter Twenty Two

The Carriage

Joey had found a bar frequented by expatriates not far from the Old Town. It was called the Carriage Bar and run by an Englishman who stayed open all day. The draught beer was cold and served in big English style pint pots. The banter was English, mostly. The lamps that gave the bar its name came from vehicles that would have gone under the name of Motor Carriages. It was a tiny piece of England, displaced. Joey spread his recently acquired map and studied the layout of Pension Lazlo.

****

Less than 50 metres away, Paige and Larry sat inside a cafe off the beaten track, by the shuttered doors.

'My friends at the Carriage will wonder where I've got to.'

'We can go to the Carriage Bar another time. Just let me enjoy my anonymity, for one more day.' Paige ran her hand over the round tabletop. Somehow its chipped paint said *France*. The miss-matched glasses confirmed it.

'Fine. Then we must get back. What are your plans for tonight?'

Paige smiled. 'That depends on a lot of things.'

'When are you going to let me cook for you?'

'Do you want to cook for me?'

'Did you like those tomatoes?'

'Yeah! Sure did. Home grown?'

'What if we watch the sun set, grab some crab rakes and then cook what we catch on the beach?'

It was Paige's turn to laugh. 'I can't wait to tell Rose,' she said.

'Who's Rose?'

'My agent. Look, our lives have obviously been so different. I think it is wonderful. If in England a man wants to impress a girl, it's a box at Covent Garden. If she is an 'A' list kind of girl, he may organise a table for two at Oscar Foxtrot's. If he wants a quick tumble in the back seat, it's a swift Chinese take away.'

'Didn't I take you to see Romeo and Juliet?'

'Yes, you did. It's just that they would really get a laugh.' Paige saw that Larry was mortified. 'At the thought of me catching my own supper,' she went on, reaching for his hand.

They haven't seen your face light up at the sight of a baby being bathed in the kitchen sink, thought Larry. A sink you passed close enough to have its water splashed on your arm; they know the other you. The 'A' list girl, on call 24 hours. I've watched you drink all this in a kid chasing a chicken in the street, a baby goat bleating for its mother. Paige was smiling at Larry, so he shrugged off the mounting feeling of pique. 'I've seen the real you. So, come on girl; we are going crabbing.'

Chapter Twenty Three

Got you Covered

The men worked on the well until the shadows grew long enough to provide shade for their backs. They could not locate the bottom of the well and left the pump suspended when they were sure it was below the water line. They ran power from an extension in Paige's apartment through the round glassless window.

As the shadows grew long, Larry said. 'That's it, leave the well cover slightly ajar. Horst can finish the job with the right gear on Tuesday.'

Larry put away the tools and wiped his hands on a rag. Luca was calling from the kitchen that they had water again. Soon it would be hot. Paige had gone to get ready. Dee Dee was off in the town with Dernavern. Larry had heard Paige on the phone as he plugged in the power cord. Now that it was quiet he supposed she was resting.

'Can I leave you and Sylvie in charge?' said Larry to Luca on entering the kitchen.

'Sure, what are you guys up to?' said Luca.

'Paige and I are going crabbing.'

'Brilliant. The usual spot?'

'That depends. If it is not overrun with tourists. Or near the airport.'

'Bring some home for our supper.'

'Will you be staying in?'

'No. It's Liberation Day. There will be fireworks in the Citadel. We met some people with a boat and have been invited to a party.'

Larry was looking forward to a long hot shower he was dirty from his labours.

Chapter Twenty Four

Glassless Window

As there was no movement and everyone seemed to rest before the festivities, Joey lowered his camera with the telephoto lens. He was standing under a shady Chestnut tree, the van about a kilometre up the road. The Pension owner seemed to be involved in some sort of emergency repairs. He was wearing overalls at any rate. Joey munched on what the bakery owner had call 'bread of the dead'. It was a flat bread with olives washed down with lots of water. This could be a long wait. He saw Paige and Larry leave in Larry's car, after first loading some equipment that looked like nets and buckets into the trunk. Then, sometime later, the tall boy and the black-haired girl walked up the lane where Joey hid in the shadows. They were dressed for a night on the town and were too engrossed in each other to notice him. They waited at the bus stop. After the bus pulled away in a plume of diesel soot, Joey emerged from the shadows. He could snoop at his leisure now and if asked, he was a tourist looking for a room. His car had run out of gas up the road. Joey got his story straight in his head and made for the empty pension. A light had been left on in the kitchen of the main house and, somewhere a television or radio played softly.

'Nice place,' said Joey, to no-one but gaining confidence.

A ten-minute stroll around confirmed the place to be in the sole possession of a middle aged couple who were talking in German and packing. Joey lifted the latch on the gate that led to the side path of the studio apartment. An inflatable pool filled the space and reflected the moonlight. Joey would not have to break in as the doors to the downstairs bedroom were open to the courtyard. A swift practiced eye told Joey this was the room of Miss Dee Dee McPhee. Booker to Miss Paige Goss. That meant the loft bedroom would be Paige's.

'Damn it,' said Joey.

There was no taller building with which to get a photograph, no cover, and the olive tree covered the front of the apartment. The courtyard provided a photo opportunity but Joey would be very exposed.

The workshop looked promising. Joey decided to move a ladder into position and, if the opportunity presented itself, shoot a photograph though the glassless window. He would hide the ladder near the wall of the studio apartment. He chose the lighter wooden ladder.

Near the wall of Paige's apartment was an empty crate, a new one that had recently been home to the inflatable pool. He stacked the ladder behind the crate lying down. Then he went into town to buy some beer.

Chapter Twenty Five

To Catch the Heart off Guard

The embers of the fire glowed a generous orange. Dry wood cracked and protested but the pot was coming to the boil. Paige, needing time to think, went for a walk. She walked south on the low-water mark and returned by the high-water mark where the sand sifted and stuck to her toes. Her beacon was a lone figure hunched over a pot. Shadows danced and he was lit red from the fire. It was Larry. It was her Larry - she felt the possessor of joy. The spirit of the moment captured: the mood captured with friends after a few drinks. She had never felt so relaxed. And the image of a man distorted by a beach fire had caused it. The reason was getting busy with their catch. Paige did not have the dexterity, or was it the killer instinct, to chase and catch the crabs in the rake. She could not keep them on her rake long enough to tip them into her bucket, so she baited a net and threw it out. Larry's bucket had ten crabs before she had one. She had held the flashlight while he sexed the crabs and threw the females and the undersized on the beach. Paige squealed as one sidled over her foot. Alive they made her flesh crawl. But she had tried to catch them and decided she preferred her seafood cooked on a plate. The man hunched over the steaming pot; Paige wanted to darn his socks. Then she laughed at the image she had conjured from nowhere.

'It must be this Ligurian air,' said Paige.

'What?' Larry had not heard her approach.

'Well, I did try to catch crabs. I might be better if it was daylight, and I was not standing knee deep in water.'

'Getting bitten hurts, but it is not a bad as the fear of getting bitten.'

'Why is that?'

'Pain is tangible; fear is infinite.'

'Who said that?'

'Lazlo Moro' said Larry, using his formal name. 'Does this mean I have to book season tickets with Covent Garden?'

'Would you like too?'

'I'd like to go - just once. How do you think I would go in your world?'

'I don't know. How would you like to have a camera in your face at every turn? How would you like to read about the break-up of your latest relationship in the daily press before it happened? People would call your mother at 3.00 am for a comment.'

'No, they wouldn't; she's dead.'

'Well, you know what I mean. Pictures of your ex-wife would appear in the paper for the whole world to ogle. Compare. Speculate. I'm prepared to pay a certain price for my fame. But what about everyone who your life has overlapped? Even briefly. Were they warned about this, are they ready?'

'Just how famous are you?'

'It's not that I'm so famous. I have been blamed for everything: the waif look, the use of younger and younger models, Heroin Chic. Anorexia, I was blamed for all of that.'

There was a lot of activity in the pot. Larry disappeared in a shroud of steam.

'They're done,' said Larry.

In the commotion a tear escaped and settled on Paige's satin cheek. Strangely, it was not self-pity; a week ago and it might have been. The tear was for Larry, his life was about to change forever.

'This is the one you caught. Yes! Definitely, this is the one.' said Larry holding up a steaming pink crab.

'What, no tartare sauce? No lemon?'

Paige wiped away the tear. The crab on the plate had created its own little puddle. She bent to drain the plate and lowered her face below the column of steam from the pot.

'This is a rarely seen culinary implement,' said Larry. 'A pair of pliers. Try it. Try the crab you caught yourself. Pretty soon you will come to realise that all those sauces and condiments are devised by chefs to disguise the fact that their food is not quite fresh.'

'Hot. Hot.' Now Paige had a legitimate reason for tears.

'Well. I've tried to cook them in cold- water but it takes too long; turn around and they've swum away!' joked Larry.

The crab was spectacular, once it had cooled. Paige overdid the oohs and ahhs.

'I'll have to catch some more now,' said Larry.

'Why? I couldn't eat another thing,' said Paige.

'I should hope not. No, I promised Luca some for his supper. These people who give you the title waif, have they seen you fall on a fresh cooked crab?'

'Not very *waify*. Not very chic.'

Larry smiled. He wished he had brought a bottle of wine now.

'What are you thinking?' asked Paige.

'I could murder a nice bottle of Chardonnay right now' mused Larry.

'Look, the moon is straight up now. Why don't I catch some more crabs for Luca and Sylvie? You get the bottle of wine before the Off Licence closes.'

Larry fell on his back laughing. 'Off Licence! This is Liberation Day, or it will be at midnight. The people who sell alcohol will have the good sense to stay open all night and go straight to the bank in the morning. Do you think you can catch them? Now you have tasted fresh crab meat?'

Paige picked up the rake and tied the rope of the floating bucket to her waist.

'Try not to let that fire go out. I'll fetch us a dozen crabs. Now go.'

As Larry made his way up the beach, people were settling in for the fireworks display. He greeted them, total strangers, in a variety of languages completely at random. With sandy feet and trousers rolled to his knee, he stood in line to pay for the wine he had selected. The wine store owner was jovial. Why shouldn't he be? It had been a long winter.

People had drawn close to the fire. Someone had rebuilt it. Larry fetched more fresh water and scanned the water for Paige. She was wading in the water and some young kids had joined in the great crab hunt.

A great lump of a man thrust his hand out. 'Dougie Moore, Manchester, England'

'Larry Morgan, Melbourne, Australia.'

'Hey! You guys really thumped us in the cricket. I tell you what we need back 'ome...'

'What?'

'Something like your AIS, in Canberra.'

Larry did not know what the AIS was, but he did not let on as the Moore family, who had inherited a full measure of the large gene from dad, settled in around the fire.

'Eh oop! Here she is, the little woman. Not only have you got the cricket sorted, you have your women out fishin'. See that pet? Now, when I want a fresh fish supper, it's no more quick-trip to the chippie. I want it straight from the ocean.'

'You'll geddit in the neck and never mind who caught it, yah bloody big lump.'

'Caught with your own fair hands as an expression of your love for me petal,' said Dougie Moore. The only thing broader than his Manchurian accent was perhaps his belly.

'Pay no mind to him, Mrs Morgan, where are you staying? Is it nice? We find the locals a bit surly.'

'The accommodation's nice and all. But they can be right snotty with it,' said Dougie Moore, in the space where his wife paused to breathe.

Paige, beaming but confused at being called Mrs Morgan busied herself with her baseball cap, putting it on backwards, while trying to wring out her wet T shirt.

The Moore's were not one to hang about waiting for an answer. Paige was thinking about nice things to say about Pension Lazlo when Mrs Moore spoke.

'Are you stayin' for the fireworks love?' she asked.

'What fireworks? No, we're getting back. These crabs are for our son, Luca.'

'Pretty name, Luca. You don't sound Australian. How old is your boy?'

'Fourteen.'

'Fourteen!' shrieked Mrs Moore. 'You must have had 'im when you were nine. I lost my figure with our Lester. Say hello, Lester. How do you do it?'

'Hello, Lester,' said Lester, and earned a cuff on the side of his head for his cheek.

Larry showed Lester and the other silent brother how to use the crab rakes. The Moore’s said they had eaten but did not protest when Larry offered to put their crabs in with his, the pot nicely steaming by way of invitation.

'Well, I never, the fresh water drowns them?'

'It only takes minutes. Then pop 'em in the steaming water. Pull them out when they are pink. Eat 'em as soon as they are cool. Don't you dear.'

'Yes darling, I burned my fingers earlier on.' said Paige. 'I was a bit too eager.'

'A bit eager to get home an' all' chuffed Dougie.

Big Dougie Moore got such a slap that his chins wobbled. Larry started packing up. He carried the steaming pot at arm’s length. Paige was running to catch up. They made it to the car and got inside before they burst out laughing. They stated talking together.

'I wonder if... '

'What did he ... '

'No, go on. You first,' said Larry.

'What did he call you?' said Paige.

'Larry Morgan. I was Larry Morgan at school, Lazlo Moro was just not fashionable. I was just trying to fit in.'

'What were you going to say?' said Paige.

'I wonder if he would ever shut up if he knew who you really were?'

'Come on husband, our son is hungry.'

Progress was slow with the lanes blocked with all sorts of vehicles. Someone stopped a truck in front a Larry and the whole family piled out with folding chairs and began setting them up on the tray of the truck. Larry reversed back and drove round the truck. He waved with good nature. The truck driver waved back.

'Do you want to see the fireworks?' said Larry

'Can you see them from Pension Lazlo?'

'If we go outside. There's a building that has a flat roof, only it's a favourite spot of Luca's'

'So, you want to be outside, secure and with some privacy. I have somewhere in mind. And I think I can guarantee you some fireworks.'

Chapter Twenty Six

A Pap Goes to Work

The German couple had gone to bed and almost every other guest was out. Joey found a lot of the doors open. An Italian couple had dashed back for a change of clothes but apart from that it was deathly quiet. Then came the car that Joey had been waiting for. A single car came down the avenue of chestnut trees, its headlights sliced rhythmically past the sturdy trunks. The canopy of green seemed to trap the car's headlights. Larry and Paige had returned alone, and from the splashes and giggles they were taking a dip in the pool. Joey looked at his watch that he had changed to local time. It was five minutes to midnight. He moved with confidence to the crate where he had stowed the ladder.

Placing the ladder against the wall, the sounds coming now from the pool sounded promising. Certain European magazines paid a premium for celebrity flesh. Joey calculated a price as he climbed.

In the pool Paige and Larry entwined limbs. Side by side they lay with a wine glass in their hands.

'Thanks for the evening, it was just what I needed.' Paige backed this up with a kiss.

'If ever you get delusions of wanting a house in the suburbs, if you ever pine for a normal life, think of Dougie and his wife. Did we ever get to find out her name?'

'He called her petal, but I think that was an affectionate term. Do you know what would make this holiday special?' Asked Paige.

'Tell me.'

'I want to be a nobody long enough that I want to be *me* again.'

'Come here Mrs Nobody.'

The sky was split with piercing white light, followed by a sonic boom to shake the windows. The expanding phosphorescence lit up the walls of the courtyard.

Chapter Twenty Seven

Is it Good When Bad things happen to Bad People?

The ladder under Joey trembled, rotten and old, it split. He fell, breaking every rung with his shin on the way down.

Chapter Twenty Eight

Out of the picture

Dernavern painted nude. That is, he did not put any clothes on. Dee Dee stayed under the sheet. He locked into the frenetic energy and sound of the fireworks and assaulted the canvas with a manic energy.

'Are you going to paint me?' asked Dee Dee.

'No.'

'Have you fucked her?'

'She's only 13,' said Dernavern.

'I was looking for a yes or no answer.'

Dernavern loaded his brush and advanced on the canvas. He was energised by the recent sex. Dernavern had leaped up when the fireworks had started and began a portrait of Sylvie from the sketches.

Dee Dee threw the sheet over her head. The door to the terrace was open and through the sheet she could see a slice of sky. Reds and chimney orange and greens ripped screaming, whistling, expanding orbs in the suede black of the night sky. One of the fireworks miss-fired - it pitched sideways with a mournful howl. It slewed sideways and was out of the picture. Dee Dee knew how it felt. She travelled in her mind to her Maida Vale flat and tried to locate her nursing certificate. It had expired. When she returned to London, its renewal would be the first order of business. The vision of the certificate was strong and the flat and its contents blurred. Herefordshire was bound to have a nice little private hospital. First Dee Dee had to clear her debts.

Chapter Twenty Nine

Champagne is Patient

Luca and Sylvie had been right under the fireworks. The boat belonged to a French couple who oozed style, even Sylvie acted in a manner befitting her designer dress. She sipped her champagne, commenting on its quality and enquiring after its vintage.

'It's an acquired taste,' she said, close to Luca's ear. 'I can get you a beer if you would prefer.'

A fountain of white flames from a ground-effect firework went off behind Luca and Sylvie. A white sheet of crackling light shot into the shy. They turned toward the display, Sylvie managing to stay close.

'Champagne, it sort of goes with the occasion,' said Luca. Conversation had to be shouted or spoken very close the ear.

'You are looking very handsome, Luca. Why don't you let your hair grow?' Sylvie's head was so close Luca could feel her breath.

'Getting it cut every few weeks is a hassle. Do you like it this length?' Luca opted for the big voice and hoped Sylvie did not move.

'A little longer maybe.'

'This takes four days to grow to this. If you like I'll leave it for a week before I cut it.' He tilted his glass and sipped in a way that suggested he had not yet acquired champagnes' taste. Never mind champagne is patient. 'Nice boat! Who are these people?'

Shrieking mortars of white hot phosphorescence went off behind Luca's head - so close he flinched.

'They are friends of Mamma's. I want them to like you. They travel a lot and could spread the word about Pension Lazlo. Besides that, they treat me like an adult.' Sylvie raised her glass. 'But pamper me like a child.'

'To one thing or the other,' Luca raised his glass to meet Sylvie's as they toasted each other.

'Will you come to Paris with me in July? Paris is double the fun with a friend.'

'For you, or for me?'

'Both' said Sylvie.

'That will leave Dad on his own.'

'He can employ someone. It will be peak season, so he could use the help. Papa also has a place in Nice. I am not supposed to know about it. He puts me up with the Corbel's. They have a daughter my age. Dull as dog shit.'

'Who are the Corbels?'

Sylvie waved at a man in a linen shirt, a shirt that looked like it cost a month's salary. He had the tanned, groomed look of a man who gave his leisure priority. Sylvie looked down at her feet, 'We're standing on their yacht.'

Corbel sauntered over. His Genoese was even and paced with a soft northern accent. 'Are you enjoying all of this?' He asked.

He meant the fireworks, which at times were desperately close and at all times loud. There was a lull but that was only to set up for the finale. Luca saw the colours and shadows projected onto Corbel's all white ensemble. He could also see from this close he was fit for his age and probably older than Larry.

'Do you sail this yourself?' said Luca

'I do, with a crew. We are sailing tomorrow for Nice. Then, in August, we run an open house. You are welcome to come. You can stay on the boat if you wish. I hear you are in the hospitality business.'

'This is true. We have been open for nine days. We are still learning.'

'You never stop learning, Luca. Why the name?'

'What name?'

'Pension Lazlo. A strange choice.'

'My father's name. He is an Australian, his father was a Czech, but the name is itself Spanish. Sort of rubs the locals the wrong way.'

'Then they will have to deal with it. In the hospitality industry your guests are not your neighbours. There is a large enclave of Corsicans in Nice. They are a tight knit lot.'

'My grandfather says that those that emigrated were the moderates. The distrust is concentrated rather than diluted,' Commented Luca.

'We are shown nothing but kindness when we come here. But I hear others echo your sentiments. This is the first time I have heard it from a native.'

Luca had no doubt that Corbel would be shown nothing but kindness wherever he went. 'Yes, then I would love to come to Nice, we could stay over on our way to Paris.'

'That's excellent, Luca. We would be honoured to have you to stay. I have a daughter of 15. She has limited contact outside her school which is in Lucerne.'

Sylvie hugged Luca's arm as Corbel bid to be excused. When he had turned his back she kissed him and then wiped away the lipstick.

'Is she really bad?' asked Luca.

Sylvie poked two fingers down her throat. After Luca stopped laughing his eyes locked with Sylvie. They shared a companionable smile. All lips and teeth.

'I have the keys to Papa's house; I know the security code and the servants are away. It will be different this time. My father won't be in the next room.'

Chapter Thirty

Capped Cries

'Shit!' said Joey to the sky as bright as midday; the fireworks display had begun in earnest. 'Shit!' So did the pain. 'Shit!'

'What was that?' said Paige.

'Did you hear something? I thought I heard something,' said Larry.

Joey tested his weight on his ankle. He hissed with pain, fell to his knees, and crawled toward the empty crate. Pain came in waves but he had to keep moving as he could hear them coming to look for him.

****

The fireworks went into a routine that sent howling projectiles higher and higher, each bursting a different colour. Red. White. Blue. Cheering could be heard between each launch.

'Jesus,' gasped Joey. He knew he had to get out of sight. Halfway to the crate, he thought he would try to use one half of the ladder as a crutch. The pain was intense. He walked with one hand on the wall to steady himself. He was under the glassless window and he chanced a look up expecting the see the courtyard awash in light. Instead, he saw it was in total darkness. He tried to look in the upstairs bedroom and took a step back onto the loosened cover of the well. The circular well cover rotated 90 degrees and Joey fell vertically down the shaft. The well cover flipped over shutting off the well and drowning out Joey's scream.

****

'Did you move that ladder? I know you thought it quaint, but did you move it?' asked Larry.

'Larry, someone or something must have moved it. Something also broke it in two - something heavy.'

'Are you coming?'

'No, I'm going to get some clothes on.'

'I'll go find a torch.'

They met back at the site of the broken ladder – it's career as quaint had been cut tragically short. Paige was dressed and Larry had found a torch.

Chapter Thirty One

A light so White

The water was so cold it took Joey's breath away. Hitting the water was like a smack from a prize fighter. Joey had never been hit but had done some of the hitting. He knew the look a man gets when he is hurt. Things can go two ways. A man fights on, or he gives in. A light goes on from deep within; you could always see it in their eyes. If Joey gave in to the pain, he would die. He was sure of it. He called for his mother and pissed himself.

At least his legs were now warm. Thankfully, in the fall Joey had held tightly onto his camera.

'Shit!' said Joey Cotz and the sound of his own voice came back at him close and harsh. He had Paige and the mystery pension manager in his view-finder, in focus, he was about to release the shutter when the ladder gave way.

A red glow from the LED showed that the flash was charged and the camera intact. Joey held the camera behind his head and pressed the shutter release. He sunk lower in the water as he raised his hand, it was cool and fresh and free of debris. That was good wasn't it?

For a moment after the flash Joey forgot where he was. A light so white it hurt, obliterated all other colours. Joey's eyes blinked involuntarily and navy blue floaters appeared in his peripheral vision. Joey's retinas ached but then so did the rest of him.

It was there, he had not imagined it. In the blue-white of the flash gun, an iron ladder. If Joey was to imagine an iron ladder he would have imagined it in better repair and within reach. It was not only a long reach it would be a blind one. He grabbed at the dark, on the first and third attempt his fingers collided with the rough stone. On the fourth lunge his inside forearm between wrist and elbow connected with a pitted rung, his hand had overshot the bottom rung in the darkness. On the fifth attempt the rung smacked his palm and it felt good. He let out a whoop, piercingly loud in the confined space. Quickly, swinging the camera around his neck, he reached for the rung with his left hand, and lifted his body out of the icy water.

Chapter Thirty Two

Welcome to my World

'We can get a better look at first light. Gaultier is always telling us how savage his dogs are. I'll bring one or two along.'

'Larry, you're not thinking. What will the other guests think? Do you want them to panic?' said Paige.

Paige looked at Larry, the man so gentle a moment ago was wound up like a warrior. The finale of the fireworks ended. The silence gathered forces with the night as the pyrotechnic smoke wafted in front of the moon. The anger bunched in Larry's trapezoids muscles between his shoulders and his ears.

'Do you think it was one of the other guests?' said Larry flexing his neck.

'I think it was a paparazzo or a peeping Tom.'

'They wouldn't follow you on holidays,' asked Larry, 'Would they?'

'Welcome to my world,' shrugged Paige.

Larry and Paige went to look at the guest list to see if she recognised any names. Larry turned the guest book round and Paige scanned the left column with a finger.

'What are we looking for?' asked Larry.

'He's an American national.'

'You know him?'

'Joey Cotz. He’s the bastard that has made my life hell!'

Chapter Thirty Three

No Getting off in the Middle

'A British photographer called Jimmy Newbery followed me from my very first gig. He was first with the photos that coined the phrase 'anorexic' and 'waif.' I think he was a little bit in love with me. He killed himself.' Explained Paige.

'He was in love with you and causing you all this distress?'

'Heroin Chic was just a photo caption until people started believing it. When I became famous all the old shots of me, he had them all. They were suddenly worth a lot of money. I bought a place in Jamaica Dock about the time his body was found in the Thames, I never moved into it.'

'Why not.'

'I'm never at home and it would take a whole swag of furniture to fill it.'

'What is it being used for now.'

'A photographic studio. It's got plenty of south facing windows. You can see St Catherine's Dock. I've lent the flat to Jimmy's brother.'

'I see.' Larry could also see that Paige was very close to tears.

'Then there was a backlash against directors using younger and younger models,' she went on. 'Thinner and thinner models. The media looked for someone to blame. Normal girls got turned down for jobs and were told to lose 5 kilos. Questions were asked in the house.'

If there was one thing that Larry observed, Paige ate heartily and a wide range of foods. She had even become enthusiastic about the crab. 'You just want to live a normal life. Earn a living and lead a normal life.'

'I couldn't find normal with an A to Z.'

'Can't you get other work?'

'This lark is a bit like a high-wire act. No getting off in the middle. Unless ....' Paige's nose was running. 'No one would hire right me now. I'm not at my most beguiling now; come back in the morning.'

Larry held his arms wide and she came to him.

Chapter Thirty Four

Creeping about in Low Places

Pain and the cold took hold of Joey's limbs. The climb with two hands and one leg was exhausting. At some point a cavern opened to the right. Joey held the camera and viewed his last shots from the Citadel and Marina. Not that he wanted to view his photo history, he knew that the back screen let off a soft light; a soft light he had found useful while creeping about in low places. What he saw was a sizable room cut in the limestone and Joey thought he saw a chair. He waited to catch his breath and make full use of his lungs. The ladder went up and so did Joey: slowly. The ladder stopped well below the top of the shaft. There was nothing for it but to go back and rest on the chair. Climbing back down his left calf muscle felt like hot steel. This accompanied the stabbing pain in his right ankle. If Joey was really lucky it would only be a bad sprain.

He would rest and see what secrets the cavern offered up in the morning. The chair crumbled like dust. The cavern felt dry and the air was sweetly clean. There was nothing else for it, Joey lay down. Did this island have rats? Joey on a stake-out to take Naomi's photograph with Heidi had seen rats as big as chihuahuas. This was in the New York restaurant district. They were well fed rats and showed only a passing interest in the pap team. It was about this time that Joey started to specialise.

Joey tried to see his ankle by the light of his camera but to no avail. He could feel it was swollen. What do you do for a sprain? Rest, elevate, cold. Well, it was certainly cold enough. Pain seeped into the part of his brain that stored these things. Lying on his back he tried the camera one more time. He had to stop doing that. The room had the sort of look of a prison or dungeon. Whoever stayed down here did not do it for kicks and a very long time ago. The side rail of the table proved a suitable prop for the ankle and the throbbing eased once it was elevated. R.I.C.E., it came to him now. The acronym for sprain care: rest, immobilise, compress and elevate. Well, immobilised that would be no problem Joey was dead tired.

Chapter Thirty Five

Too Late

'Do you think Luca will come home tonight?' asked Paige.

'No, I don't. It's a pretty big celebration. Are you sure you don't want to go into town again, Mrs Morgan?'

Those wide eyes that were used to sell so many products were a little puffy. Larry had forgotten the love of Genevieve from so long ago, he had nothing to compare his feelings with. Inarticulate feelings rose and found no purchase in a long dead heart. And he, a writer. Larry got confused and angry with himself and Paige saw this in his eyes and let the tears fall. From the sunken herb garden where they had moved, she saw a light go on in her apartment.

'I have to go home now.'

Larry swore silently when she had gone.

Paige padded into the apartment where Dee Dee was packing.

'What happened to you?' asked Paige.

'The French artist was painting. I was just in the way. Paige, when we get back to London, I'm quitting. I'm going to get a normal life.' Then she turned around. 'Paige, what the hell happened to you?'

'I don't want to ruin his life,' she said between sobs. 'What was it you said? Normal life.'

'Paige, what happened?'

'A pap, I think. During the fireworks. He's got enough on his plate raising a kid. I can't do it to him.'

'Who was it?'

'Who do you think?'

'Joey Cotz? That bastard.'

'Did Larry chase after him?'

'He got away in all the confusion.'

'Oh Paige! I was going to go on some walking tours. I picked up some brochures in the town today.'

'Why don't we hire a car and get away? Let's get away to the other end of the Island.'

'The truth is I'm broke. Cards are maxed out. Why do you want to get away? You and Larry not working out?'

'I think he has fallen in love with me. And I had this plan when I saw him; he was going to be my rehab project. Ten days of hot sex, toast crumbs in the bed, tea and midday movies.'

'It hasn't happened?'

'No! And I think I've fallen in love with him!'

'So! What's the problem?'

'Larry, Luca - I can’t do it to them. TV crews camped out under the chestnut trees. Every guest stopped and questioned. Every trip into town a commando raid. I think Sylvie could handle it, but not the men. They’ve had nothing but each other for so long.'

'Sylvie would love it. Can you hold out until Luca's grandparents are back?'

'I think it’s better it ends before it begins. Before anyone gets hurt.' Paige thundered up the stairs and threw herself down on the bed.

'Too late,' said Dee Dee.

Chapter Thirty Six

I am not Without Influence in This Town

Rose Underhill never slept more than four consecutive hours. Her four hours usually came after midnight. She was often at her computer and on trans-Atlantic phone calls at 4.00 am and she would be sharp and refreshed for breakfast at 6.00. She would work until ten then nap to be fresh again for her round of lunchtime meetings. She was reading when the call from Dee Dee McPhee came through.

'Hello, Rose. Did I wake you?' said Dee Dee.

'No, I was reading a novel and not getting into it. What's up?'

'Joey Cotz. He has followed Paige on holidays and climbed a ladder to take a photo of her in the pool.'

'Right. It's time Mr Cotz got his due.'

'His what?' asked Dee Dee.

'What is coming to him.'

'Can you complain to the Press Council?'

'I could, but he is not a member. It would do no earthly good. And there is no chance of reasoning with him?'

'What are you going to do?'

'You leave Mr Cotz to me,' said Rose confidently, 'I am not without influence in this town. I have heard he lives at home with his mother and father in New York. There is a certain ex-assistant Mayor who has a score to settle with our Mr Cotz.'

'What are you going to do?'

'Watch and learn. We can give him some of his own medicine. He has been doctoring photographs of Paige and others. I have had experts study his photos. In the meantime, I'm sending someone down to keep a lid on things.'

Dee Dee would miss all this. The butt kicking, the bustle, being a cog in the system. Somewhere in her nursing brain she saw how a fall from that height would produce an injury.

Rose was talking about chartering an aircraft.

'Rose, I think he is injured.'

'What makes you say that?'

'He fell from a ladder.'

'Good. That'll slow him down. Listen how's the weather?'

'Fine. Hot and balmy nights. Can't move on the beaches but I hear it quietens down after Tuesday.'

'It's raining here. Is there a room for me if I can get there?'

'If not, there is another empty bed here. You missed the fireworks but come, it'll be fun.'

'Dee Dee, I did *not* miss the fireworks, I can assure you. I will make my own fireworks. The public has started to tire of the paparazzi after the whole Diana thing. I'll will come after I have rattled some cages here in London. See you.'

'OK, bye!'

Rose put her book down, not bothering to place the bookmark inside. She pondered, if a man lived at home when he was 28, he was either lazy or terminally dependant. Rose would to ring the Cotz family home when it was daylight in England, she calculated it would be early morning in New York. Just the time to find out your son might be injured in a foreign city with no visa and no health insurance. Rose would ring her friend in the French Consulate in the morning. If her suspicions were correct Joey Cotz would have travelled without a visa. Then it was time for an exposé on a certain maggot.

Rose would ring a producer she knew who worked for American 60 Minutes at a decent hour. Next she rang one of her own photographers, despite the late hour. She could not stop Joey Cotz from taking photos but she had it within her power to make them less valuable. After that, the book lost all interest for her. She put it back in her bookshelf. The real life happenings of people she knew and loved were more exiting and made more sense than what was on the page. Before retiring Rose found her passport. Thank God for the EEC she thought, I can travel to France without a visa.

Chapter Thirty Seven

Fitful Sleep

Paige did not sleep well. This morning she would have to break it off with Larry. She wanted to have the hire car ready with its engine running, Dee Dee at the wheel for a swift getaway.

Larry had not slept much either. The weather had turned hot and oppressive. There was going to be a storm. He saw Paige come down the steps in the herb garden. He knew what was coming. He stayed on his stool. She opened the door quietly and stood with the light behind her. They viewed each other from about 15 feet.

'Larry. I can't see you,' she blurted.' I can't put you through all this. I'm going away for a while. I'll still stay on the island. Do you want me to come and see you before I leave?'

With every bone in her body Paige wished the answer would be yes. She hoped against hope that he would get up off the kitchen stool and sweep her off her feet and tell her he could not live without her. She knew the options for that she had calculated them in her sleepless hours to be very slim.

'No.'

The door closed silently on Paige's back and the steps and the green herbs became a blur. Tears blinded her. She made her way to the car by the sound of its running engine and collapsed in the front seat and cried. She was aware of Dee Dee reaching across her prone body and shutting the car door. Then she let the motion of the car lull her, finally, into a fitful sleep.

Chapter Thirty Eight

A Twitch Upon a Thread

Genevieve was nervous about returning home. All the flights were booked and she could not face the arduous train and ferry. The travel agent had to tell her twice that this weekend was part of the Three Cultures Festival. In some recess of her mind, she knew this, but now her priorities were to return home to ask her husband for a divorce. She decided to wait until after the long weekend.

She looked long and hard out of the taxi window to try and find something familiar. The town had changed or was not as she remembered. 10 years and 15 cities had all become a jungle. Bonifacio's beautiful images had not lodged in her mind because she thought she would never return. She hoped she would never return. She prayed she would never return. The rain on the glass was a fitting veil to her view. A tangible screen that blocked out the visions of a past she tried so hard to forget but fought hard to remember.

Chapter Thirty Nine

A Field of Wildflowers

Larry got in his car and just drove. Blindly drove. He passed the familiar avenue of chestnuts and noticed a white van on the road to Gaultier's farm. It did not register, nor did the direction he travelled or the purpose. Larry just drove. He left the pension in effect, without a manager, with no one at the helm.

Clouds massed malevolent mauve. Piling, rolling and gathering with foreboding purpose. Larry pulled over when he could no longer see. Tears blinded him. Something was about to burst; it might just be his heart. He staggered blindly into a sea of wildflowers. The first sob racked him to a standstill; the second, more of an animal wail, robbed him of breath. He arched his back and sucked a lung-full for the third bellowing wail. He howled his chest empty and the effort seemed to take him to his knees. The first fat drop of rain stung his arm. The next hundred thousand drilled him to the spicy earth. Larry lay prone in the rain in a field of wildflowers and cried his heart out.

'Stop the taxi,' yelled Genevieve. The taxi driver shrugged. He kept driving in impertinent silence. Genevieve had to remember the

Genoese phrase. She waved a fist full of francs, the international language, 'Stop the fucking taxi.'

Genevieve piled out and was instantly soaked.

'Wait here' she commanded over her shoulder and bundled the offered money inside her bra.

The heaving lump she had seen had looked familiar because she had slept next to it for four years. A little sturdier now but it suited him. And a little less leonine. He wore it well. Even face down. Her husband, the man she had not spent a night apart from until she stole away forever. But it was not forever. She was here, wondering what or who, had made her husband cry.

'Larry?' Genevieve shouted above the drumming rain.

Larry lifted his head. The wind and rain were playing tricks he thought. He swore he heard his name.

'Larry. It's me.' Genevieve was soaked to the skin, the wad of money in her bra was fast becoming a damp soggy mess.

Larry rolled over. His face was shockingly distorted from crying, but her Larry just the same. Genevieve jolted herself with the notion that this was the man she had travelled 1,500 kilometres to divorce.

'You?' said Larry, 'why don't you piss off and leave me alone.'

Chapter Forty

From Another Life

Genevieve stopped and asked a chamber maid dressed in black and white what was going on. The answer only baffled her.

Larry had collapsed into bed saying he had not slept all night. He took a bottle of whiskey. Genevieve sat in the kitchen. Her kitchen from another life. It might seem more like home if her parents were around. The nervousness she felt was stored away for another time. In the absence of anything else to do she made herself a cup of coffee. None of the plates were familiar. The coffee pot was new. The kitchen had been remodelled. The one constant was the Aga. She lifted it's lid and placed the coffee pot on it just as a white Mercedes van pulled up. Genevieve walked out of the kitchen door, the new part, where land had been excavated to extend the kitchen, and where someone had planted a herb garden.

'Hello,' said Genevieve.

'Hello, who are you?' said a voice in French with a strong German accent.

'I could ask you the same question.'

'Are you a guest?'

'No, I am not. I am Genevieve du Plessier. This is my parent's farm.'

'Was your parent’s farm.' Horst saw her alarm. 'It's all right nothing has happened to them. They have gone on a bus tour of Italy for ten days.'

'My father would never leave the farm.'

'That's just it. It is no longer a farm. This is Pension Lazlo.'

Genevieve turned on her heel and banged on Larry's door.

Horst smiled and thought of his own wife back in Dresden. She had a wild temper too and he looked forward to a time when this contract was over. 'And good bye to you too,' said Horst and made his way to the van.

Genevieve stood at the end of Larry's bed. 'I don't care if you have had no sleep; I want some answers.'

'Go away. Go away and stay away,' said Larry. 'Your timing is impeccable; I'll say that for you. You’re programmed to cause maximum grief, maximum destruction.'

'Where is my mother? Where is Pappa?'

'I can't say exactly. It's a mystery tour.'

'Larry. What the hell is going on?' asked Genevieve.

But Larry never got a chance to answer as Horst was back, shouting for someone to call an ambulance.

Larry stood in the kitchen wishing he had not had that slug of whiskey.

'I have an idea who it might be' Larry said to Horst. 'Does he speak English?'

'Yes,' said Horst. 'Was he a guest Mr Moro?'

'That's right, chuck your guests down the old well.' Genevieve said. 'It could catch on. Be the new hospitality craze to sweep Europe.'

'Shut up Gen.'

Gen was a name no one but Larry called Genevieve, usually after lovemaking and at other tender moments. It took the wind out of her sails, even the agitated Horst could see that.

'I have an idea who it is. A vicious low life pap. He was spying on me and my fiancé.'

'Fiancé?' Genevieve suddenly felt the need to sit down. This she did on the nearest chair.

'How long till the ambulance arrives?' asked Larry?

Horst was not about to answer and Genevieve seemed to be stunned. 'I have some questions for him before the ambulance arrives,' Larry went on. 'Horst, is the ladder in good repair?'

'I brought my own rope ladder. It’s already hanging in the well and it's new.'

Larry turned to Genevieve. 'Why don't you make yourself useful? Cook breakfast. Do you think you can manage that?'

Larry sprinted up the steps. The world seemed like it was just back from the cleaners after the storm. His first stop was at the workshop to fetch a torch. He walked sedately to the well as he did not want to arouse alarm among the other guests. He bid the young Scottish couple a good morning. They said they were on their honeymoon but they had different names on their luggage and worked for the same Law Firm in Perth. The real Honeymoon couple in unit 3 had that dreamy look and walked and talked in unison on the brief appearances when they actually left their room.

'Are you alright?' Larry shouted in a voice thick with scorn.

Larry shone the torch down the well. When it looked like he wouldn't get a reply he swung his legs over the well and tested the rope ladder. Larry switched to the metal ladder about two metres down.

'What's that noise? Where did that German guy go?' came an American voice from below.

Larry stopped and listened. There was a noise. A noise like running water. He reached the cavern and saw Joey lying on his side. He shone the torch on Joey's face for a full minute before answering.

'Did you hear that storm? That noise is the sound of the well filling up.'

'How far does it come up? The water.'

'I don't know, we don't come down here much.' Larry was shining the torch around the cavern. The beam stopped on the camera.

'We haven't rain like this in living memory.' He swung off the ladder and landed on the floor of the cavern. Little swirls of dust eddied around his feet. 'The caves around here are all limestone. Do you remember limestone?' Larry bent and picked up a fragment of broken chair. He turned to the well shaft and dropped it. It made a splash but not a large one. 'We need something heavier.' He picked up the camera.

'Not the camera,' cried Joey.

'Well if you can't remember limestone, I will tell you how it works.'

'Get me out. Don't fuck with me. Get me out.'

'Limestone is porous. Like a sponge. Water will permeate - don't you love that word? Permeate - it will find its own level.'

Larry had removed the long lens as he was speaking. It was the next to travel down the well. It made a louder splash.

'No, man, not the lens. That was brand new.'

'Does that water sound closer to you? It sounded closer to me. Just as well there is a nice strong ladder for us to climb.'

'I can't climb. I've sprained my ankle. I can't put any weight on my foot. It's bad. God it's bad.'

Larry continued to look around the cavern. He saw its spine first. Wedged into a crack and high above his head and above a high water mark, a book. He took it down and blew the dust off it.

'Well, looky here. The water has been up as far as this ceiling.'

'For Christ's sake, get me out of here.'

Larry detached the flash gun from the camera and made sure the prone American saw him do it.

The splash came sooner and was louder.

'Now that was definitely closer. Was that closer?'

'Jesus Christ!' Cried Joey.

'Tell me what is on the camera?'

'What?'

'What - is - on - the - memory - card?' Larry drew out every word and in the spaces in between the sound of gushing water was definitely getting louder.

'Some pictures of you and Paige through the long lens. Nothing I could use. That girl with your son, one of them at the bus stop.'

'Any of us in the pool?'

Joey missed his old camera. By now he would have changed the roll of film and they would be safely in his bag in the rental van. But the guy at 42nd Street Photo had assured Joey that digital was the way to go and all Joey’s lenses were compatible with this new age technology. That’s Canon EOS for you.

'No, the ladder broke just as I had you in focus. I swear.'

'I want you to know this before the water laps around your ears. You are a low life scum. You are lucky the builder found you. I suspect no one knows you are here and if I had found you ... well, let's just say we would be looking for an alternative water supply. Fear of going to jail is the only thing keeping you alive at the moment. I'm keeping this.' Larry meant the camera. 'And if I ever see your sorry face again, I will rearrange it.' In the confined space of the cavern, Larry's calm, even delivery chilled Joey to the bone. Joey had seen Larry's face in the reflected torch light. Larry's hair had dried haphazardly as he lay trying to get to sleep. His eye sockets were sunken and dark. He looked like a mad man.

He was.

'You're not out of the woods yet? How long have you been on the Island?' asked Larry.

'About two days.'

'Did you notice the traffic?'

Joey did not trust himself to answer.

'The ambulance has to come from Calvi. It could take half a day.'

'Get me out. Winch me out. Do something' pleaded Joey.

'Do you really want to be hauled to safety by the man whose relationship you have just fucked up? I was just starting to feel alive again. For 9 years I have raised my son: alone. Give me one reason why I shouldn't ring the emergency services and tell them it was a false alarm.'

'I'm in pain man!' Joey recognised that voice. He had heard it often enough when he was collecting debts. The voice of a frightened man.

'What effect do you think your photos have had on Paige? Don't talk to me about pain. You deal in misery.'

From a long way up, the shaft came a disconnected female voice. 'Is everything all right down there?'

'Who is that?' asked Joey, glad to hear another human voice.

'My wife,' said Larry.

Joey’s face was an entire play, in several acts, he ran through the whole gamut of emotions from A to Z. But mostly F: fear, fatigue, fascination.

'Hey Lady! Save me, this guy is crazy. He wants to let me die.'

The stream of language that followed was lost on Joey but exasperation is the same in any language. Genevieve had had a long day. She had travelled with her heart screwed up in anticipation of seeing her parents and her husband again. She wanted a divorce. She knew there would be a price to pay. The hardest part she thought would be Larry. She half wished he had left, bailed out, years ago. Something had kept him here. But something in him had changed. Snapped. It was a change she was unprepared for.

'What did she say?' asked Joey.

'The world has gone to shit.'

'You can say that again,' said Joey Cotz.

Chapter Forty One

Too Well Fed for local

When Sylvie arrived for work she went straight to reception and started to attend to the morning mail. Luca went and had a shower. Horst popped his head into the office.

'When will the ambulance get here?'

'What ambulance?' asked Sylvie.

'For the man who fell down the well.'

'Sorry. Who has fallen down the well?' asked Sylvie.

'I don't know, I came to attach permanent pipes to the pump and a man yelled to me. I nearly fell of the ladder. He was an American.'

'Sorry, what is your name?' enquired Sylvie.

'Horst. I am the builder. Larry has climbed down after I heard shouting.'

'Horst. Can you watch the desk for a moment, I'll get Luca.'

'Sure,' said Horst.

Sylvie knocked on the bathroom door, opened it a crack and put her head into the billowing steam.

'I think you had better get down to the well and give your father a hand.' Sylvie told Luca.

Luca shut off the taps immediately. It was something in Sylvie's delivery that had an immediacy. 'What's happened?' asked Luca.

'A man has fallen down the well.'

'Who?'

'I don't know,' said Sylvie. 'An American.'

'We don't have any Americans staying here.'

'Go! Find out and I'll watch the phones and the reception desk.'

A door to the reception led off the kitchen. Sylvie and Luca's paths diverged in the kitchen. Luca bounded up the stairs. Genevieve, looking for an apron, turned in time to see the back of a large red-headed man. Nowhere in her brain was she prepared to equate this to the small chubby baby she had walked out on. Horst left via the office door as Sylvie slipped behind the desk. Genevieve, who had no luck with the apron stood with a large cook's knife in her hand, her face was a study in confusion.

Horst almost collided with one of the guests, a lawyer, at the door.

'What's happening?' He asked in his soft educated brogue.

'Someone has fallen down the well' Horst explained.

'Could it have been the guy we saw snooping around last night?'

'You saw someone, an intruder?'

'Well, we thought it a bit funny he was on his own and he had a big camera. We thought he was getting ready to take some photographs of the fireworks. Earlier, he moved a ladder down to the wall, the wall with the round window.'

'What did he look like?'

'He looked too well-fed for a local. Big, broad and dark.'

Sylvie, who was eves-dropping, had lots more questions but English was not her best language. Quite a crowd was gathering around the old well cover. Sylvie, on impulse, pushed the buttons on her new mobile phone.

When Paige answered, her voice was thick from crying.

Chapter Forty Two

Four Tonne winch

Gaultier's dogs were mud caked, but just as vociferous. Luca, at a canter, excited them more. The relationship building from last-night's walk was forgotten and the rust coloured bitch barked as loud as the rest of them.

'Henri, can we borrow the cart-horse collar.'

'It will be filthy. Why?'

'A man has fallen down our well.'

'It is better that you wait for the experts. A man could slip from the collar. You need a special harness.'

'There is no time. The well is filling, after the rains.'

Gaultier for an old man could move fast. 'I'll fetch it, you back the truck; it has a four tonne winch.'

Chapter Forty Three

What is Your Name, my Lovely?

A deal was struck. One of Gaultier's friends would get Joey to Sardinia. With his Italian ancestry Joey had a better chance with the authorities there. The Scottish solicitor, whose name turned out to be Dixie Dean, drew up an agreement stating that Joey Cotz would not come within one thousand metres of Paige Goss and never publish or take her photograph again. Part of it was an admission of trespass, with intent to commit a criminal act. The final paragraph absolved Pension Lazlo from any civil action. It also looked as if Joey had broken a bone in his foot and it had swollen to twice its normal size.

'He bought it,' said Dixie Dean, not bothering to hide his astonishment.

'He's an American,' said Larry. 'Americans are paranoid about the cost of medical care overseas. Illegals over there are thrown in jail, I believe. He was shit scared.'

'He entered the country illegally?' said Luca. It was more of a question. He sloping off to the office periodically to keep Sylvie updated.

'Shall we cancel the ambulance?' said Larry.

'I did not order an ambulance; did you?' said Horst.

'No. Did you Genevieve?'

Horst shrugged.

'Just as well Victor and Clara are away. They don't need this stress.' said Larry.

A taxi pulled up and a woman and two men got out. The woman was well dressed with expensive dark glasses and a large hat. She looked around appearing to find her bearings. Then she went into the office.

'Hello. I'm Rose Underhill. Do you have two rooms? A single and a double. You don't mind sharing, do you boys? And who, may I ask, is this pretty young thing. And do you have an agent?'

'We only have a three bedroom studio,' said Sylvie.

'I'll take it.' Rose said emphatically. 'How old are you my darling?'

'I will be 14 on August the first.'

'Can you make it to London?' Rose Underhill produced a thick personal organiser and flipped it open. 'On let's say the 15th.'

Sylvie was lost for words. One of the men took a registration card and began to fill it out. No one spoke. It was as if they were all waiting for Sylvie to say something.

Rose's pen hovered. 'What is your name, my lovely?'

'Sylvie Murat.'

Rose wrote and the men seemed to approve of the name. 'Do you know Laetitia Casta?'

'No, but I've heard the name,' said Sylvie, gaining confidence with physical action. She had the guest register ready for when the man who appeared to be Rose's assistant finished with the registration card.

'She was a local girl, found on a beach.' Rose continued. 'By someone on holidays. She is now working in Paris, Milan, New York. Do you want to know the tragic thing?'

'No! Yes! Tell me.'

'She was *not* discovered by me.'

Sylvie's face split into a smile. It seemed to jolt her back into her realm. 'How will you be settling your account here at Pension Lazlo?'

'Visa.' And Rose produced one with flourish. 'Can you make it? I need to set up a photographer and some studio time. Arrange for a chaperon, I will fly both of you in and put you up near Green Park. Would that be convenient?'

Sylvie cleared the screen. The last thing on it was the agreement drawn up for the lawyer for Joey Cotz.

'Is that hair natural? Of course it is. I think we can get you hair work. Have you finished growing?'

'I'm sorry?' Sylvie battled with the combs that attempted to tame her hair.

'What size are your feet? Oh look! They are tiny. Your mother, is she tall?'

'Yes. One sixty eight,' said Sylvie more confident with plain facts.

'Your father. What nationality?' asked Rose?

'French. My mother has Spanish on her mother's side.'

'Excellent. Now chuff along boys. I want to speak to Sylvie alone.'

'Do you want a Polaroid?' asked the registration card man.

Rose Underhill' eyebrows went up. 'That depends, is London absolutely out of the question?'

'No,' said Sylvie, sounding enthusiastic. 'Yes to London.'

'Forgive me, I can be a little like a runaway locomotive when I see such raw beauty. You'll do! Won't she lads?'

'Absolutely!'

'You bet!'

'I discovered Paige Goss. I understand she is staying here.'

'I went shopping with her the day before yesterday. She is out at the moment, but I have just spoken to her on the phone. She is on her way back.'

'You're the one.'

'I'm sorry?'

'You're the one she told me about.'

'She has also mentioned you,' said Sylvie.

Rose waited until the men had left. They were making noises about the light and photo opportunities here at Pension Lazlo. Rose leaned forward conspiratorially.

'Can you stay a week? I want to get you fitted. Do some make-up tests. Have you been properly fitted?'

'For what?'

'A bra. I can get you into a corsetiere at Harvey Nicholls. When you are sixteen, we will get you swim-suit work. All sorts of work. The sky is the limit.'

'No. Fitted for a bra, I mean. I live with my Papa at the moment. I model now; or when I am in Paris. I do swim-suits and catalogues.'

'Does anyone represent you at the moment?' asked Rose.

'No.'

'That's the long road, sweetie. Do you want to be a supermodel? Ask yourself that. If you do it your way, there are plenty of pitfalls. Men who don't care if you are underage. They will want to use your hunger, your ambition and make you believe that the way to the top is between their sheets. Ask Paige.'

'I will. I did. We had lunch.'

'What seems to be happening out there?'

'The men have just winched an America out of the well. He fell in it trying to take a picture of Paige and Larry.'

'Who is Larry?'

'He is my boss. He is my boyfriend’s father.'

'Do you happen to know the name of this American?'

'Joey Cotz.'

'I see.' The atmosphere changed. It was as if someone had opened a deep freezer's door.

'Is there a problem?' asked Sylvie.

'For Joey Cotz there is. Where is he now?'

'He went with a neighbour to the next farm.'

Rose's face went into what those that knew her called composure mode. She adjusted her bag on her wrist, arranged her face pleasantly and stood still and erect. Then the smile escaped from within.

I want to be one of Rose's girls, thought Sylvie. I have had enough with indifference.

'I will just freshen up, and I wish to speak to your employer. It has been delightful to have met you.'

They left just as Sylvie was about to get Luca to help with their bags. Luca would need to collate certain information while he was in the room. If Luca was good at anything, it was observation.

Larry came into the office, he looked haggard and wound up the way athletes are. 'Sylvie, I need a favour. It will test your skills as a receptionist. And as the girlfriend of my son.'

Sylvie liked the sound of that.

'His mother has shown up. Has Luca mentioned his mother?'

'Briefly,' said Sylvie.

'There is no subtle way of putting this. I don't want her here.'

'That won't be a problem as I have just let the last studio to Rose Underhill and two other gentlemen.'

Larry turned the registration card around and perused it. 'Are we fully booked?' he asked.

'We are fully booked.'

It sounded good.

'Good. She probably has some business with her parents. It is a shame she turned up when they are away.'

'Where shall I send her, Mr Moro?'

'Hotel Des Étrangers, Hotel Le Royal. Think you can manage that?' Larry's face twisted into a wry smile.

'I think so,' said Sylvie.

'Good, I'm taking siesta today. Luca's in charge.'

'Mr Moro, I telephoned Paige and told her about the American down the well.'

The tiredness behind Larry's eyes set up camp in his body. He appeared to change shape in the space of one sigh. 'And what did she say?'

'She said she would return earlier than she had planned.'

'If she and Dee Dee check out, try not to let Mrs Moro know. And Sylvie, I am not to be disturbed. By anyone. Are we clear?'

'Yes Mr Moro.'

'Good! And how long are you going to keep calling me Mr Moro?'

'Until Mrs Moro leaves' confided Sylvie.

Sylvie had made her new employer smile. 'Would you like a permanent job here, Sylvie?'

'I would like to work here until I am 16 and then I want to go to London and pursue a modelling career.'

'Good for you. And as your boss and your guardian I am asking you to stay here tonight. OK!'

'Fine!'

Larry closed the door to his bedroom. He undressed but despite his tiredness, when he lay his head on the pillow he was smiling. Sylvie caught on fast.

Chapter Forty Four

The Bureau of Missing Eye-Line Pencils

True to her word Sylvie did not allow Larry to be disturbed. It was an afternoon in which he was in great demand. Horst dropped off an old dusty book that Larry had put down while they winched the American out of the well. Luca had gone down the well and wanted to tell his father about a cavern there. He had to be physically headed off as he ran into the kitchen calling his father's name. Genevieve Moro had taken a walk to see the changes to her old home, grown bored, and wishing to speak to Larry. Paige rang. She wanted to speak to Luca to get a firsthand account of the well incident. All sorts of people rang from London and New York for Rose Underhill. An Art Agent rang from Paris and wished to speak to Dee Dee. It was urgent, Dernavern had been arrested, apparently. Sylvie recognised the Parisian accent and revelled in it. She pressed the agent, called Paul, for details.

'What has he been arrested for.'

'Improper dealings with a minor,' said Paul.

'Who, where?'

'A teenage girl. He painted her portrait and her father found out.'

Sylvie became alarmed. 'Do you know who the father is?' she tried to keep her voice level and moderate.

'I know nothing, except he buys directly commissioned works from Dernavern, and he buys for a bank, with bank money. He writes it off as a tax loss and hangs the pictures in his home,' said Paul. 'And they call me a crook! I must say it is nice to speak to someone down there who speaks French. I could never make myself understood with Dernavern's housekeeper.'

'No, problem. If Dee Dee returns can I have her call you?'

Sylvie switched her voice to the office voice, the one she had been trying out. Genevieve had entered the office.

'If you would. She is his alibi.' said Paul in Paris.

Sylvie wanted to find out more but not let Paul know that this man might be her father. Her heart was beating in her chest but her mind was keeping pace.

'This is a small community,' she said. 'If you want someone, a local who speaks French and you can't get hold of Dernavern, I will give you my mobile telephone number.' Sylvie stroked its new sleek shape, aware that Genevieve was listening. Now it was time for the big gamble. 'How did the father find out?' she asked after dictating the number.

'I'm sorry?'

'How did the father find out, if he was in Nice at the time.'

Paul's tone changed abruptly. 'Who said he was in Nice? I never mentioned Nice.'

'I told you it was a small community,' Sylvie recovered. 'Less than 3,000 souls in the winter, that's why you can count on my discretion.'

The line went silent in Sylvie's ear. She had to hook Paul again. His main concern, his reason for calling was to locate Dee Dee. 'Of course, we get about 30,000 visitors a day in the summer. That is why I need to know. This, Dee Dee, is she one of the visitors? What if I can't locate her?'

'Then Dernavern is in for a little jail-time. Good day.'

'No don't hang up!' Sylvie spoke fluidly in her own language. 'How can you let one of your artists go to jail?'

'It will send his prices up,' said Paul. 'Particularly if the girl is 13, as they say.'

Sylvie felt as if she was being ripped in two internally. This is what it was like to run on pure adrenalin. If it were otherwise, Genevieve might have asked some awkward questions. As it was Sylvie detested her hovering.

Genevieve had spotted the pock marked book. She approached the reception desk. Sylvie took a huge gamble.

'Paul, I have another call coming in.' And she cut him off before he could protest.

The other call was completely fictitious, but Sylvie went about it as if she was making a booking. She and Larry had practised while Clara watched. It was role-playing to see if she could handle a guest enquiry and learn the telephone equipment. She only hoped Genevieve could not hear the dial tone on the empty line. Sylvie spoke in English, as if the person on the other end of the line was a bit little deaf.

'A double, on the week starting the 18th, I will see.' Sylvie pulled the reservations book across the old battered one that Horst had entrusted her with. It was covered. 'No, we have a studio at 1,000 F a day. Well, if that is too much we can recommend, the Hotel des Étrangers or the Hotel Le Royal. Would you like their number?'

Sylvie looked up and rolled her eyes dramatically for Genevieve and this only served to add to her anxiety.

'There is always the camping ground at the Camping Municipal Arepos.' She said, wondering if Genevieve spoke English and hoping she sounded a little patronising. Under the reservations book, Sylvie slid open a drawer and pretended to look for a pen. She found one, tested that it wrote and slipped the old musty book in the drawer shutting it with her hip. A nonplussed face told her that Genevieve's English was not up to scratch. She was becoming very impatient on the other side of the counter. Sylvie finished with her imaginary caller and prayed that Paul was still on the line in Paris. She shot Luca's mother an 'I can't help it' look that was pure drama.

'Hello Paul, thank you for waiting,' said Sylvie smiling so the feeling carried down the line.

'Does everyone know everyone's business in Bonifacio,' asked Paul after the shortest of delays.

'Let's say that I dropped my eye-line pencil once, when I was rushing to the hairdresser, it was returned to me before I noticed it missing.'

'If that happened in Paris,' said Paul, 'you would need to buy another, that's for sure.'

Paul had relaxed. He was possibly even flirting with Sylvie.

'My manager's son worked closely with Dernavern. Do you want to speak with him?'

'What's his name?'

'Luca Moro,' said Sylvie, watching to see of Genevieve picked up on a familiar name. 'It would help if we knew why this accusation has been levelled by a client of Dernavern's. You did say he was a client.'

'All I know is that this guy pulled some strings in Nice and Dernavern was picked up by the local police this morning. The client is on his way back now to file a civil complaint.'

'Wow!' Sylvie hoped she was flirting. 'He must have got someone pretty pissed off.'

'Hell hath no fury... Now, if you are ever in Paris, I can be contacted at the Department of Missing Eye-line Pencils. I will buy you dinner.'

After more pleasantries, Sylvie rang off. She was certain that someone had squealed to her father about Dernavern. The question was: who?

Genevieve would be stalled no longer. She leaned on the high part of the counter. 'Where is my husband?'

'He is sleeping.'

'He's a bloody Australian, he never takes a siesta.' Genevieve did not even try to conceal her pique, 'Where is my son?'

So, this was what it was like to be a receptionist. It was just like dealing with an indignant parent. 'He is getting some guests settled at The Studio.'

'Where did they take that American? They said they had to wait for an ambulance to come from Calvi. I happen to know there is a hospital in Bonifacio. What's going on?'

'Did they? I was here all the time. As you can see it is busy when the phone goes. I wouldn't know.'

'There is something going on and, I intend to find out,' said Genevieve, and stormed out.

It was time to use the intercom. Nothing scared Sylvie more than having to use the intercom. Your mistakes would be broadcast. Would she be able to hear her own voice? She took to the telephone system like a bird to flight but the intercom terrified her.

LUCA MORO, TO RECEPTION. It was not as bad as she had imagined so she repeated it in French. Sylvie thought her amplified voice sounded dignified. Very grown up.

'What's up' said Luca, appearing from the kitchen and startling Sylvie?

'Your Dad's asleep and your mother is snooping. Luca, do you think you could drive a Bentley?'

'I can drive a tractor; a Bentley can't be hard. Why?'

'Dernavern has been arrested. My father is on his way back and I think the shit is about to hit the fan.'

'What for, and where does driving come into it?'

'He has been arrested for improper dealings with a minor. I think he has turned those sketches of me into a painting. I think it would be wise to find out who has it in for Dernavern. I think it might be Dee Dee.'

'No! Not Dee Dee, she's pretty cool. Do you want me to go to Dernavern's house?'

'Yes. If he has been falsely accused there has to be a reason. I don't care what happens to Dernavern, I just don't want to end up in a boarding school in Zurich.'

'Is it a good idea to turn up to a man's house who is in jail, in the car belonging to the man who put him there?' said Luca. 'A Bentley does not exactly go unnoticed, you know.'

'All right what do you suggest?'

'I can get a look inside Dernavern's place, if you think that will make this whole thing go away. I can't see us convincing the police he is innocent.'

'We don't have to convince the police. It's my father; we need to get him to withdraw the charges. But most of all not send me away. I have used up all my get out of jail cards, Luca.'

'I see! I see there might be an urgency. I'll ride my bike.'

'And ring me from Dernavern's. I might ring Dee Dee. Go, before your mother returns and your dad wakes up.' Sylvie stood to kiss the towering Luca. God he was cute. Now she had met his mother she could assemble him from his genetic building blocks. His mother may not have had much to do with his daily life but she had not been stingy with the handsome gene.

Chapter Forty Five

A slashed Painting

Luca stood on Dernavern's sun lit terrace. Four folding glass doors led to his studio. When Dernavern washed at the water butt, he put his keys and change on a pot plant saucer. Luca hoped Dernavern was creature of habit. He was. A key to the back door was in a potted Monstera plant.

The picture that Luca suspected was causing all the calamity was missing. An empty easel stood ominously among pinned sketches of Sylvie. Luca felt a sudden flush a jealousy, until he saw a slashed painting of a flaxen goddess. She was angles of serenity, planes of radiance, and flaxen blonde with dark, velvety skin that made you want to touch it. And this was just the painting. Luca knew this to be the Norwegian girl. He punched the Pension Lazlo numbers into the phone as he tried to remember her name.

'Hi, Sylvie it's me. The picture of you appears to be missing. There is a picture of a girl and it is slashed.'

'Is the face slashed, Luca.'

'Why?'

'No woman could dare to slash her own face,' said Sylvie. 'Even if it is an image.'

'No, the canvas is slashed from top to bottom. Where could the picture of you be, do you think?'

'If it is not there then maybe it has been taken for evidence, or something. We can't ask any of the adults as they will want to know why.'

'All right, I'll head back as soon as I can.'

'Luca. The slashed painting? Is it anyone we know?'

'Dernavern told me of his last summer's subject. A Norwegian, looks like her. Stayed with him all summer and it shows in the suntan.'

Chapter Forty Six

A Dreamer's Dream

Paige and Dee Dee had eaten a picnic lunch by a steam that was urgently swollen with the rain of yesterday. Paige's phone rang again.

'Leave it. This is so idyllic. Let's just listen to nature's sounds for a while,' said Dee Dee.

'You can get so much of nature's sound that it makes you want to pee, 'Hello, Paige Goss.'

Dee Dee broke off some biscotti and threw it to some curious but skittish ducks. The female was more brazen and waddled up the grassy slope towards the piece of biscuit. 'Got a sweet tooth, ducky?'

It was a dreamer's view. If the dreamer dreamed they had themselves woven into a carpet of mauves and lilac and greens of every hue. This dreamscape was complete with its resident ducks. These were not like the ducks in St James' Park, they were wild ducks with survival high on their agenda. They appeared by the same unwritten lore as their St James' Park cousins observed: just after the food came out.

'You can't have any of this canistron, I'm saving it for my tea.' said Dee Dee, taking a lung full of wafted scents as she reclined.

Her friendship with the ducks was motion dependant. The act of lying down had undone ten good relationship building minutes, and the wild duck put half a metre between herself and Dee Dee.

'It's Sylvie, for you.' said Paige.

'For me?' Dee Dee sat up and the duck flew off, its mate followed a wingbeat behind.

'Hello, Sylvie how are you?'

'Fine, good. Listen, there is no easy way to say this but Dernavern has been arrested.'

'Oh my God! What for?'

'Have you seen a painting he was doing of me?'

'I certainly did.'

'He has been arrested for improper dealings with a minor. His agent has been on the phone from Paris. Dernavern is naming you as an alibi.'

'Shit!' said Dee Dee.

'Exactly. I had nothing to do with these pictures. He sketched me as we ate in the evenings, but I had my clothes on.'

'How did he get caught? His studio is up a narrow street on the edge of a forest.'

'Someone who wanted to get at Dernavern told the police,' explained Sylvie.

'He's good in bed and handsome in a roguish sort of way, but not worth the aggravation of involving the police.'

'I'm glad to hear you say that. I sent Luca up there and a picture has been destroyed.'

'A picture of who?' said Dee Dee.

'A blonde sun-worshiper.'

'One that positively oozes sex?'

'I was not about to ask Luca that. But it sounds like one and the same person,' said Sylvie. 'Do you suppose this woman - girl really - returned and tried to patch things up with Dernavern?'

'That's one possibility. She could have asked who I was. Is Dernavern the type to brag? He is a male, isn't he?' said Dee Dee.

'He must have mentioned my age. She has tried to hurt him using my age and probably involved my father to seal the deal.'

'Your father, how?'

'The person who rang from Paris said that whoever was involved got the local police to arrest him. I guessed Nice. My father is not without influence.'

'What would be the charge?'

'I'm not sure, Luca and I don't want to involve adults. It's all happening here. Hand me to Paige. Rose Underhill has turned up with two other guys. They have taken the family studio.'

'Can't talk to Paige. She is communing with nature.'

'I'm sorry?'

'She has gone off to have a pee. We are doing our own thing. We are letting the dust settle. We are sitting at the moment in a valley at about 2000 metres above sea level. We went into a bakery, stood in front of the glass counter and just pointed at things.' Then Dee Dee added conspiratorially. 'Paige is very fragile at the moment.'

'Rose wants to see you when you get in, she has a plan.'

'A plan? Did you happen to see a magic wand?'

'I was stuck in here when it was all happening - pulling the American out. I would have loved to have seen him. He was in a lot of pain.'

'Pulled who out? Which America?'

'Joey Cotz. Mr Moro confiscated his camera.'

'Joey Cotz! He followed us from Connecticut?'

'Did Paige not tell you? I rang her this morning.'

'No, she went all dreamy. I thought it was all these narrow roads and sheer drops. The scenery can take your breath away.'

'Listen Dee Dee. You, me, Luca and Paige need to get together, it seems we all have a piece of this jigsaw.'

Chapter Forty Seven

Fresh Gnocchi

Aldo Cotz had worked hard in the new country. He maintained a garden despite the walls of his garden being factory walls three stories high on all sides. He grew tomatoes in olive oil cans, painted black to get the most out of the short burst of sunshine his garden got each day. He grew red peppers. He grew cherries. He grew everything. If you couldn't eat it, he didn't grow it. If there was one thing Aldo liked more than his home grown produce, it was his sleep. His sleep was disturbed last night with some awful news about his only son Joey. Aldo had gone to the new country to make a new life. He had hoped and expected to raise a large batch of dutiful children and by now he had hoped to have grandchildren. But it was not to be, on both counts. Aldo had returned to his native Sicily to select a wife. One with childbearing hips, a good Catholic, a good woman, a *paesano*. His wife Maria had failed to produce again, the telltale swell that had come so suddenly after their marriage vows.

Now this good woman was making gnocchi, her antidote for stress. A beefy forearm rolled, scraped and flicked to produce the lightest fluffiest dumpling west of the Hudson. Aldo sprayed for bugs on his cherry tree. He considered again converting the basement for Joey. Stairs would be difficult to negotiate on crutches. The basement was full of ladders. Aldo never quite knew why Joey kept purchasing brand new ladders. He always returned with them and in the basement they stayed.

Aldo kept an Australian Cockatoo in an aviary. His name was Charlie. Charlie flicked his head left and then rolled it right. He followed this up with a little dance along his perch. Then he lined up Aldo with his black beaded eye and raised his yellow crest. In twenty five years the bird had never spoken. It could however imitate a telephone. This it did now. Not the home phone; Joey's cellular phone. The latter being shriller and a newer sound to Charlie's ears.

'I'm gonna throw that bum out, Charlie.'

In the kitchen his Sicilian bride wiped her hands on her apron letting a mother's tears fall onto fresh gnocchi.

Chapter Forty Eight

Pole-Axed Parent

Rose Underhill had changed; the hat had gone as had the glasses. She wore a simple linen shift and strappy sandals of gold and black. She was used to pretty girls, haughty girls, but this level of self-assurance was rare. It would need to have the edges knocked off, or it could come across as arrogance.

'What exactly am I to be an expert witness for?' asked Rose

'I depends if Dernavern is arraigned or formally charged. You see, you seem to be a bit of an expert on breasts' explained Luca.

Luca shifted. He wore his naivety like a garland. He blushed when he mentioned them earlier, and Rose suggested they all wait until Sylvie had finished her shift and they could all have a lemonade on the terrace.

'And Luca can vouch that the breasts in the painting, are not yours?'

Luca chose this moment to study his shoes.

'He can' she said shyly.

'And Dernavern took it upon himself to paint you, as he paints all women: nude. He filled in the blanks, so to speak.'

Next Luca spoke. He gathered himself. The terrace went silent. It was a huge effort for him and he had won Rose over earlier with his obsequious good manners. He was the son she wished she'd had. 'We don't want to involve our parents,' he said.

Rose and Sylvie allowed space for his words to fall. There was possibly more to come.

'I would like, one day, to get to know my mother. Not now. Not today.'

An ice cube chinked as it melted.

'I think my father deserves a second chance at love.' The terrace waited for Luca to finish. 'I think he is a little protective of me. I learn in my own way, at my own speed. Our friend Dernavern, the other day, used the expression worst case scenario and I have never heard it before. I use it now. The worst case scenario, is that Sylvie gets sent away for something she has never done and Paige returns to England. They both continue with this obligation, that only they see. It takes a certain bravery to cause the least amount of pain.'

'How do you see this ending, Luca,' asked Rose.

'My mother gets whatever it is that she wants, and gets the hell out of here. Paige to return, or Dad goes to London. They meet, just as two people.'

'Paige could have any man in the world. Don't get your hopes up. I usually read about her new boyfriends in the papers.'

'Then if it was not meant to work out, let it be for the right reason,' said Luca.

Rose turned to Sylvie, 'He doesn't say much. But when he does, he draws on a wisdom greater than his years. As I see it you want these incidents to be treated as two separate issues, yes?'

'If I get sent away, it would be awful. I love my job. And I could be ready to start modelling in two years' time. For you,' said Sylvie.

'So, it's definite then. You have just talked yourself out of a trip to London. Nigel some photographs please.'

'My father would have to agree,' said Sylvie.

'Actually, we have a house policy that means both parents will have to agree.'

'You will need to get my parents to speak to each other then.'

'Simon, this is why I did not have children of my own. All my girls, all of them, are like kids to me. They need their Rose, at some point or other. Fetch me the standard contract Simon.'

'But you just said that you have a house policy that needs both parents' consent,' said Sylvie.

'And your father is a banker. He deals with contracts, figures, returns on investments.'

'He would consider me an investment?'

'He will face the prospect of educating you in Switzerland. Airfares, uniforms, an allowance, telephone calls. He will weigh this up against tangible evidence of your...' Rose searched for a word. '... net worth. All those outgoings don't guarantee any sort of return. An increase of exposure. I know bankers darling; I have been married to two.'

'Three,' chimed in Simon, as he went inside.

'No, Charlie was a Turf Accountant, he *lent* money to the banks,' said Rose, raising her voice, to continue the conversation with Simon inside.

Simon, in all black, glided back gracefully with a slim leather folder, he unzipped it silently. He began filling in the date and the blanks for names. He handed the semi-prepared document to Rose. His all black contrasted her white ensemble.

'Now, I propose a party in Paris. We can invite Paige, Naomi, Tyra, Christy. After the Paris fashion show and before the girls all leave for their next assignments. Do you think you can get your father to Paris for that?'

'He can't resist a party; he's been living like a hermit for ten years.'

'That's just what we need, the kids acting as adults and the adults acting as kids.'

'Will Paige return?' asked Luca.

'She is hurting, sweetie. She will lay low, and come back in her own time. She doesn't even want to speak to me. But I suspect she won't come back until your mother has gone.'

The telephone rang. Simon took the call, out of his chair at the first ring. Luca suspected out of these flowing black clothes, he could lose these feminine affectations, in a sports strip he would be quite an athlete. Simon put his hand over the mouthpiece.

'The police are here. They wish to speak to Sylvie.'

'We need Dee Dee here,' said Luca. 'I'll go and get rid of my mother.'

******

Larry was awake and returning calls. He saw his son and waved to him. Luca diverted to the office. Now he could meet with Genevieve. No sense it putting it off.

'Your mother is in the sitting room,' said Larry. 'She wants a word with us.'

Genevieve had paced, smoked, arranged nick knacks and thought about how she was going to tackle this. She practised to the mantle.

'I know it's going to be hard ...' She tried looking solemn again. No, contrite; that was what was called for.

'I know I don't deserve ...' Too self-centred. Focus on the men.

'You seem to have done an excellent job with our son ....' No leave yourself out of it.

'You have done an excellent job with Luca ...' *Sounds like a King Charles Cavalier that's done well at obedience school.*

'You men have done without me in your lives. I must now ask you to dig further and beg for my freedom ...' *Too dramatic?*

A knock on the door startled Genevieve. Two men stood in the door of her parent's sitting room. It was a formal room with stiff unpleasant furniture. Most of it wedding gifts - all of it new. It had merely gained the patina that came from being under plastic for most of its life.

When did Luca get so tall? He towered over his father.

'Come in,' Genevieve said. 'I was just going over what I was going to say. How long were you there? Never mind. It has gone right out of my head. I don't know what to say.'

Luca and Larry entered and sat on the unfamiliar furniture. Both settled in as if they were waiting for teeth to be drilled.

'I didn't think about tea. Or coffee, do you prefer coffee?'

'Nothing for me thanks.'

'No, I'm fine,' said Luca.

'Well then!' Genevieve paused. 'I haven't been much of a wife, or mother. Less of a mother. In fact, no mother at all.'

Luca looked at his father. Larry looked at his wife. The sleep had done the trick for the dark circles under Larry's eyes but this hair was not its best. Today was not a good hair day.

'I have met a man.' Genevieve began. 'No, that is, I have found a life for myself. I live in Brussels these days.' Genevieve paused for some sort of response. 'I have often thought of writing to you. Luca, do you know where Brussels is?'

Luca responded in what must have been perfect French with a Belgian accent. Genevieve was stumped and stared in total amazement. Larry ran his hand down his face. His bristles against his palm were the only sound in the room. He had forgotten to shave this morning.

'He is a diamond cutter,' Genevieve continued. Both men were staring at her benignly.

'He is a good man. He has been married before. But it was over before I came along.'

Nothing. No one moved.

'I am still young enough to have children.' Genevieve drew her breath. 'I have come here to ask you to set me free.'

Larry looked at his son, he was perplexed. 'If it's a divorce you want, bring me the papers and I will sign them,' said Larry.

'This is not how I wanted it.' Genevieve gushed. 'I want your blessing.'

'I wish for nothing other than what you and your diamond cutter deserve,' said Larry, swiftly.

'Thank you! I just want to be free.'

Luca spoke, 'When have you been anything else?' and it was as if the air had been sucked out of the room.

Larry had nothing to add, so he stood to leave.

'Where are you going? Larry what are you going to do?'

Larry had a devilish look on his face. 'Me? I'm going to have a shave. Then I have a business to run. Luca, do you want a lift into town?'

'Luca, where are you going?' Genevieve sounded more hurt than alarmed.

'To the police station. I need to verify a painting and a pair of breasts.'

Genevieve sat on the musty lounge as if she had been pole-axed. Indeed, she had. Before, while she was waiting for Luca and Larry, she had gone into the room she had expected to sleep in. In it she saw things belonging to a young woman. Her old room: occupied and no longer hers. This was *not* how she had planned it.

Chapter Forty Nine

An Old Woman Knitting in the Courtroom

Because Rose Underhill was an out of town visitor and partly because someone behind the scenes was pulling strings to expedite events, Dernavern was in front of a magistrate in the morning. The Magistrate was a wise old bird and he recognised this for what it was: someone manipulating the law to their own end. But he was not without a sense of humour, so the portrait was sent for and Rose and Sylvie listed as witnesses for the defence.

Dernavern had engaged a lawyer fluent in Genoese, but need not have bothered as the magistrate spoke French, Corsu and Genoese.

Dee Dee saw her first, putting her back pack through the security scanners in the foyer of the courtroom. The Norwegian, because it could be no other. Her hair was pulled back and she looked drawn and tired, but it was her. Her hair was the colour of summer grasses. Even tied back, it was all one colour as were her eyebrows. Her arms were not tanned as in the picture, but this was Dernavern's girl.

'Luca, is that her?'

'I only saw her at a distance last summer.'

They all turned to look. Paige felt a tinge of jealousy. She had tried that hair colour, and thought she had got away with it until now.

'Luca, can you remember her name?'

'Yes...'

'You're closest to Dernavern, go up and talk to her,' said Dee Dee, before Luca could go on.

'What should I say?'

'You and Dernavern talked about her. What sort of things did you talk about?'

Luca coloured slightly.' Boy things.'

'This is ridiculous,' said Sylvie, 'why are we whispering?'

'Shall I go? She may recognise me,' said Paige. ut Luca had already got a shove in the back from Sylvie.

When they had gone through the embarrassment and settled on English as the language with most common competence for them both, Astrid actually relaxed.

Sylvie dragged Paige and Dee Dee behind a column.

'Hey! I thought you were the jealous type,' said Dee Dee to Sylvie.

'Luca has a bumbling charm, no?' she said not taking her eyes off Luca.

Luca saw that Astrid's eyes were pale blue - when this girl cheered up they might even be called luminous.

'Piers mentioned that you are from Bergen.'

'I am a student in Oslo. But now I have dropped out. I cannot study.' Astrid's singsong voice played the English words out like a poem. 'I did not mean things to go this far. I just rang the girl's father. I made Dernavern tell me his name, and a man at the bank, his name was Paoli, gave me the telephone number in Nice. He insisted that Murat would want to know.'

'Do you want me to sit with you during the trial?'

'Yes, that would be nice. I have done a stupid thing.'

'Come on; they are going in,' said Luca.

It was immediately obvious that this was not a single hearing sitting. All around, those that looked like lawyers tried to behave like lawyers. Those who were answering to a charge looked like they wished they were somewhere - anywhere else. The newspaper men sat together and muttered and sent messages back and forth. The ones Luca could not place he assumed they were friends and relatives of those appearing before the magistrate. One lady sat in the front row with her legs crossed in front of her and knitted. To do this she needed to slouch and sit on the edge of her seat.

The bailiff called the first case - it was a motor vehicle ownership dispute. An estranged couple suddenly wanted to claim ownership of something they did not show a whole lot of attention too. Including its road worthiness, and road tax which had not been renewed.

The magistrate banged his gavel and ordered that the cost of the car's repair be split, then sold and the proceeds divided 50 - 50. 'Next'

'When are we going to get to the sexy artist and the school girl?' called the old woman who was knitting. On closer inspection, Luca decided she was not that old. She was just possibly wearing everything she owned.

'In a minute, Gilda,' said the magistrate in a good natured tone. 'First we have the case of M Cortiichiato and her failure to pay her road taxes. Driving without a licence and driving under the influence of alcohol.'

The newspaper men showed an interest in the 'sexy artist and the schoolgirl' case too. Luca looked over at Sylvie, from this distance her eyes look luminous. Compared to Astrid, Astrid's eyes looked hollow. Piercing, but hollow.

M Cortiichiato was quickly dispensed a good deal poorer. This magistrate did not hang around. Luca looked for his name. The courtroom was warming to the antics of Jean Bernard Cirendini.

Dernavern was next.

He was led in from the holding cells. He had not shaved and he looked haggard. Astrid let out a little whimper. Luca squeezed her hand. Astrid, when she had composed herself, held onto Luca's hand.

Jean Bernard Cirendini greeted him warmly. He asked if his stay had not been too uncomfortable. Gilda stopped knitting. After the case was read out, Jean Bernard Cirendini addressed the gallery and told them of the special circumstances of Rose Underhill's evidence. He addressed her in English and welcomed her. A photographer stood and took her photographer and was immediately ejected from the gallery.

'Some of the evidence you will here today concern breasts, and ownership thereof. A man's career hangs in the balance. I want to take this opportunity to warn you that I will not tolerate any outbursts in this courtroom.' Then he turned to Dernavern. 'You have heard the charges as specified?'

'I have.'

'How do you plead?'

'Not guilty.'

'The charges brought against you deal with the age of your subject. Indeed, she is listed as a witness in your defence.' Jean Bernard Cirendini looked over the top of his spectacles and gave Sylvie a big grin. 'We will get to you, Mlle Murat.' He turned to Dernavern. 'This is not a case of you denying that you are the artist responsible for this portrait.'

'I would not call it a portrait your honour.'

'Yes, yes we will get to that in a moment. It is not also a matter of disputed ownership.'

'It is not.'

'The charges relate to Improper Dealings with a minor. The age of the subject. Your solicitor has informed this court, that no sitting was undertaken by the subject in the creation of this painting. What say you?'

Dernavern cleared his throat. 'I began this painting as a series of little sketches. One night, with the warm spring weather, I was suddenly inspired to make a painting. It has become a major works. One of my best yet.'

'You're a French national?'

'I am.'

'We'd better hear your story.'

'I am an artist, your honour. I have lived on the outer edge of Bonifacio for five years and I sell my paintings in Paris. I paint the nude. The female form. My work is highly sort after in the right circles.'

'What would a painting of yours fetch?'

'In Paris, one of my paintings might fetch 120,000 F. A small one around, 90,000 F.'

'So, you are well compensated for your efforts?'

'You could say that.' Dernavern could not hide the pride in his voice.

'Why do your paintings fetch so much money?'

'Because I don't paint landscapes, your honour. Landscapes fetch a lot if you are dead or famous.'

'Do you consider yourself famous?'

'No. The word recluse has been used to describe me. The word passionate has been used to describe my art.'

'Do the words Improper Dealings describe your art?'

'No, your honour.'

Dernavern's solicitor stood up. Luca only got to see his back. 'As my client has an unblemished record your honour, as he is a celebrated artist, a national icon, if you will, we intend to discredit the charges and have them quashed. As the charges were not bought about by the subject herself and as a special clause exists to protect the identity of him or those that brought these scurrilous charges against my client, we intend to defend them vigorously.'

'Vigorously! I have come to expect nothing less from you M Billet. Are you ready to call your first witness?'

'We are your honour.'

The bailiff stepped forward. 'Who do you call?'

'I call, Sylvia Emmeline Murat.'

Sylvie stood erect in the dock. If she was nervous, it did not show. After she was sworn in, she answered her first question in a loud clear voice. The newspaper men sat forward in their seats.

'Now, I have to ask this for the record. Are you aware of what we say when we say improper dealings with a minor.'

'Having sex with, or doing anything that might be thought of as sexual, without the consent of the individual. It means basically, sexual predators.

'Concisely put. And why would a minor be a special case.'

'She, or he, might not see an advance, gesture or act as sexual or improper because of his, or her, tender age.'

'Exactly! What is the nature of your relationship with the defendant?'

'He works, or worked for my employer.'

'You are working? At 13! That is very enterprising.'

Dernavern's solicitor stood. The newspaper men scribbled away. 'Did you ever work with the defendant?'

'No, he was involved in the construction of the Pension where I work. I am getting experience at reception. It is just for the holidays, you understand.'

'Sylvie is in the process of negotiating a contract with Rose Underhill Management. A London based agency that only handles the top models,' said Dernavern's solicitor. The smile vanished from Jean Bernard Cirendini's face. While he was on his feet the solicitor pressed on. 'It is our intention to give joint evidence, privately in chambers your honour.'

'Yes I saw that. Highly irregular. What do you hope to achieve by this?'

'To prove she did not pose for this painting, your honour.'

'I see. Bailiff, bring the painting. Miss Underhill needs to be sworn in. And the court will adjourn for ten minutes.'

A groan went up from the gallery.

It was obvious that a major story was in the making. Several news crews had OB vans outside the court building. Outside cameramen kicked their heels and waited for word from the other half of their team from behind the tinted glass revolving door.

Paige and Dee Dee stood together. Astrid and Luca were deep in conversation. 'He does have a boyish charm,' said Dee Dee of Luca.

'Do you want to rip her eyes out?' asked Paige.

'No. Men like Dernavern can't help themselves. It was dirty and mean of him, but I remain unscathed. Do you think we will get out of here unnoticed.'

'No. I think that we haven't been recognised because none of the journalist have turned round. They must have a special room or gallery they go to.'

'Why do you say that?'

'They all left together and turned left at the foot of the stairs.'

'You miss it all, don't you?'

'Does it show?' said Paige, her face splitting into a coy smile. 'I have been out of the media for a week now, my public misses me.'

Dee Dee was looking at Astrid and Luca. 'What is it about attractive women and pricks? I don't mean you. I don't mean you!'

'Yes you do. And it's all right. Yesterday, when I was sulking in the car, a thought came to me. I have been doing it all wrong. From now on a bloke gets a quick once over and a quiz. Then I will ask, what is your favourite movie?'

'What does that prove?'

'Most people want their life to be like their favourite movie.'

'Yeah! So?'

'The guys I've been dating's favourite movies are Space Vixens from Mars.'

In another part of the foyer, Luca was explaining his relationship with Sylvie to Astrid.

'So, this language teacher sat you two together?' said Astrid.

'Yeah and I was bragging about all the languages I can speak. Keep in mind I had just had an assignment thrown back with re-do and an F. She said, *'Call for me then, and be sure and tell Papa that you are a pig farmer's son.'* She works for us now.'

'There is some bad feeling in that family and I have gone and thrown a spanner in the works.'

'Look at the media. I don't think you will be buying any cheap paintings from Dernavern.'

'I slashed one.'

'Yeah, I know,' said Luca.

Chapter Fifty

A Body of Evidence

In chambers, Jean Bernard Cirendini became more relaxed. He settled in behind his large mahogany desk to hear evidence from Rose Underhill. He gestured hospitably to the deep leather chairs. Dernavern sat with his solicitor. Rose and Sylvie on the chesterfield.

'Your honour I represent many girls who begin their career at this age. We send them to a trained corsetier. Then they go again once their breasts have stopped growing.

'I only have sons,' he said.

'It is often a strong bonding moment for adolescent women to have this first fitting with their mother. It's a sort of rite of passage.'

'What do you intend to enter as evidence.'

Rose looked at Sylvie and she removed her blouse.

The chambers were filled with the sound of three men exhaling. The face of M Jean Bernard Cirendini became less than poised. His collar suddenly felt tight.

'The adolescent breast is a different shape.' Rose said. 'The areola is swollen and often, at odd times during the month, quite sore. The mature breast, as in this painting, has flatter areola, with the nipple more centrally located. It has, you could say, settled. It has arrived at its given shape.'

Rose placed the painting next to Sylvie's chest. 'The adolescent breast takes on that plump look while it is still growing. A man arrives at manhood like an express train. Only then does he begin to grow. A young woman grows first and develops hips and breasts later. The whole process can take four years.'

Rose had the rapt attention of her audience, so she went on. 'They call you a judge. I ask you to make the judgment. Do you think this girl posed for this artist?'

'I'm no expert,' he blurted. 'But if this is the painting and this is the subject, at first glance there appear to be differences. Many differences. I will say that this is a very compelling demonstration.'

'As a woman your honour, I ask you to remember the first time you gazed on your young bride's breasts, if I may be so bold. Then I would ask you to look at the faces of the men here in this room. Do you see anything but wide eyed amazement? Ask yourself if one of the men in this room is witnessing this magnificent spectacle for the first time, or two.'

The judge looked at some papers on his desk. 'And you handle all these women?'

'One of them. Paige Goss, is in this building as we speak. She started with me when she was 14.'

'Well, I never! On the strength of the evidence and the fact that the subject has appeared as witness for the defendant, I rule in favour of you, Dernavern. Case dismissed. I rule that you have no case to answer, and that no conviction will be recorded.' Turning to Sylvie, 'You can put your clothes back on now Mlle.'

Chapter Fifty One

A Party to Which One Is Not Invited

Genevieve slept fitfully. This was her parent's sitting room. The camp bed was impossible and it creaked at her every move. The noises from the kitchen did not help. There was a small party going on, and she was not invited.

****

The assembled group included all those at the court. Dernavern and Astrid, Luca and Sylvie and Dee Dee, who was keeping a distance between herself and Dernavern. Paige and Larry stood close to the alcohol – Larry acting barman. Simon and the other man, whose name turned out to be Ross, were both gay but not a couple.

Dernavern proposed a toast, 'To Luca, who had the money for the bail, but did not know how to go about posting it.'

'I didn't want to involve the adults. They always assume the worst. I had it all in cash, in different denominations.' With that he lifted the lid off the shoe box.

'How much is in there, Luca?' asked Rose.

'$7,800. It's a lot to change into French francs. All in one go,' said Luca.

'Too big even for Dimitri?' asked Dernavern.

'No, Dimitri will give me 300% for my Greenbacks.'

'Wouldn't it be better in a bank?' asked Simon.

'Dimitri needs hard currency. He is prepared to pay over the odds for it.'

'Why so?' asked Simon.

'He is a Greek. He can sell it on the black market. Or buy consumer durables.'

'What do you call consumer durables?' asked Simon.

'Deodorant, sanitary napkins, condoms, shampoo, the sort of things that are not made here or in Greece, but tourists cannot do without.'

'It seems that Luca has a head for business!' said Rose.

'Why are these things so expensive?' asked Simon.

'They are items used by young people with disposable incomes. They are exactly the type of people we see here as tourists. And I imagine in Greece.'

'Why is this Dimitri here? Why not in the Greek isles?' asked Simon.

'He does the rounds. He considers the Eastern Mediterranean to be his territory. He has his own plane,' said Luca 'and his own yacht.'

'Why don't we order some food in and move out to the terrace,' said Rose.

'This isn't London,' said Larry. 'If you want any food you will have to go and get it. Come back next year and we will have the bistro up and running.'

'Oh! We will. I will give myself more time to do some sightseeing.' Rose did not want to let the bonhomie die and keep the victory spirit going. 'Who's for going to into town and having a cheap and cheerful Pizza?'

The only takers were Ross, Simon, and Rose. When Dee Dee saw how the numbers stacked up she put her hand up too.

'I don't want to stay and be the third wheel,' she said.

Dernavern and Astrid where the first to leave. Luca and Sylvie went to Luca's room.

'Well if there is only this small number, I can drive you all,' said Dee Dee. 'Is that all right, Paige?'

'Fine, take the car,' she said.

Larry and Paige were left alone in the kitchen. Silence settled like a blanket. A scratchy rough blanket, but the alternative was less palatable for Paige.

Larry was the first to speak. 'I think my wife has attached a foal alarm to my heart.'

'What's a foal alarm?'

'When a horse is pregnant, the farmer or horse owner, attaches a foal alarm and if the horse lies down for a certain period, the alarm sounds. Only Genevieve had this one set to calibrate feelings. It's a pretty accurate contraption.'

'How does the horse sleep?'

'Horses sleep standing up,' said Larry.

'How convenient.'

'For who?'

'The maker of this foal alarm.' A sly grin, an alluring one, had crept to the corners of Paige's mouth.

'Damn obliging of the horse however.'

'It's just a common courtesy, someone goes to all that trouble to invent a foal alarm. The least you can do ...'

'... Is read the instructions.' interjected Larry. It got the desired result: a pair of liquid eyes.

'Exactly.'

'My wife came here to ask for a divorce. I think she expected a little more gnashing and wailing.'

'If she had come a week earlier, would she have got it?'

'Possibly. A week is a long time in the hospitality game. I gave her the acid test.'

'And what is the acid test, Larry?'

'I told her to cook a breakfast.'

'And she did?'

'Yes,' said Larry. Pouring the last of the wine in Paige's glass. The procedure took him within arm's length of Paige. It felt comfortable but Larry sensed his limit.

'Pretty standard stuff. Married people do it all the time.'

'Do you know that, or have you read it in the manual?'

'The manual!' Paige shrieked, 'If there were such a thing, I should throw it out.'

'Exactly. When I told Genevieve to cook a breakfast, I did not say for who, or how they might like their eggs. The thing is, she did it without question.'

'And this proves, what?'

'It proves two things: for years I have been the guest in her house, a sort of interloper. This proves she feels like an outsider in her own kitchen. And when she left she was a domestic cripple.'

'And?'

'It proves she has compromised. The old Genevieve would have given me a string of abuse and told me to cook it myself. But more importantly, this is a farm. Food is never wasted as people under this roof probably had a hand in producing what went into that meal.'

'Tough test,' said Paige.

'I told Joey Cotz that if I had found him, he would be dead. I said that the fear of going to jail was the only thing that kept him alive. How's that for tough?'

Paige answered with a grin.

'So don't think I am not tough. If you decide not to see me, do it for the right reasons. If you think me too ugly, tell me. I might not be good for your image. Part of your mystique, as an international model, could be the fact that you are so available.' said Larry.

The air seemed to crackle with a supercharged energy. Paige was so close. All he had to do was reach out and touch her. Paige was wearing one of the new dresses she had bought with Sylvie. The red one. She had tried all three on and settled on the red one. Although cut from the same pattern, the red one clung to her skin and plunged deeper. Paige knew the mole on her left breast showed in the red dress. Her newly acquired sun tan would bring out the colour and the shape in her eyes. Paige was trying very hard to be irresistible. She was calling on nine years of experience and giving her first live performance.

'OK! Tough guy, what's your favourite movie?'

'The Big Chill.' Larry said without hesitation. 'Now, when I say tough, I mean robust. And there are probably more modern movies than The Big Chill but I have yet to see them.'

'No, they haven't made a movie to top The Big Chill. Kiss me.'

'What?'

'I said kiss me.'

Larry and Paige embraced on the century old flagstones cut by Victor's father. Larry ate Paige's lips in small insatiable bites.

'Hold on tiger, you've got my motor running,' said Paige. 'You've passed a little acid test of mine.'

'I have?'

'You have. Now I want you all to myself but my stomach is empty. How about we ask Luca to mind the fort and we go out to dinner?' Paige smoothed her red dress and swung her small bag to her shoulder.

'Good idea. What do you fancy?'

'I fancy squid. Who does a nice squid?'

'Who's paying?'

'My treat. For threatening the life of Joey Cotz, it's my privilege.'

'U Castille. Expensive! It's in the Citadel. It's time to get drastic with the plastic.'

'Oh! How well you know me. But first we have a problem with the water in the pool, it is starting to pong.'

'Why don't we get Luca to drain it? He can syphon the water to the vegetable garden.'

Larry turned and headed for Luca's door. Perhaps it was a long time since Larry had been a teenager but Paige knew to stop him. 'Hey! If I am going to shout you dinner, the least you can do is shower, change and do something about that hair. I'll tell Luca to drain the pool and ask him if he can keep an eye on the place.'

Larry changed direction and in a few minutes Paige heard the noise of the faucet. Instinct, or was it part of her brain tuned into the sexual frequency told her that Luca and Sylvie were making love. At the door, Paige heard the sounds of lovemaking. She closed the door quietly; her instinct was right. From the sounds, the very skilful sounds, she would not have to wait long. She listened at the bathroom door - Larry was still under the shower. His mood had improved from this morning, he was singing.

Paige tapped quietly and entered Luca's bedroom.

'Don't turn on the light!' Luca did not try to disguise the panic in his voice.

'Larry is under the shower. Listen, he was on his way in here to ask you to drain my pool and use the water for the vegetable garden. I am taking him to U Castille for dinner so the place is yours for the evening. And you are taking a hell of a risk with your mother in the next room!' When Paige was met with held-breath silence she went on. 'You're in charge, OK?' And with that she shut the door as silently as she had the first time.

She decided to touch up her make up in Sylvie's room. She chose a dark red lipstick to match her mood and the tingling between her thighs. She swept her hair back and decided on an up style for the evening. She borrowed one of Sylvie's combs and took in her full-length reflection in the dresser. She liked what she saw and considered herself to be suitably irresistible. From her bag she got out her eye shadow and made her upper lids a dark umber, it brought out the colour in her eyes. She wondered again if men knew the lengths women went to allow themselves to be seduced.

She heard pillow talk from the next room and thought of Sylvie's career with Rose. Sylvie was ready, but was Luca? When she started in this business she still thought boys to be pretty yucky. Her own deflowering had been pretty perfunctory and it came in the same week she had been asked to portray innocence for the camera - a look she pulled off with a sort of stunned denial. A look that later became her signature. How much she had learned. Sylvie would go far. From the sounds she had heard from the crack in the door Luca and Sylvie were fast learners.

Chapter Fifty Two

Dumb Questions

Sylvie sat at Luca's elbow. The reception was quiet but from the sounds coming from the sitting room, Luca's mother was still not asleep. They shut the door. The object of their attention was the old book from the well. In all the activities Luca had nearly forgotten it. It was brittle and cracked when they eased open its pages.

'What does it say, Luca. Can you translate?'

'It is written in Corsu and Genoese.' The book was handwritten and had been started from the back as well as the front.

'The front is a journal of daily events except the names of the people were all animals. The back section is a list of people and how they died and on what dates....

'*Carillet, Gilles. Died during questioning, Cardiac infraction 28 years old. Billiet, Vincent. Shot through the head, Luger 9 mm.* Both of these happened on the same date. But the book is too fragile to examine.'

Then a look came over Luca's face and he no longer cared for the fragile nature of the book. Its bindings cracked as he read from the front journal section. It was one of the last entries.

April 20th 1942

12.45 - The Eagle after 20 hours of sustained questioning is weak. Schultz is running out of patience.

14.40 - Schultz loaded his pistol with nine bullets. He told the Eagle to shoot nine of the village's men. He lined them up. Repeated his command under threat of death. The Eagle can hardly see out of one eye. All his fingernails have been removed. Schultz forced the gun into his hands and reiterated this is the only way he will see this day out. The pain causes the Eagle to pass out.

14.55 - Schultz himself shoots the nine men and reloads. He places the barrel of the gun to The Eagles head and asks once more for the names of the Maquis. The Eagle spits a bloody gob into Shultz's boot. He is shot six times though the head. The Bear is now senior resistance movement leader, she takes over as team leader of the gang.

Then followed the kind of silence reserved for church.

'My great grandmother. That's why they call her the Bear. I knew she was involved in the resistance movement but she was the leader. How about that?'

'She will want to see this book,' Sylvie let her enthusiasm show.

'No, it is a national treasure. I mean, of course she should see it, but this could be used in the War Crimes Tribunal. It could be evidence.' Luca was visibly moved.

'Luca what is it?'

'My great grandfather was killed during the German occupation. Victor's father. The handwriting is possibly The Bear's. I think The Eagle was my great grandfather.'

'How could you prove it?'

'I don't know. I don't want to confront the Bear; she is old and frail.'

'In the meantime, what are you going to do with the book?'

'Put it in the safe.'

******

Luca, true to his word attempted to empty the pool. That is, he emptied half. The ground around the vegetable garden was saturated and would take no more water. He moved the hose around to the herb garden and was surprised to see the kitchen light on.

'It's your mother,' Sylvie whispered at his ear. 'She can't sleep. Do you want to talk to her?'

'No. I want her to leave. When she re-marries I hope she looks me up.'

'Luca, I have it! Come, come, finish here and put the hose away.'

'What is it?' Luca hissed, but Sylvie had gone back into the office. He closed the hose off and went to Paige's studio to take the hose end out of the pool. The pool was half empty and reflected the rising moon from its still surface. Luca disturbed the reflection and the still night air as he coiled the hose, getting wet in the process. Back in the office, Sylvie was nowhere to be seen.

The office door opened slowly and Sylvie slipped in with her finger pressed to her lips. She was dressed all in black with soft rubber sole shoes.

'Shhh!'

Luca chuckled and Sylvie tried to look angry.

'You're all wet,' she whispered into his ear and then bit it. 'Get changed, we are going to the cemetery.

'The cemetery?'

'Don't let your mother hear you, or she will ask dumb questions.'

'Am I allowed one dumb question?'

'Sure.'

'Why are we going to the cemetery?'

'We have the date of the assassination. Your great grandfather is buried there?'

Luca got it. The penny dropped. 'But I am meant to stay here and look after this place.'

'Silly. The time to go to a cemetery is midnight; everyone knows that.'

'Why don't we go in the morning?'

Sylvie lifted her up black long-sleeve top. She wasn't wearing anything underneath.

'I'll get out of these wet clothes,' said Luca.

Chapter Fifty Three

Whispered in a Way that Could Part a Sheep's Fleece

The moon was visible and it made the headstones luminous and sharp. Shadows took on depth and a life that did not exist by day. It could have been romantic, it could have been eerie, but Sylvie held Luca's hand and whispered in a way that could part a sheep's fleece.

'Shhh!'

'Why are we whispering, Luca.'

'You might wake them.' Sylvie pretended to shiver. 'Shhh! No, I'm serious this time. I thought I heard something.'

'You're imagining things. Do you know where your great grandfather is buried, Luca?'

Luca led the way.

Sylvie skipped and sang to the stars. Overhead, the trees seemed closer to Luca. Luca thought he heard something again but did not say anything. Sylvie would only tease him.

'Here it is.'

Sylvie leaped on top of the tomb. 'It's a family vault. You didn't tell me it was a family vault.'

'It's our family vault.'

Sylvie rolled over and looked down at the carved letters playfully. 'You read it; it makes me go cross eyed.'

'du Plessier, Jacques. Born December 11th 1896, died April 20th 1942. You were right. He is the Eagle. Wow!'

'You're the great grandson of a war hero. Come here war hero.' said Sylvie rolling onto her back.

Luca kissed the upside down form of Sylvie.

'Rose says my breast are still growing. And they are very sensitive.' Sylvie took Luca's hand and pushed it down her top. 'Do you like my breasts, Luca?'

Then they both heard it. Luca snatched his hand away as Sylvie sat up. All her playfulness had gone. Sylvie swung her legs off the marble tomb and felt its coolness for the first time. They both listened for the sound. The marble felt clammy, Sylvie felt clammy. Sylvie's black comfortable clothes now begun to cling to her.

Luca was never so aware of all the night sounds. They were thunderous, whereas he had not heard them before. A cricket chirped near his foot and he suspected another insect was climbing up his shin as his bowels shrank.

Then it came again, a low mournful wail. Luca and Sylvie ran at full tilt. Wildly. They dodged headstones and fought for purchase on the gravel. They were making such a racket that Astrid stood and Luca nearly ran headlong into her.

Chapter Fifty Four

What Fully Booked Meant

When their hearts had returned to their chests, when the feeling of nausea had subsided, when they had their breath back; only then, did they ask Astrid what she was doing in the cemetery. Astrid began to cry again and it was Sylvie and Luca that had to calm her. Her eyes pully and swollen, she was barely recognisable from this morning. No one would want to paint a face in such turmoil.

'What is it, Astrid?'

'I am locked out of my hostel.'

'Is that all? We can fix that, can't we Luca?' Sylvie embraced the taller sturdier woman. Luca was aware of the strands of hair that mingled. The tangle of limbs entwined. The different textures. The contrast.

'Of course we can.'

Luca was going to have to explain to Sylvie what fully booked meant. But Astrid's wailing snapped his mind back to matters at hand. Luca had never seen anyone cry like this.

'He does not love me. He used me and threw me out.'

'Dernavern?' asked Luca

'Of course, Dernavern,' said Astrid.

'Do you have a return ticket?'

'No, I used all the money I had to buy a one-way ticket.'

'Well, you can earn your board and enough for a trip home but I think that Dernavern should help you out. You can work in the laundry.'

Sylvie looked at Luca. The look said: are you mad?

He shrugged and said, 'Well, Dad did leave me in charge.'

It was close to 1 am before Astrid had composed herself and looked like taking Sylvie up on her offer.

'What were you guys doing in a cemetery anyway?' Astrid's English had an American twang. Luca shouldered Astrid's pack as he saw the girls' heads go together conspiratorially. Astrid raised her head. Her mouth was a perfect oval. 'Oh! You guys want to fuck.'

Had it been happening to someone else Luca would have laughed. Had it been happening in a movie or a book, it could have been entertaining.

'Not now. Look! We'll put you into Sylvie's room. You are next to my mother so you will have to be quiet, OK! We will be in the room next to my father. That's if he comes home.'

Larry was not home. Luca read his note. Getting into U Castille at short notice would take some doing. Perhaps Paige would finally flex her celebrity muscle. He put Astrid's backpack into Sylvie's room, went to the kitchen to see if a light was on in Paige's studio. It was, but Luca had no way of knowing if that was Paige and his father or Dee Dee.

Rose's terrace was very secluded, he could see no lights and hear no sounds. By now, it was close to 2 am.

He laid down next to Sylvie. She was not asleep.

'No! We can't. What if my father came home?'

'I just want to spend the night in your arms, Luca.' Luca knew those words to be false as soon he heard them. Sylvie curled her body next to his and Luca stirred. Sylvie's hand accidently brushed Luca's groin.

'What do we have here?'

'Sylvie!'

'We'll be quiet. I'll be quiet. I want to taste you, Luca.'

The last shred of Luca's resolve evaporated as a shock of thick black hair brushed his abdomen.

Chapter Fifty Five

First available Flight

Astrid's crying had exhausted her. She fell asleep immediately and heard nothing. Genevieve was consigned to a very sleepless night. She tossed and rolled in her noisy camp bed. She would be on the first available flight in the morning.

Chapter Fifty Six

Our Time Together

The stone walls of U Castille reflected their 600-year patina in the flicker of the five-candle chandelier. Paige was recognised by Georg and shown to a premium seat. Larry brushed the linen with his fingertips.

'Expensive!' he said and that was before he saw the menu.

U Castille was an establishment taken to the pre-feminist notion of male and female menus. Paige's menu had no prices. It was broadsheet in size and handwritten. Calligraphically - a work of art.

'No prices. Should I be concerned?' She asked, her face a mask of contrived horror.

'Well! How well do you get on with your bank manager?'

'Very well. And I've eaten at Oscar Foxtrots', so I keep the smelling salts handy when the bill comes in. Actually, I've never met my bank manager.'

'Well, if it's time for confessions, I told my wife that you were my fiancée.'

The wine waiter arrived, and it was obvious he was going to do the whole thing properly. He poured a small taste for Larry. Larry hammed up the tasting process, drawing it out, for Paige's delight. She stroked the stem of her wine glass as it was filled. The waiter, sensing a sexual tension in the air, melted away.

'Fiancée?' repeated Paige when they were alone.

'Actually, it was a moment of high drama amid telephoning for ambulances and she had just hurled an accusation about losing guests down wells, I sort of dropped it into the conversation.'

'Did it have the desired effect?'

'It did. My wife suddenly felt the need to sit down.'

'You are a cruel man Lazlo Moro.' said Paige beaming.

'Am I ready to face the world's media; do you think?'

'You are, but that's just my point. We can face most things if we can prepare for them. What you might not be ready for is the relentless nature of the British media in particular. Or perhaps that's just me. Because I am British.'

The entrées arrived and Larry sat silently as a huge white plate was placed before him. The lamb cutlet looked small and lonely in a verdant puddle of parsley sauce. Paige was having the risotto.

'They should have said 'risot'. Or whatever is the singular for risotto,' she said, lifting her huge fork.

'A ris?' suggested Larry.

'You know Rose has suggested an article to go out on the wire. She is talking in the region of 30 thousand.'

'Dollars?'

'Pounds.'

'An article about you and me?' Said Larry.

'With a photo it could be worth a bundle. I thought I would be spotted at the courtroom. But the local press mustn't have been alerted to the fact that I was here. It won't last long though.'

'How do you know?' asked Larry, refilling Paige's glass.

'Did you see the look on Georg's face? He bumped someone for us to get this table. Someone from one of those super yachts in the marina. I saw the look in his eye. He's probably on the phone right now.' Said Paige.

'What? Would he get a kick-back for the information in the local press? Asked Larry.

'Possibly. Is there local press? But publicity for his restaurant is his main motivation.'

Paige had finished her tiny morsel. 'I hope main course is a bit more substantial.'

'So do I. Well, what am I in for? Give me the Paige Goss media survival course.' Larry laid down his knife and fork.

'Well, you have used the word fiancée; don't be surprised to read that in the press. Along with photos of anyone else you have ever been engaged to. Who was there when you said this?'

The waiter floated in, and plates were removed. Larry saved his answer until he had gone. Just as he was about to answer Paige thought of something else.

'That's good with the waiter. Trust no one. I saw you mulling over your answer until he was out of earshot.'

'I was thinking. I was thinking who was there. I'm pretty sure it was just Genevieve and Horst. One lives in Brussels and the other in Dresden. Neither knows many people here and both will go home soon.' Said Larry.

'It doesn't matter that you have said it. I was once told to give an interview to this sleazy tabloid journalist. He said if I didn't talk to him, he would just make it up anyway. That was when I was new in the business. Now, I would just refer him to Rose. This is a multibillion-dollar business. One advertiser or agency, threatening to pull their advertising and the journalist backs off. Rose says to think of them as a pack of hungry dogs, they have no manners, but they have to eat. So! Throw them a bone once in a while.'

'Damn! The waiter has taken my chop bone,' mused Larry.

'Seriously. What are you going to tell the world's press? 'We are just good friends' just doesn't cut it I'm afraid. It will just incite them.'

'What is the current expression of the day?'

'Well, that depends on what continent and what publication. I like that we are an item. Don't for God's sake say we are in a relationship!'

Larry cringed and once again hammed it up for Paige. She mimed sticking two fingers down her throat.

'That's so American,' said Larry. 'The whole dating thing. They have institutionalised sex.'

Paige’s shriek of laughter drew stares. It did not go with 120 F a plate and candlelight - people who paid that sort of money for a main course had very little to laugh at.

'How have they, the Yanks, institutionalised sex?' asked Paige.

'We call them Septics.'

'Septics?'

'Septic tank: Yank. That was back in my university days. I, and I think I can speak for most males of my generation, hung out in groups. We paired off, in a sort of tertiary natural selection.'

'Darwin would be proud.' Said Paige.

'I can't speak with any authority on dating as I have never done it myself. If I was interested in a girl, I could seek her out. Uni students are poor anyway, a cask or a flagon of wine, talk and things just went from there.'

'You smooth devil. No wonder you swept me off my feet.'

'I used to have a special trick. Shall I give away my trade secrets?' said Larry.

Paige wiped her mouth and sat up straight and attentive. She tossed her fringe out of her eyes. 'I'm all agog.'

'Well, my world was inhabited by lots of people my age. And the mix was about 50 - 50, boys and girls. Women, lots of them, flowed through my life daily. Tall ones, thin ones, pretty ones, smart ones, ambitious ones and if I got some sort of rapport going and don't forget, there were just as many eligible men, I made it my business to seek her company on her own. Now! Most men would ask for a date or a phone number and that whole date thing can range from ecstatic to excruciating. But the whole relationship thing, whatever gets off on the wrong foot. You end up spending a whole three hours, pretending to be something you're not. You try and be interesting, enigmatic, engaging.'

'How would you find them?'

'My world then was Melbourne University. Not hard to find a person with no or little disposable income and a daily routine similar to your own.'

'What if your scheme backfired?'

'It did once. She was an American. She wanted the whole courtship dance, complete with at least three rejections. I had to prove my worthwhileness. I couldn't see the point. I wouldn't play Rhett to her Scarlet.'

'Was it just the once, that it backfired?'

'Yeah! Sometimes I fancied someone and did not get a bat-squeak of interest.'

'You rely on your charm you silver tongued devil. No wonder I fell under your spell. But what do we tell the press? What if I say this is a holiday fling, try and deflect some of the attention away from you and Luca?'

'Do you think we need saving? Alright! What you say makes sense. But I hope you don't mean it.'

Larry lifted his glass and held it out for Paige to chink glasses.

'What are we toasting?' asked Paige.

.'Time together. Our time together. However, and whenever we can manage it.'

'Our time together.' Paige looked around the restaurant. Older couples mostly, well-heeled tourists, and regulars. 'I'm so glad I've been spared the 'I'm just out of a relationship, not ready to commit' speech or the 'I'm going through a me' phase. '

'Jesus, do people say that?'

'When you say that sex is institutionalised, so are the excuses for breaking up. It's like someone wrote the fucking manual, or something, and it is distributed on the old boy's network.'

'Well, I've only had one relationship and that was a marriage. It is no fun being married to a ghost I can tell you.'

'How did you cope?' asked Paige.

'The first year was the hardest. I have only had my one interest and those old feelings came back. My Italian teacher made me horny. Apart from that the volcano was dormant. And to save you asking, I have been celibate for all that time.'

The main courses came out and Paige's marinated squid brought noses to attention with its aromas, and eyes with its spectacular presentation. Larry was having the local equivalent of a Caesar salad. The menu gave very little credit to international influences despite Georg relying on their trade. Mainland tastes and those North American and Japanese tourists had to be satisfied while balancing regional allegiances. Two types of people lived in Bonifacio: millionaires on the yachts in the marina and the locals. Georg catered for the tastes of the former and the latter were excluded mainly on price and had to book in advance. Six months in advance.

'How did you get started,' asked Larry.

'I was young. Very young. I had done some shots for Steven Meisle in New York and met Patrick Demarchelier. Then I met Calvin, and he said, 'I want her.'

Larry's eyebrows went up. Even he had heard of Calvin Klien.

'I was fourteen. They have changed the rules now and a model has to be sixteen.'

'So, you are ten-year veteran.'

'I am.' Paige got a look in her eye. 'Are you telling me you have not had sex in ten years,' she asked.

'Nine.'

'Don't worry,' Paige said, 'it's like riding a bike. Only you're less likely to graze your knee if you fall off.'

In spite of the fine linen, the oversize flatware, the pewter candelabras, and the scorn of Georg, Larry roared with laughter. The stone walls that had seen six centuries bounced the joyous sound like a newfound toy.

That is how the flash caught Paige - laughing and eating. A tanned arm resting on the white linen tablecloth. Her torso was décolleté red and floated above the table and her plate like it was an arranged window dressing. Larry was in profile and the cause or object of Paige's mirth. The wide and fresh-faced Paige who had been out of the papers for some time appeared relaxed and gloriously happy. As most of her tabloid photos had been doctored for over a year, the photo made the 6 o'clock news on the major networks on two continents. The Australian networks picked up on Larry's home-grown content and he was splashed on three of the free-to-air networks.

The whole world wanted to know who had made Paige Goss smile again.

Chapter Fifty Seven

You and me Alone Together, on an Island

Eating late was quite the norm in this climate. The Citadel was crowded and the shops still open. The Castela was lit up from below and it felt like the perfect night to stroll along the marina.

'Hadn't you better pop in there,' said Paige. They had slowed walking passed the chemist. 'Safe sex! And all that.'

'No, we have those in the bathroom cabinet; that is if Luca has left me any.'

'No! I was talking about knee pads in case you fall off!'

The mood from dinner spilled over into the evening. The kinetic energy of goodwill trampolined by a cognac and a bottle of wine carried them to a place very close to heaven. Larry felt unburdened after he spoke of the years bringing up Luca alone. It felt like a noble surrender to fate when recounting familiar things to an eager listener. It turned out that Paige's parents had separated, and she spent most time with her father.

'I'll ring Dee Dee,' said Paige, with a wicked look in her eye. Larry heard her negotiating to have the apartment to herself.

She snapped her phone shut. 'I woke her' said Paige to Larry.

Taking his arm, they commenced walking.

'She will stay with Rose - Rose never sleeps. They can have a catch up over a bottle of wine.'

'Shall I hail a cab? Or shall we wander over to the taxi rank in our own time?'

'I'll be swamped at Heathrow, you know?' said Paige. 'I'll have microphones and cameras thrust in my face and someone will say: what's your relationship with Mr Moro?'

'And?'

'I need to get you home,' Paige said. 'The answer could be a holiday bonk, or the next big thing in my life.'

'Talk about pressure. Putting a guy under pressure.'

Paige bit her lip and framed her question. 'What about this: you and me alone, together, on an island?'

'No, a big city,' enthused Larry. 'Near a river or a lake.'

'Silly me! You've been stuck here all this time. Of course, you want to get off the island.'

Larry stopped and the natural momentum swung Paige around.

'London,' said Larry, his eyes bright. 'I love decorating. Pension Lazlo just whet my appetite. I could fix up your place; the one you have never even spent a night in - in London.'

'It's on the river. Don't tell the media you have come to London to decorate. It will sound like I have hired you, or something. I love what you've done at Pension Lazlo by the way. What will you do about Pension Lazlo? Can Luca run the place?'

'He can. But it takes two,' said Larry, 'even if there is someone there just so you can get a meal break.'

'Don't tell Dee Dee I told you this, but she is looking for a change of career. She bailed me out and I owe her financially. She was there for me while my world fell apart, keeping the media from the door when I was not up to facing them. It is all part of her job description. She told me she was putting her place on the market, so I will have to move anyway.'

Chapter Fifty Eight

Welcome to Sicily

The boat bobbed and at times the motion was in sync with the throbs from Joey's foot. The water was a lazy turquoise broken only by the occasional white wind-whipped wash. In shallower water it would be clear but they were in deep water and had been for a day and a half. Joey had given up trying to talk to the skipper. His rheumy eyes were probably once blue and looked out from a face that looked like a sponge cake left out in the rain. The chin was brindle, the moustache yellow from tobacco smoke. The whole thing looked like a scrubbing brush, a scrubbing brush that you would want to throw away.

If it was five days since that chin had seen a razor and it was longer since the whole body had seen warm soapy water. Deep creases near the mouth were black with grime and gave the face the appearance of a ventriloquist doll. A cap topped off the picture, once black or dark blue it was now salt stained and white in patches. The hat was coming apart at the peak, the piping hung to one side like something that once lived and had died ingloriously. The mouth was permanently clamped around a cigarette, lit or unlit, the hand on the tiller and the stare at a spot just over the horizon.

Occasionally all the effort went into rolling another cigarette and at this point the tiller flapped freely. The horizon ignored. The cigarette engaged all the skipper's attention. With no navigation equipment at all Joey wondered what course they were on, if any, and how the silent, smelly skipper navigated, if at all.

'Look, where are we going? Sardinia is just 12 kilometres. We have been at sea for a day and a half, now!'

The skipper kept his gaze on objects unseen, as if he had not heard at all. It was the same each time Joey asked. Joey thought of his money in a secret compartment in a camera bag, in a rented van, on a farm road.

Joey laid his head down again on rough timber. The smell was of oil and dead fish. Smells old and rank, too numerous to catalogue. At least here he was out of the wind. He covered his head in his light jacket and studied the paint chip contents. Once the boat had been black but it had been painted, quickly, roughly in a coat of cheap cream paint. These had cracked and were now peeling. These shapes, in the absence of clouds, had amused Joey as he tried to stay out of the sun. For a while they had been lakes and he picked feverishly at a large paint chip to fashion it like the shape of Lake Michigan, Chicago and a large chunk of Gary, Indiana had come away in his hand after the first morning. He tired of that game. His arms and neck felt burnt and the skin contracted to make him forget the pain in his foot. Laying in the bottom of the boat offered a bit of shade. It must be afternoon thought Joey, but he would have to lay in filthy diesel. There was nothing for it. He lay on the bottom of the boat. The chug, chug chugging of the engine became Joey's new pain. He wore it like a wet suit.

Joey must have dozed off, because he heard voices. A shadow crossed his face and the boat jarred as a larger vessel tied off. Its algae encrusted buffers protested mournful groans as the boats rode the swell. Both engines cut and the tied boats found a collective rhythm. For the first time in day and a half there was silence. It mocked Joey now as he found he could not speak.

It was within his mental capabilities to hear the clear, measured, American accent and how the owner switched so effortlessly to regional Italian. The skipper of the small wooden boat ascended the ladder without word. Why would he? He had said nothing in 36 hours. Joey followed up the ladder sheepishly. Every molecule in his body was responding to a common alarm. Joey did not need a neon sign to know this was Deep Shitsville.

'Allow me to introduce myself. I am Peter del Gatto,' said a voice that had studied at a red brick university.

Joey would have guessed law. Joey would have been right.

Joey was offered no refreshment but was standing downwind from where his shipmate of the past two days was tossing back Rye Whiskey in a manner that did not involve his lips getting wet.

'I am to understand that you wish to re-enter the United States,' said Peter del Gatto.

'Yeah!' Joey tried to clear his throat aware he had only two sips of rancid water in the last day and nothing the day before. 'Yes, I am an America citizen. Can you help?'

'Of course. The question is, are you in a position to pay?'

Joey hated to ask but why put off the inevitable? 'How much.'

'$40,000.'

'Jesus, fuck, I'm a bit flat till pay day.'

'$40,000, US dollars. Cash.'

'You're crazy! Who has that kind of money in the middle of the ocean?' Joey was shouting. It hurt his throat, but he was shouting.

'Of course! How rude of me. Welcome to Sicily.'

Joey was worried. Sicily was not good - he was not sure why. Joey noticed that Peter was dressed in a lounge suit, had taken one concession to matters nautical and removed his tie. Perhaps they were near land. Joey looked around and took in the gleaming chrome and white of the boat. Its deck had the look of being cleaned today, yesterday and the day before. Every day. Joey scanned the horizon for land. Something in Peter's demeanour told him it would be just over the curve of the earth: seven miles, and not much more, Peter looked like a busy man.

'Perhaps we can discuss a payment plan.'

'It would seem I have no option.'

'No,' said Peter del Gatto folding his arms. 'You can go back with Christophe.'

'No offence but the guy was getting on my nerves. Does he ever shut up?'

'You are a brazen, vulgar man. My uncle was right.'

A look of thunderous dread spread over Joey's face. The word 'Uncle,' escaped from his lips which were suddenly very dry. His tongue chose this moment to stick to the back of his teeth.

'Christophe here is a simple man of the sea. He has been paid and sees you as 190 pounds of useless ballast. He would be calculating, in his own simple way, how much less fuel he would expend if he threw you overboard. He could open your stomach and use your blood as burly.'

Christophe said something and threw back another whiskey.

'He says he has not bought his large hooks; let the sharks eat you.'

Peter del Gatto brought his attention back to Joey. 'I suspect you are hungry, thirsty and tired.'

Christophe downed two more shots in the silence that settled like dust.

'You are welcome to use this vessel and all its creature comforts, but they do not come cheap. I think you will find our chef up to international standard. And our selection of wines par excellence. Shall we discuss a payment plan? Quickly now, Christophe has a family to feed.'

Chapter Fifty Nine

A Swiss Boarding School

The morning was a mild one. Morning sounds wafted their way into the loft bedroom in Paige's studio. In a wreck of fine cotton sheeting Paige wrapped herself around the sleeping Larry. A lover's nest. A voice was raised in angry French - Sylvie swore. A door slammed. Larry and Paige were anaesthetised to the outside world. Their bodies ached pleasurably. They woke and slept fitfully. A heartbeat or the sound of breathing, satisfied them. A touch, it had not all been a dream, they snoozed in utter contentment.

One strident accusatory voice was calling for Luca. It could not penetrate his happiness bubble, Larry slept. Paige curled into his back.

Sylvie was bundled into a car.

Larry shifted as Sylvie screamed and scratched Saunders on the face. The sound of her throwing away the keys to the Bentley was woven into the fabric of Larry's dream. Rose's was the voice of reason but M Murat would not hear of it.

By the time Paige and Larry had showered, made love again, dressed and come down, Sylvie was on her way to a Swiss Boarding School.

Chapter Sixty

If My Life Were a Video, I'd return it

When dressed, Larry had suggested to Paige that she call a cab for Genevieve. They were acutely aware that something had gone down outside the office. Fragments and half remembered pieces of argument had permeated but had not yet been assembled. Larry was steeling himself to go out and face his family.

'No, drive her. Can you think of a better time to spend alone than after you have just pleasured a supermodel?'

There was a certain logic to this, and Larry had grown to appreciate Paige's sense of humour.

Paige kissed him on the nose, 'I'll come down when the coast is clear.'

'Put some clothes on first.'

Larry was met by a babble that had been building. He found himself agreeing to take Genevieve to the airport. She must have been waiting for him to come into the kitchen. Larry felt nothing but pity for the fuddled face that begged for sleep and longed for order. The feelings of anxiety from yesterday had gone, they were strongly anchored in duty. Larry realised that he had a forty-minute drive on his own with his soon to be ex-wife.

Luca appeared, 'Can I be relieved on reception?' but he knew, from his parent's faces that he was too late. 'We have just lost our receptionist.'

'Lost our receptionist. How?'

Larry had to be told, twice. At first the awful truth could find no purchase in Larry's filled and tingling senses.

'M Murat came and had Saunders man-handle Sylvie into the car.' Luca said. 'She scratched him.'

'I'm surprised you didn't hear it,' Genevieve's voice made it plain she wished to be anywhere but Pension Lazlo right now. 'She fought like a wildcat.'

'He had his day in court. You'd think he would be satisfied. I was hoping you would come with your mother and I to the airport,' said Larry to Luca.

Luca knew he should have felt something, but he did not even register the void. His mother was leaving, possibly for ever and he felt nothing. He went to the larder of dutiful love, and it was empty. He knew she was witness to the worst moments in his life. He played his trump - 'someone has to look after reception.' What he really wanted to do was find out where they had taken Sylvie.

'I have to drive your mother to the airport.'

At that moment Astrid was promoted from laundry to reception.

'Alright, I'll stay here,' said Luca.

Rose caught Larry loading Genevieve's luggage into the car. It struck Larry that Genevieve had packed for more than two days, and she was leaving without seeing her parents. Larry's mind was full of Luca - he'd given in too easily. There had to be a catch.

'I'm going to open a branch office down here,' said Rose.

'Yeah! Great,' said Larry, with a careworn vagueness.

'That was a joke, Larry. I have just met your new trainee. Is being drop-dead-gorgeous a job requirement to work at Pension Lazlo.'

'What?' Larry stood as the quizzical look on his face turned to anger. 'Stay here. If my wife comes out, tell her to stay here and not move. Use physical force if you have to.'

And with that he stormed back into the office.

This was how Astrid met her employer.

It was a full minute before Larry could speak. 'Luca! What the fuck are you up to?'

'Dad, this is Astrid.' Luca did not have time to be shocked by his father swearing. He had to find Sylvie. 'If this works out, I can go and find Sylvie.'

'Are you totally mad?'

'Dad, I may never see her again,' cried Luca

'Luca, no!'

'I only need ten minutes.'

'Luca you have to stay here and look after the Pension. It is not fair to leave a person on their own, on their first day. That was your intention; I can see it. Luca, I know you.'

'Why do you have to drive her to the airport? I hate her. She messed up everything.'

Genevieve stepped back from the door to the office and glided silently into the kitchen. She had taken a few stolen moments to watch her son explain the telephone system to the blonde girl. She was astounded at his patience, his even measured English. His voice never wavered, even when Astrid got it wrong. Astrid's raw beauty made even Genevieve uneasy and her son was comfortable and confident standing at her shoulder. She left the kitchen door ajar and ascended the few steps of the herb garden and strode to the waiting car, looking straight through the hovering Rose Underhill.

A door slammed, Larry's body language implied urgency. Rose did not delay him with small talk.

'I have got to take my wife to the airport, and I am told to expect paparazzi.'

'Do you want Simon to drive her?'

'No! She is still my wife. Sorry, this is just too weird. If my life were a video, I'd return it.'

'No, you wouldn't,' said Rose.

Larry at some level knew Rose was right. He was dreading the trip to the airport. Then, in two days Victor and Clara would be back. All the events of the past few days did not stack up well. At some point he was going to have to ask Luca what happened while he slept, again!

Genevieve appeared to be focusing on a point about half a kilometre in front of the car. 'Just drive,' she said.

'Teenagers can be ...'

Genevieve silenced him with her hand. All words of comfort and praise were banalities now. She had a family in Brussels, good obedient little girls who loved her. Oh, why did she come?

Chapter Sixty One

American Rescued in High Seas Drama

From a round glassless window, one of the world's top ten supermodels watched as a man opened the car door for his wife. A gesture borne of manners and breeding. Larry scurried around to the driver's door, the tyres scattering the gravel as he selected reverse. That was good. He opened the door because he was trying to get her to hurry. The next hour and a half in Paige's life would be punishment to balance last night's pleasure.

****

On the Figari-Sud-Corse, the silence had mounted and fallen in on itself like a mushroom cloud that the wind steadfastly refuses to disperse.

'Luca has a shoe box full of money.' Larry said, he was leading somewhere. 'He also collects names and addresses. I thought, we all thought, he would follow you. I watched the mailbox to see if there was ever a letter from you.'

Silence was Genevieve's reply.

Six more kilometres passed in dappled sunshine. Larry thought the tension could burst his insides. Silence was insurmountable.

'I hoped he would leave,' said Larry. He did not trust himself to look at his wife. 'I was waiting for him to leave.'

The early summer riot of wild flowers inspired by the recent rains drifted by the windows. Larry had to drive onto the hard shoulder to let other vehicles pass. Stones hitting the under-tray of the car ruptured the silence.

Larry's meaning was tacit. If you don't speak I don't drive.

'If I hadn't left, would you have left?' asked Genevieve 'eventually, I mean.'

Larry's answer was unqualified. 'Yes.'

'We were Love's Lost Dream for a while there,' she said.

'I know. It was hard to live up too. I was waiting for Luca to ask why you left,' said Larry, 'But I think he has worked that out for himself.'

'Say goodbye, for me. I screwed up all my courage to come here. That's why I didn't ring, I might have chickened out again. If I had come another week, would the outcome have been different.'

'No,' Larry lied.

'I think you should ask that young woman to marry you,' said Genevieve. 'She's besotted.'

'Two people besotted, that doesn't guarantee a future. Look at us. You have got to be ready.'

'And are you ready, Larry?'

'No,' Larry lied again, 'I'll need to get away from time to time from Lazlo's. Otherwise you are working from sun up to sunrise.'

'You were already with the pigs and film scripts, Larry.'

'People are much harder working, at much more unpleasant things.'

The magnificent scenery was lost on Genevieve. She had long ago tired of trying to match the images she saw with those in long term storage. It was wearing her out. Nothing was the same as she remembered, and the bare beauty was lost because she was not quite seeing this for the very first time. It was like seeing a movie out of sequence: entire sections in the wrong order. She found her reactions did not match the images, because the facts had changed or were unknown or had become scrambled. She would bring her new husband and two daughters here and forget what she knew. Drink it all in like a tourist. The only way to really escape, is to return on your own terms and let Corsica smack you fully in the face.

'God this is beautiful,' she sighed.

'Here we are,' said Larry. 'Why did you fly into Aero de Figari?'

'I wanted to get a taxi to the farm.' Genevieve said gathering her hand luggage. 'Larry, I have a confession. I have done this before. I got right to the gate.'

Larry said nothing, mainly because he knew this as soon as she had said it. A park, quite near the terminal, was about to become available. If Larry hesitated, he would lose out to a waiting Renault.

On entering the Terminal, Genevieve bought three French newspapers.

'I'll take these home for Ann and Freda; they love to follow the gossip from Paris. They think Brussels is a dreary little town.'

Larry picked up the Paris Match while Genevieve became engrossed in the Globe. Reading was good; if Larry read, he might get through the rest of the day without lying again. It was there on page seven. The photograph caught his eye.

AMERICAN RESCUED IN HIGH SEAS DRAMA.

Italian American businessman, Peter del Gatto plucked his fellow countryman and paparazzo, Guiseppe Cotz from the seas off Sicily. Cotz had been adrift for two days, suffering the effects of exposure and dehydration, Cotz was rushed to a private clinic part owned by Mr del Gatto in Palermo.

'It was lucky we found him when we did. It was touch and go,' said Mr del Gatto. 'Mr Cotz is a business associate of my brother in New York. We are showing him every hospitality: it is the Sicilian way.'

'Can I have this,' said Larry, but on second thought got up to buy his own paper.

Genevieve read the story from the newspaper that Larry had left on the seat. 'That was the American down your well. How unlucky. He gets rescued from a well and then lost at sea!'

Chapter Sixty Two

Beatrice Fleur du Plessier

The proud old woman sat at her dresser. The curtains were drawn back as far as they would go. A small crowd, some with cameras, had assembled near her front door. She had not worn makeup for a long time and had dispensed with the notion of trying to make the parchment planes, creased from years of delight and sorrow, a different shade or shape with powders and scented creams. She had forgotten how. Lulu, a girl from Scola Corsa University had volunteered to lend her own makeup kit. The old woman's eyebrows had remained black but her hair had turned white. She had thickened her brows with a pencil at Lulu's suggestion and she liked what she saw. A beret; that was all she needed. She was told to wear something with a lapel as Mitterrand wished to pin the medal on her himself. Clara had offered a military style jacket with a row of shiny buttons. This the woman, known as The Bear, opted for, as it was similar to the one worn by her husband the day he had a 9mm Luger placed to his temple. And don't be fooled by what doctors tell you, brains are not grey, they are pink and yellow and very, very sticky.

Then there had been the delay in the paperwork as confirmation from Paris came on her birthdate. Beatrice Fleur du Plessier was 103 years old.

The opening line in her speech thanked the authorities for unpacking very tender memories and for letting the whole world know. But her speech needed work and there was duty to perform before she went to Paris. Larry was in London and Victor and Clara were getting settled in their new house in Porto Vecchio. She had ordered a taxi but when the taxi company heard who they were to be carrying, the director sent his own private car and driver. Beatrice hoped the media circus would follow her to the bank where Murat worked.

The civic reception for her in Paris would not go ahead while family matters hung in the balance. She would not be driven down the Champs Elysees while her great grandson's heart ached with misery.

A dab of perfume and the black beret raked at a jaunty angle over her right ear. She was ready.

Her battered front door opened onto the street and the flash guns started before the door was fully open. She paused and smiled a little smile for Jacques, he would have wanted her too. A small wave and she started the few paces to the waiting car. The crowd parted with a wave of cheers and applause. Someone yelled bra*vo* and the whole world replied.

The Bear's heart swelled with pride. She had waited her whole life for this. Somewhere in a shallow scrape, in a corner of a flax field the Eagle's spirit was laid to rest. This one is for Jaques she thought.

The door was closed by the driver and the crowd closed in. Hands placed up to the tinted glass and the light of whole world died from the press of their hands and faces. Later when these people re-told their stories they would say they were there and touched The Bear, the Hero of Bonifacio, leader of the *Maquis*.illiners sold out of black berets that day.

Chapter Sixty Three

Never Summon a Member of my Family Again

Murat had made the appointment fifteen minutes before the bank closed at one o'clock. The streets of Bonifacio, normally busy at this time, played host to a flotilla of tooting scooters and motor bikes. Young people had been taught this as history, with one exception: that *all* the members of the *Maquis* were dead. Young people now formed a guard of honour, to witness an immortal.

At the bank, Beatrice Fleur paused again for photographs. In some photographs Bertrand Paoli could be seen waiting to close the door. Some say he is anxious in the presence of The Bear. Others, that know him, say he is eager to get home for his lunch.

'Murat is waiting. He has waited for 15 minutes already,' said Paoli.

'Then let him wait one minute more,' said Beatrice Fleur.

Beatrice was hoping that Murat would come into the banking chamber, perhaps to the door. It was well known in the town that his tart was visiting from Nice. Let her wait too. A specially chartered plane was waiting to take The Bear directly to Paris. She had no schedules to keep until tomorrow. Where she would have The Legion of Honour pinned to her lapel by Mitterrand himself.

Bertrand Paoli showed The Bear to Murat's office letting his skittishness show in the process.

'Close the door,' she said to his departing back.

The Bear wanted to take control from the start. Murat must have been expecting Larry or Victor, it showed for a split second in his face. He greeted her cordially but made no mention of the fact that she was on the front cover of every national paper.

'You were expecting Larry, perhaps?'

'No! Yes, maybe. Please, sit down.'

'This won't take a moment. I will stand.' And this she did, at the window behind Murat's desk. Murat, in his chair would be at her chest level and at very close range. He would have had to turn and look up at her. A disadvantage: which was exactly the reason his high-backed chair was placed in front of the window. Murat stood and a flashgun fired from the street.

'Perhaps you will be more comfortable over here,' Murat chose a wing chair leaving the impossibly low velvet ones with their stark angularity.

Beatrice du Plessier made Murat wait a full minute and a half before she spoke. 'Firstly, never summon a member of my family again. We are not in your employ; we do not owe you any money and we are not related to you.'

'I wanted to speak with Mr Larry. It was convenient as this is where I take my meetings.' Murat's voice pared off at a squeak

'Larry is in London if you had taken the trouble to find this out otherwise I would not be here now. Victor and Clara are getting settled into their new home. Barking orders at a fifteen-year-old is part of your character and pivotal to your problem. After I am done you may wish you had been more circumspect and waited to speak to the men.'

'Problem?'

'Shut up. Another is that you don't listen. I am going to make a request, after I have finished you will be a fool not to comply. Oh! But you are a fool, I have allowed for that contingency.'

Murat was about to speak but then a shadow of doubt clouded his face but not this reason.

'I am head of this family. And over the next few days we are all meeting up in Paris. I arrive early to rest and put the finishing touches to my speech. We consider - I consider, Sylvie to be part of that family. Before you protest she has made more progress in the last ten days than she has in the last ten years. It's emotional growth I am speaking of, so I don't expect you to understand. I need Sylvie to help me to put the finishing touches to that speech. If she chooses she can live with us.'

'But...'

Beatrice raised her hand and Murat forgot his posture, he positively slouched.

'My speech needs work, it contains a section where I ask the French people, 'What is the point of so many giving their lives and standing up against the tyranny of the SS? If men take a wife merely to gain promotion and keep a whore in luxury in Nice. What also is the cost in human suffering if they produce a child and ignore it? It's needs and emotional growth?'

'Sylvie! Write a Speech! Sylvie needs discipline. That is all.'

'She can work the machine, the word processor. Discipline! That is the point I was coming too. Thank you for bringing it up. You dumped her on Larry and Luca, at a time when we were opening for business. Clara, Larry and Luca have invested time and effort in training Sylvie as our receptionist. She mastered the European languages and was showing great promise, I only say this because we are having the devil of a time training her replacement.'

Beatrice Fleur turned and waved out of the window. A cheer and shouting floated up from the street. 'I believe our children hold the future of our proud country; this is a central theme of my speech.' Beatrice turned back to face Murat. 'The president has sent a plane for me, a pilot waits for me at the airport. A driver waits outside this very bank. Here is the offer: I will stay here until you agree to rethink your treatment of Sylvie.'

'This is blackmail!'

'Is it? I wonder what the young people think. Come here and look. I am a bit of a novelty to them. I was born in the last century, I will see this one out, and I will see that the last of my days are spent right, if I have to. Sylvie was on the verge of a brilliant career and you are holding her captive; yes that's the word - captive. Holding someone captive is in the same league as blackmail. How do you think the papers will see it? I can't go to Paris to collect my award because an infidel holds our receptionist captive. I'm not very good at making up headlines; I'm sure they will do a better job.' Beatrice used the Corsu word for infidel, it translated into French as unfaithful. 'Of course,' she went on, 'the whole business of her having sex with Luca could come out, and people would wonder what kind of father you are.'

Murat sat forward, placed his hands on his knees, hung his head below his shoulders; every bit the picture of a man defeated. 'Don't bring her into it,' he pleaded.

'Who? Your tart! It is funny that your first concern is for her. Where is Sylvie?'

'With her mother in Paris.'

'Then, she will be joining us in Paris.'

Murat nodded. He looked like he might speak, so, for a moment the sound of the restless crowd outside was the only sound in the room.

'Did she work? How did you..... she would never do anything we asked. She was impossible!'

'I am only guessing, but I would suggest that she modelled her behaviour on your own. Telling a child to do something, and doing the opposite is a quick way to lose respect. My daughter-in-law says she is bright and quick to learn, she took to the job like a bird to flight.'

'What will you tell my wife?'

'I will tell her you listened to well-reasoned argument,' said Beatrice.

'She will not believe you.'

'That is not my problem. It could be the start of a new beginning. You don't look like a happy man. Ring her and let her know I am coming; she knows me as, The Bear.'

Murat's phone rang. 'I said no interruptions.' He relaxed a little. 'Put her on then.'

The conversation that followed was not employee or client focused. Murat was speaking to close friend. Then he held the telephone out for Beatrice. 'She wants to speak to you.'

'Hello! The name is Beatrice but I am known everywhere as The Bear.

'Luca has spoken of you. I wish we had met. What did you tell my father to make him change his mind?'

'I reminded him of his responsibilities, I hope you will come back and work for us. Astrid is hopeless at Corsu and Italian. She is not at all self-assured; I like you.'

'That's the nicest thing to say. Thank you,' said Sylvie.

'I want you on one side of me and Luca on the other, as we drive up the Champs Elysees. With you two there no one will be looking at my tired old face.'

'How do you know what I look like?' asked Sylvie.

'I mentioned it might be worth persevering with Astrid as she looked like a Nordic Goddess. Everyone agrees that you, my dear, are prettier and more capable.'

'Do they?' the delight crackled down the telephone line.

'You may have to live with us,' said Beatrice, in what Luca called her 'That's the way it is,' voice. 'I think I can get your father to agree to that. What about your mother?'

'He is warm compared to Mamma! She can be pretty reptilian. Can I really live with you? And Clara and Victor? It would make things easier for me. It might just make it possible.'

'My dear child, it will be like a ray of sunshine. And I think I have your father's vote on being very persuasive.'

Murat looked as if he had just had his first lesson in parenting. He was sitting up looking like he wanted to take notes.

Chapter Sixty Four

The Wrong Road

The earth was scared a deep, rich brown and the white seam of PVC lined the trench like an artery. A line of chestnut trees stood like a sentinel in the silence of the lunch hour and provided shelter for the workmen. The lone tourist had wandered by and taken the road to Gualtier's farm. She had the look of a journeyman and a strong proud stride. She was alone with lustre behind her eyes that took in the view. Many tourists travelled alone, fewer stayed at Pension Lazlo; fewer still had this air of confidence.

The moment passed until the cacophony of Gaultier's dogs broke the still, well-fed quiet.

'She's taken the wrong road,' said the foreman.

'The smelly old man will come out to chase her off,' said another.

Luca, running a message to Basil the night manager at his residence heard the dogs and wondered what had disturbed them. A detour to the slaughterhouse roof and Luca saw the brown legs first. Their sandalled measured pace leisurely reduced the distance back to the pension.

Luca forgot about the lone Belgian woman in unit 4. The Dutch couple wanted to extend and with some last minute shuffling they would not have to change rooms. Luca delivered the good news personally.

He saw the Italian girl slouched over the reception counter and noticed the dust on her sandals.

'I see you have met our neighbour's dogs,' Luca said in Italian. He used a Venator dialect, his favourite.

'I have, I took the wrong road from the village. Sylvie here, was just recommending Simoni. They stay open all day. My name is Gina.'

'Welcome Gina'

'I like it here; it is a very different pace from home.'

'Don't you take a siesta?' asked Luca.

'Sometimes, but I slept a little on the ferry

Luca thought this odd because the ferry from Santa Teresa took only twenty minutes.

'Now I want some lunch and some fresh air.' It would be a very late lunch.

'Well, Le Royal is open all day as is another half dozen cafes and restaurants on or near the marina.'

'But Sylvie recommended Simoni,' said Gina.

'Just follow the avenue of chestnut trees, the workmen may whistle at you, but ignore them,' said Sylvie.

'I'm from Roma; I'm used to it,' said Gina, backing out the door.

****

'Why did you recommend Simoni? Said Luca, 'You know Dernavern hangs out there.'

'A challenge for Dernavern perhaps? '

'Sylvie you are wicked. If this one ends up lost and heart-broken, you will have to be the one to lend her the money to get home.'

Chapter Sixty Five

Assignment Dropped off by a Chauffeur

Astrid relieved Sylvie at reception and asked to use the phone to ring home. For someone being thrown in the deep end, she was doing well.

'Of course.'

What you had was a new pension run by young people and word spread far and wide. Basil and his family had been installed at Pension Lazlo as Larry now spent most of his time in London. He was due back to oversee the final stages of the building of the bistro. A faxed menu from Larry had arrived from London this morning. Luca was reading it now. Sylvie slipped her arms around him as he bent over the counter where the fax machine was installed.

'We have a history assignment due tomorrow.'

'I know, and I haven't even started,' said Luca.

'I can stay here tonight and Saunders can drop it in tomorrow,' suggested Sylvie.

'We must be the only students who drop their assignments off by a chauffeur,' said Luca. 'Do you think he can be enticed to do one of his omelettes?'

'Saunders loves it here, he will stay at the slightest provocation.'

The shadows drew depth from the departing sun at the west-end of another day at Pension Lazlo. In a room in the old farmhouse two teenagers sat doing their homework.

****

Basil, former head of house duties at The Savoy, settled in for his night shift. In Paris, papers were finalised for the divorce of the Murats. Fabien Murat rented his villa in Bonifacio to a Spanish film director and moved to Nice.

In London, Larry, spending the night with friends because the Jamaica Dock flat smelt of paint, caught up with Paige's day via a phone call from New York.

Chapter Sixty Six

Lived in Three Centuries

In Porto Vecchio, Victor snored and his wife, missing her evening talks with Luca: read.

In the small hours and at the end of a long and fruitful life, Beatrice du Plessier slipped away. She had lived in three centuries, but she did not outlive Fabien Murat.

On the currents above a valley, The Bear and the Eagle where reunited and the country would mourn for a week.

Chapter Sixty Seven

Dernavern's Nemesis

'Buy you a drink?'

'I buy my own drinks thank you.'

'Where are you from?'

'Do you mean today?'

Dernavern nodded. Gina was not forthcoming. Dernavern tried another tack. 'That is a lovely tan.'

'Thank you,' said Gina.

'I have a lovely South facing terrace.'

'Look; cut the shit man.'

'I am only being hospitable!' cried Dernavern, 'when did you get a tan like that?'

'Oh! Aren't you a silver tongued fox?'

'Just asking; that's all.'

'Sardinia. Are you happy now?' There was a pause as Gina studied the wine options.

'You're not from here, where the hell is that accent from?' Dernavern allowed himself a little smile, 'I am from Paris.' This usually worked.

Gina didn't have a handbag or purse. She had a little zip bag at her waist and a small backpack. She opened the zip bag and Dernavern saw no makeup, no wallet, not even eyeliner. From the pouch she produced her passport and flicked it open to the last page.

'France. When I can't make myself understood. I find Italian works better. But this stamp definitely says France.'

At least she was talking. 'Do you mind if I get another?' raising his glass.

'Knock yourself out?

Dernavern's drink arrived before Gina spoke. 'So where can I get some Lira changed?'

'I know a guy who won't rip you off'

Gina thrust out her hand: 'Gina'

Dernavern just smiled. Let her wait. Sometimes the fish liked to fight.

'Ok I'll have that drink now. But allow me to pay you in Francs – handy you know - for when you get back to Paris.'

Dernavern had no intention of returning to Paris. 'Knock yourself out.' Was that a wry smile? An exchange of currency was executed with scant regard for exchange rates. A Chardonnay was procured. One thing was for sure, Gina carried wads of cash.

'Cheers!'

'Shalom'

'L'chaim.'

They both smiled. This girl was different. But what was it? 'How did you get here?' asked Dernavern?

Gina stuck her thumb out. Dernavern affected alarm. 'Don't you know there are all kinds of weirdos out there?'

'Weirdos like you?'

'No! I am but a humble artist' If Paris didn't work humble and artist might.

Gina's hand flew to her mouth' Oh My God! You're Dernavern.

Dernavern was sure he had not mentioned his name. 'How do you know that?'

'The girl that gave me a lift was a hairdresser and she mentioned you by name.'

Dernavern thought he had an arrangement with Caroline.

'So, do you know good place to stay?' asked Gina.

'I know a place but it's four star.'

'I think I wandered in there today, just now. Is it Pension Lazlo?

'Yes it is, but it's four star.'

Gina opened her little zip bag and showed Dernavern a wad of cash: Pounds, Marks and Francs.

'How do you have so much cash?'

'I have skills'

Dernavern shrugged in what he hoped was his best Parisian smirk. 'What do you do? And where?'

'Never you mind! I am on holiday. Or do you say vacation in whatever you call this place?'

'Bonafacio. It translates as *beautiful face*. So, you are obviously not a struggling student.' Dernavern got a pout as a reply. What was it about this girl? Much prettier girls would be in his bed by now. Especially ones who had obviously just landed on the island and might be looking for a warm bed and a local with special talents.

'So...' the word hung in the air like soaring hawk, 'what do you want to do? Fuck me or paint me?'

Dernavern thought long and hard and answered from his heart and not his groin; his head came along for the ride. After the appropriate pause, he simply said: 'Talk'

'You want to talk big-fella?'

'Yes, yes I think I do.'

'Alright. Where? that's the next question. And don't think you are going to knock me off on a pile of etchings.'

'I paint in oils and they take a month to dry.'

'A month?'

'If I'm in a bit of an expressionist mood, yes! A month. And I dry them standing up.'

'How 'bout this? You take me to this four star place and we get a bottle of wine?'

'Cognac?'

'I'm buying.' It was a statement not a question.

'I painted the signs there, so you have already seen an example of my work.

'I met a tall guy there - a bit of a hunk. Is he the owner?'

'Technically his father is. But it's a family run thing. That guy, the tall one, he's actually the guy who changes the money.'

'Perfect. Lead the way.'

'How about a stroll first? It's quite beautiful on the marina.'

They walked side by side, close but not touching. Gina had slung her sandals over her shoulder. If Paris, artist and sundecks did not work, let's see what the marina at night would do to soften this girl's resolve.

****

Gina had worn her feet red, then sore. It had been a long day since the ferry ride this morning. Along and back, in a giant semi-circle with every vista a sideshow for free. People ate on their poop deck with cabin doors and hatches flung open. People sat around in groups on the low marina wall or on its flagstones, hewn when Napoleon was emperor.

There were deep pockets of shade were lovers murmured honey-sweet nothings point blank range right into the ear. The flood lights, above head level, made night insects dance and flit. A ballet for the senses. Everything was bathed in calm, reflected light. Spilled light splendid and soft. Gina wore Dernavern's jacket around her shoulders as the breeze had grown cold. Dernavern carried Gina's sandals. Gina heaved a deep sigh and her eyes, large and luminous, had lost the hollow shadows of before.

****

Gina only had a small back pack, so unpacking took no time at all. Dernavern was nervous and he didn't know why. Sitting on the bed, Gina opened with,' So; let's talk stud.'

Dernavern took the chair, linked his fingers and smiled. Why was he so happy? He locked eyes with Gina and felt at home.

'So, what do you paint and why?

'I paint women.'

'Girls?'

'Women.'

'Not what I heard. And then you fuck them.'

'Sometimes, actually most of the time.

'That's a good boy, confession is good for the soul.'

Dernavern sat back in his chair. He stretched his legs out and kicked off his shoes.

Gina crossed her arms and said,' Ok, spill. Go right back to the start.'

Dernavern took a deep breath.

Chapter Sixty Eight

They talked all night

And they talked all night.

Chapter Sixty Nine

Lammas Eve

Sylvie's first modelling assignment was for Louis Vuitton. It was scheduled on her sixteenth birthday - and she got to keep the bag! She now lived in Paris in a flat owned by the agency with a chaperon appointed by Rose and was due to split a bottle of champagne with Paige who was in town for the day. She had been nervous and thought the photographer could see her heart beating in her chest. She had a no nudity contract until she was 18, but the dress was backless and Sylvie thought she gave good back. They got the shot done in half the time and she felt happy. So, this is what contentment felt like.

Three well-chosen words, 'Good job Sylvie.' *Those three words are said too much or not at all.*

****

Now at home, Sylvie threw the windows open to the autumn Paris breeze. It was the first of August.

'Hello!' She called to a man and his wife studying a map at street level. She was feeling so special she added a little wave. They had trouble locating the voice. Their clothing screamed retired American couple.

'We are having a bit of trouble locating The Metro.' said the female of the couple. The man's body language told Sylvie that asking directions did not sit well with him.

'Down there, one hundred metres, on the right. I'd show you myself but I am waiting for my friend: Paige Goss.'

'Thank you! Did you hear that George, a Supermodel right under our noses. Will you stay there for a photograph?'

'Me, from my window? Sure.'

'What is your name dear?'

'Sylvie Murat, I'm going to be a supermodel. I'm sixteen today. Remember my name.'

'We will, won't we George. Wait till we tell Meryl, and she said all Parisians are rude.'

'Got to go, that's the door.' Sylvie disappeared inside while the American couple bickered about the missed photo opportunity.

It was Paige. They bear hugged with manic energy and then Sylvie started bunny hopping around the room shouting, 'I'm a model, I'm a model.'

Sylvie had not seen that Paige had brought a friend; it was a young effeminate male model. He snapped off a picture with a disposable camera - it showed two of the world's most sought after faces in a candid cheek-to-cheek pose, Paige with her tongue poking out, Sylvie laughing open mouthed.

The male model picked up the Louis Vuitton bag and slipped it on his shoulder.

'No, you don't,' said Sylvie in a mock stern voice,' I'm taking that to Gina and Dernavern's wedding.'

'Are you going with Luca?'

'Yeah, we're just friends now but he will always be my first,' said Sylvie.

'Who would have thought that they would get married before Larry and I?' Paige said soberly.

'I think fame has gone to his head! Ever since Dernavern painted that picture *The Seven Crowns of Luca Moro* and won the Kennedy Art Prize for Beauty he's found his stride.'

'His agent now asks fourfold prices for an original Dernavern. He is short listed for the Claude Monet prize for portraiture,' said Paige.

'My beautiful Luca! Maybe he painted something and not someone he was trying to get between the sheets and found his true vocation'.

A playful note in Sylvie's voice told Paige and the hovering Jonathon that it was not quite over between Sylvie and Luca.

The end

Printed in Great Britain
by Amazon

46608387R00215